THE CREATIVE CAPITAL OF CITIES

Studies in Urban and Social Change

*Out of print

THE CREATIVE CAPITAL OF CITIES

INTERACTIVE KNOWLEDGE CREATION AND THE URBANIZATION ECONOMIES OF INNOVATION

Stefan Krätke

WILEY-BLACKWELL

A John Wiley & Sons, Ltd., Publication

This edition first published 2011
© 2011 Stefan Krätke

Blackwell Publishing was acquired by John Wiley & Sons in February 2007. Blackwell's publishing program has been merged with Wiley's global Scientific, Technical, and Medical business to form Wiley-Blackwell.

Registered Office
John Wiley & Sons Ltd, The Atrium, Southern Gate, Chichester, West Sussex, PO19 8SQ, UK

Editorial Offices
350 Main Street, Malden, MA 02148-5020, USA
9600 Garsington Road, Oxford, OX4 2DQ, UK
The Atrium, Southern Gate, Chichester, West Sussex, PO19 8SQ, UK

For details of our global editorial offices, for customer services, and for information about how to apply for permission to reuse the copyright material in this book please see our website at www.wiley.com/wiley-blackwell.

Library of Congress Cataloging-in-Publication Data

Krätke, Stefan, 1952–
The creative capital of cities : interactive knowledge creation and the urbanization economies of innovation / Stefan Krätke.
   p.   cm. – (Studies in urban and social change ; 33)
   Includes bibliographical references and index.
   ISBN 978-1-4443-3621-4 – ISBN 978-1-4443-3622-1 (pbk.)
   1. Creative ability.   2. Technological innovations.   3. Urbanization.   4. Cities and towns.   I. Title.
   BF408.K73 2011
   307.76–dc22

                                                    2011013465

A catalogue record for this book is available from the British Library.

This book is published in the following electronic formats: ePDFs 9781444342246; Wiley Online Library 9781444342277; ePub 9781444342277

Set in 10.5/12pt Baskerville by SPi Publisher Services, Pondicherry, India
Printed and bound in Malaysia by Vivar Printing Sdn Bhd

1   2011

Contents

List of Illustrations

Figures

Tables

Series Editors' Preface

The Wiley-Blackwell *Studies in Urban and Social Change* series is published in association with the *International Journal of Urban and Regional Research*. It aims to advance theoretical debates and empirical analyses stimulated by changes in the fortunes of cities and regions across the world. Among topics taken up in past volumes and welcomed for future submissions are:

- Connections between economic restructuring and urban change
- Urban divisions, difference, and diversity
- Convergence and divergence among regions of east and west, north, and south
- Urban and environmental movements
- International migration and capital flows
- Trends in urban political economy
- Patterns of urban-based consumption

The series is explicitly interdisciplinary; the editors judge books by their contribution to intellectual solutions rather than according to disciplinary origin. Proposals may be submitted to members of the series Editorial Committee, and further information about the series can be found at www.suscbookseries.com:

Jenny Robinson
Neil Brenner
Matthew Gandy
Patrick Le Galès
Chris Pickvance
Ananya Roy

Introduction

Over the last decade, urban theory has been strongly shaped by a heated debate concerning "creative industries" and the "creative class," which are said to undergird the "creative city." However, the notion that the cities and metropoles of the urban system function as major centres of creativity and innovation – playing, in turn, a decisive role in social and economic development – is not a new idea (cf. Hall 1966, 1998, 2000; Jacobs 1969; Heßler and Zimmermann 2008). Throughout history, large metropolitan cities have fostered "innovative milieus" (Camagni 1999), that is, creative systems composed of a diversity of actors and knowledge resources that multiply the capacity for networking and encourage the generation of knowledge and innovation. In a globalizing economy, large cities and metropolitan regions are attaining ever-greater significance due to the fact that "economies of urbanization can be consciously exploited in a worldwide-reaching spatial division of labour" (Thiel 2005: 19). The recent proliferation of publications on creativity and cities might be related to the current prominence of new urban growth theories in the public debate, a phenomenon that is crowding out the insights and contributions of critical urban theory. The "creative city" can be regarded as the newest place-marketing slogan to be exploited in interurban competition. Particularly at the urban level, the concept of creative industries today is being taken as a message of hope and inspiration for future successful development. This heated debate, however, has led to a highly questionable usage of the notion of creativity and an increase in uncritical urban and social theory. The widespread trumpeting of the "creative class" might be best understood as the marketing of misleading terms in order to create a new urban growth concept which is based on the self-idealization of particular elites within a

The Creative Capital of Cities: Interactive Knowledge Creation and the Urbanization Economies of Innovation, First Edition. Stefan Krätke.
© 2011 Stefan Krätke. Published 2011 by Blackwell Publishing Ltd.

neoliberal model of society. Richard Florida's claim that cities are "cauldrons of creativity" could be countered with the thesis that cities today are more accurately characterized as "cauldrons of neoliberals" acting in concert to undermine the world economy. The rise of the dealer class in contemporary capitalism has led to the invention of diverse "weapons of financial mass destruction," which have been deployed very effectively at the expense of people all over the world, a fact that imbues the catchy thesis of a "creative age" (Florida and Tinagli 2004) with a highly ambiguous meaning. The "age of greed and fear" might be a more precise term for capturing the driving motives of the dealer class that dominates today's capitalism (cf. Anderson 2008). While "creativity" has a generally positive connotation, it is quite a fuzzy concept (Markusen 2006a). It is worth noting that creative acts can also serve negative ends (Howkins 2001; Krätke 2004b). Creativity fuels the productive activities of the real economy, yet also played a key role in the creation of the risky financial products that triggered the economic crisis of 2008 onward.

The booming debate on "creative cities" can be traced back to the increasing interurban competition in contemporary capitalism (Harvey 1989). Creativity is at the heart of innovative capabilities, and successful innovation activities positively contribute to an urban region's economic competitiveness. However, there are different pathways to urban competitiveness in capitalist societies. Besides an innovation-oriented path that focuses on the development of innovative capabilities, the space economy of capitalism offers – at least for a number of major urban regions – the option to rely on economic command and control relations for attaining superior competitiveness in the urban system. The economic strength and competitive power of urban regions thus may stem from quite different sources (including different functional and sectoral structures as well as different development paths). The "creative city" growth ideology ignores the fact that urban economic development is embedded in the basic societal framework of a capitalist economy. We have to keep in mind that the unfolding of creativity and innovation activity represents a particular strategic asset in the framework of increasing interurban competition. Thus, this book argues that the debate on the general role of creativity and innovation in urban development, interurban competition, and urban economic "regeneration" should be based on a deeper understanding of how creative work that yields technological as well as artistic innovation is organized and embedded in urban socioeconomic settings.

This book intends to furnish an alternative perspective to the uncritical and superficial notions that currently dominate the creative cities debate. This alternative perspective is theoretically and empirically grounded in research on urban and regional economic development, urban innovation networks, and the function of the cultural economy of cities. The term "creative capital of cities" denotes the ability of urban economic actors to produce scientific, technological, and artistic innovations on the basis of relational assets that are socially produced within a city or urban region. A locally bound creative milieu of cultural producers might constitute one example of a city's creative capital, the knowledge networks between an urban region's research establishments and businesses yet another. By focusing on the socioeconomic context in which creative activities are embedded, this conception deviates from the standard notion of creativity as a uniquely individual quality. In our approach, creativity denotes the capability of individuals and of interacting groups of workers both at the intra-firm level and the level of interorganizational cooperation to create new knowledge that entails the variation of existing forms or the creation of novel forms which are applied to generate new technologies, products, and organizational forms. Hence creativity functions as an essential "input" in the process of innovation. The formation of interorganizational knowledge networks in a regional economy and the emergence of a locally bound creative milieu of cultural producers in the urban economic space are the hallmarks of an urban and regional socioeconomic environment that enables creativity to flourish. In short, beyond the specific capabilities possessed by individuals, creativity is embedded in relational networks of social and economic actors.

With respect to its ability to generate meaningful new ideas in collaborative contexts, creativity "is not necessarily an economic activity but may become so when it produces an idea with economic implications or a tradeable product" (Howkins 2001: x). Creativity is present at all levels of the economic process and can flourish in every kind of organization open to innovation. As the creative process is dependent on a specific socioeconomic context, there is a weak basis for developing a general theory of creativity which encompasses the activities of both the artist and engineer. Creative capabilities are relevant not only in the sphere of cultural industries, but also in a wide range of other industries, particularly the research-intensive branches of high-tech and medium high-tech industries. Since the unfolding of creativity depends on specific socioeconomic contexts, we will emphasize in particular the difference between scientific/technological creativity that draws on localization economies and knowledge networks, and artistic creativity that draws on urbanization economies and a continuous reconfiguration of project networks. Thus we do not intend to offer a "general theory of creativity." The main emphasis is on the diversity of organizational and spatial contexts for the unfolding of different kinds of creative work. These will be the subject of analyses in Chapters 3, 4, and 5.

Yet clearly, only human actors – not things or territories – are creative. The "creative city" as such is a fiction. The creative capital of cities or regions has to be understood as an expression of the aggregated collective capability of its economic and social actors, which also comprise particular occupational groups specializing in creative and innovative activity, to yield new forms, products, and problem solutions. Creativity depends on human actors *and* their interlinking (yielding knowledge networks of industrial innovation and project-based networks of artistic production), which creates a "collective" innovative capacity within particular regional and urban settings. Terms such as the "creativity of urban regions" or the "creative capital of cities" have to be understood as representing rough generalizing terms which do not imply that territories or cities as such can be creative. In the term "creative capital of cities," "capital" should be understood as representing a "capacity or capability to" perform creative work that leads to successful innovation activity. This kind of usage of the term "capital" is quite common, for example in the literature on "social capital," yet it differs from the classical notion of economic capital that prevails in the theory of political economy and in economics. The creative capital of cities thus denotes the capacity to create value from interactive knowledge generation in urban economic settings which are at the same time characterized by the geographic clustering of specific subsectors (i.e., the formation of local clusters) and by the presence of a diversity of industrial activities and knowledge resources. This creative capacity can be unevenly distributed (e.g., geographically concentrated) in the urban and regional system. The so-called "creative economy" (Howkins 2001) is predominantly an activity concentrated in urban economies, particularly in metropolitan regions.

The debate concerning "creative industries" and "creative cities" has for the most part focused on a selection of economic subsectors in which creativity plays a key role (see Hartley 2005; Kong 2009). However, the delimitation of these "creative subsectors" is still a subject of debate. Gibson and Kong (2005: 552) emphasize the dominance of selective interpretations of creativity, which is mostly discussed with reference to those forms which can be harnessed in productive ways for economic growth, while ignoring others that do not automatically contribute to economic development. Landry (2000) offers an unusually broad interpretation of the creative city that concentrates on innovative ideas for developing and running urban life. Landry addresses a wide range of topics, including the creative use of culture in urban revitalization, as well as imaginative solutions for the organization of urban transport systems, garbage collection, etc. The nearly forgotten realm of "social creativity" – understood in terms of the renewal of social institutions – is another topic addressed by Landry. On the whole, he aims to surmount the challenges to creative urban policies by offering a "toolkit for urban innovators." In this way, his approach diverges considerably from typical assessments of creative subsectors in urban and regional economies. Landry's approach has been extended by contributions that intentionally depart from the debate on market-led models of technological innovation in order to explore notions of community development based on *social innovations* as an alternative interpretation of the creative capabilities of the city (see Moulaert and Nussbaumer 2005). This book, however, deals more specifically with the creative and innovative capacity of urban regions from a multi-sectoral perspective. It encompasses a wider range of activities than the prevalent "creative industries" approach, but doesn't attempt to develop all-encompassing policy prescriptions for urban development.

In order to delimit the "creative subsectors" of the urban and regional economy, we draw on the approach taken by Howkins (2001). Most participants in the current debate restrict the term "creative industries" to the arts, media, and cultural industries while deliberately excluding the sciences and R&D activities (which are relevant to all economic sectors, particularly the "knowledge-intensive" subsectors of the economy). Yet this view of creativity is rather one-sided. Indeed, Howkins (2001) notes that

> the output of creative products has tended to happen most publicly and obviously in the arts, which has caused the arts to be seen as the core creative activity and for creativity and the arts to be treated as synonyms (or, at least, creativity and good art). But artists have no monopoly on creativity, nor are they the only workers in the creative economy. The difference between creativity in the arts and elsewhere is not that artists are more creative, or more successfully creative, but that because they deal in a specific range of ideas and aesthetics, they create specific kinds of works and work according to identifiable business models with their own patterns of supply, demand, values and pricing. Creativity flourishes equally in the sciences, especially in research and development (R&D). There is little difference between the creativity of the scientist and of the artist.... Put simply, the creativity is the same; the creative products are different. (2001: x–xi)

In contrast to a narrow categorization of creative industries that only includes sectors of "artistic" creativity (see Scott 2000), Howkins (2001) offers a broader definition that is based on the *tangible* products of intellectual property and a distinction between "copyright industries" and "patent industries." The copyright industries consist of the prominent subsectors of the media and cultural economy (the advertising, film, TV, music, publishing, and performing arts industries, etc.). The patent industries, by contrast, consist of all industries that produce or deal in patents, which are the most important form of intellectual property for creative products (i.e., inventions) generated by research and development. However, the term "patent industries" is applicable to all manufacturing subsectors. Patent-producing R&D is particularly widespread in "knowledge-intensive" manufacturing subsectors such as pharmaceuticals, information technology, mechanical engineering, aerospace, and vehicle manufacturing.

Limiting the discussion to a narrow range of cultural products and industries prevents the formulation of an accurate definition of the creative capital of cities and regions. Yet the inclusion of all of the above-mentioned subsectors under the term "creative industries" would be misleading, as it would encompass an excessively broad range of economic activity. In an era of economic development increasingly driven by innovation-related competition, every industry makes efforts to generate new products and manufacturing techniques. There is only a gradual quantitative differentiation of industries according to their average shares of research and development expenditure or employment. While most scholarship on creative cities focuses on cultural production, our approach to creative capital embraces cultural production as well as industrial research and development. Both are constitutive components of the creative capital of cities and regions. In our analysis, a distinction is drawn according to occupational categories; creative activities in artistic and cultural domains are grouped together and contrasted to activities in scientific and technological domains. Thus, in contrast to Howkins's approach, R&D activities are not viewed as a distinct industry within the traditional range of economic sectors. The generation of new products, processes, and patents is a function within the value chains of various industries (which are traditionally distinguished according to their final products), but does not constitute an industry of its own, even if there are firms and organizations which specialize in R&D functions. R&D activities are included in our analysis with a particular focus on the "collective" generation of industrial innovations in urban and regional settings. Here, the formation of regional knowledge networks plays a decisive role. Networking and creativity are symbiotic. The capacity for interorganizational learning and innovation in a regional innovation system is directly proportional to the number of actors and interrelationships encompassed by it, as innovation is based on the interlinking of diverse knowledge resources. In this way, our analysis underscores a dimension of urban creativity mostly neglected in the current debate on creative cities. It should be noted here, however, that this topic is not neglected in the literature on urban and regional economic development, where a prominent area of research concerns creativity in industrial innovation and its territorial embeddedness in regional networks and local innovative milieus.

The theoretical framing of the book includes, first, the embedding of creativity and innovation in the capitalist imperative of accumulation and the unfolding of interurban competition, and, second, the classical economic geography concept of "localization and urbanization economies" that are at the heart of urban regions' particular creative and innovative capabilities. This economic geography concept will be applied to the technologically and artistically creative capacities of cities and combined with empirical analyses of the functioning of these agglomeration economies in terms of the embedding of creative work in relational networks of socioeconomic actors at the level of cities and urban regions. By applying social network analysis to urban innovation networks (Chapter 3), a new and detailed empirical analysis of knowledge networks that might extend the understanding of urban and regional innovation networks will be presented. The literature on the regional and urban dimension of innovation has been most influential to the approach presented here.

This book is divided into five main chapters. Each deals with a separate aspect of creativity in urban economic analysis. The chapters cover different levels of abstraction and focus on different scales of spatial contextualization (with empirical analyses moving from the national to the regional and intra-metropolitan local scale). This way of bringing together complementary theoretical concepts and different levels of investigation seems appropriate for achieving a differentiated understanding of the creative capital of cities.

Chapter 1 offers a basic contextualization of the issues of creativity and innovation that draws on David Harvey's theory of capitalist urbanization, wherein the capitalist imperative of accumulation subordinates creative work and innovation activity to the continued race for competitive advantage and the appropriation of surplus profits. Harvey's theory emphasizes the role of different circuits of capital and places innovation activity and technological change in the framework of interurban competition. We will suggest modifications of Harvey's account with regard to the rise of a finance-dominated model of capitalist development. While technological innovation remains a significant source of competitive advantage and surplus profits, the capitalist economy today can privilege different pathways and investment options that comply with the imperatives of capital accumulation. The unfolding of creativity and innovation activity represents a *particular* strategic option in the framework of a finance-dominated regime of accumulation.

Starting from the thesis that creativity can be exclusively assigned neither to a particular social class nor to a particular selection of economic subsectors (i.e., the so-called "creative industries"), Chapter 2 engages in a macro-level analysis of the impact of creative occupational groups on regional economic success within Germany's urban and regional system. The chapter starts from a critique of Richard Florida's notion of the "creative class," which has been wholeheartedly embraced by many policy makers and social scientists. Florida's theory is criticized for its ideological affirmation of widening social stratification and detrimental economic trends as well as for its disregard of relevant urban economic development factors. In the deconstruction of the "creative class" concept, empirical research is also presented concerning the relationship between regional economic success and the distribution of particular occupational groups in Germany. The chapter ultimately concludes that the "dealer class" (or, in Florida's terms, the class of "creative professionals") does not enhance the ability of urban regions to pursue sustainable economic growth. The findings at this macro level of analysis indicate that a specifically delimited creative workforce indeed has a positive impact on urban economic development. However, the findings simultaneously indicate that prominent factors of capitalist economic development such as entrepreneurial control capacities and capital concentration in large firms still have a "greater" influence on the cities' economic performance. The macro level of comparative regional analysis does not address the important question of how creative work generates innovations in the institutional setting of an urban region's economy. The following chapters will go beyond the level of macro-analysis and present an analysis of the functioning of creative work in different subsectors of the urban economy.

Chapter 3 presents a meso-level analysis of the interactive basis of creative activities within the context of a metropolitan region. The analysis draws on existing studies regarding the sources of regional innovative capacity and includes a detailed investigation of the knowledge network employed by regional actors in a selected "medium high-tech" manufacturing sector of a metropolitan region in Germany (Hanover-Braunschweig-Göttingen). The capacity of technologically creative occupational groups to develop new products and solutions manifests itself in a specific regional context. The case study deals with a type of metropolitan region that is shaped by technology-intensive manufacturing industries and related innovation activities, still representing the backbone of the German economy. Within the framework of a regional innovation system and its *relational* aspects – that is, the knowledge networks employed by economic actors in particular economic sectors – "creativity" or creative capacity appear to be a *socially produced* locational advantage and regional economic success factor. Looking at regional or urban innovation systems in relational terms is a basic premise of much economic geography research on innovation. Yet prominent scholars in this field of research frequently emphasize the lack of empirical analyses of the structure and functioning of urban innovation networks that provide the framework for the unfolding of creative capabilities particularly in the sphere of technological innovation. Against this background, this chapter aims at a presentation of the specific socioeconomic context of technological creativity in a selected metropolitan region. The conclusion can be drawn that *in the realm of technological innovation* the creative capital of cities depends on the properties or "strengths" of their knowledge networks in specific branches of economic activity. This implies that the creative capital of cities has a specific "sectoral profile" in terms of one or more specific sectors with "strong" knowledge network properties. Due to their size and internal economic diversity, large metropolitan regions are able to develop a "strong" creative capacity in a variety of subsectors. In sum, the chapter deals with creativity in terms of the dynamic agglomeration advantages of knowledge creation and the interactive social framework of technological innovation.

Chapter 4 focuses on the institutional order of the cultural economy, underscoring the impact of commercial imperatives on artistic creativity. We present an analysis of the functioning of artistic creativity under the command of capital and the imperatives of entrepreneurial success. The conclusion is reached that there is little justification for speaking of "creative industries" exclusively in terms of the capitalist culture and media industries to the exclusion of creative innovative activities undertaken by other industrial branches. The chapter also deals with the globalization of the cultural economy and the emergence of global centers of the culture industry.

Chapter 5 concentrates on urban cultural economies and, in particular, on the "urbanization economies" of artistic innovation. The cultural economy of the Berlin metropolis will be taken as a case study area. The Berlin case is a good example of the local clustering and rise of new "city industries" that prefer to concentrate in the densely built inner-city area. However, a specific feature of Berlin is the mismatch between flourishing creative industries and regional economic growth. The Berlin economy is comparatively weak even while the creative industries are expanding. Hence the Berlin case undermines Florida's causal claims regarding the relationship between creative industries and growth.

We present a micro-level analysis of the inner urban clustering of the cultural economy sector in the Berlin metropolis that illustrates the functioning of the "urbanization economies" of artistic innovation. The clustering of artistically creative workers at the local level (i.e., in particular inner-city districts of a large city or metropolis) and the related emergence of a locally bound creative milieu of cultural producers again highlights the fact that "creativity" is in part a socially produced asset. The setting within which the cultural economy's creative actors interact is the local "creative milieu," which represents a key asset of the creative capital of cities, as it provides networking opportunities between firms or in non-work settings. The analysis draws on the large body of "pre-Florida" studies on urban cultural economies.

The misleading term "creative industries" has encouraged the self-glorification of actors in the cultural industries (comparable in many ways to the near-forgotten hyping of the so-called "New Economy"), and – even more crucially – currently operates as a disarming catchphrase for dominant urban growth ideologies ("creative class cities"). Nevertheless, the cultural economy makes a positive contribution to regional economic development, particularly in large cities and metropoles. The cultural industries employ a comparatively high and growing share of the workforce in global cities such as New York, Los Angeles, London, Paris, and Berlin. Yet creativity and growth of culture industries cannot be regarded as a "fix for urban ills."

The discussion of the implications of "creative industries" for urban regeneration will firstly emphasize the creation of "low quality" employment and the sector's limited potential to solve a city's labor market problems. Second, the expansion and local concentration of creative industries and actors contributes to the unfolding of gentrification processes in inner-city districts that are leading to increased sociospatial inequality and polarization. These arguments contradict most of the salvation promises of the "creative industries" urban growth ideology.

Chapters 2 and 3 draw on rather "rigorous" statistical analyses requiring a mode of representation and outlining of hypotheses that differs from Chapters 1, 4, and 5, which entail a predominantly "qualitative" way of presenting theses and conclusions. The empirical analyses presented in the book are related to the urban and regional system of Germany. On the one hand, this is the context within which the author works; on the other, the German case studies are relevant in a European and global context, too. The polycentric urban and regional system of Germany contains a range of metropolitan regions that compare with the different types of metropolitan urban economies across the European territory (except outstanding "extremes" such as the global city regions of London and Paris). This includes metropolitan regions thriving on an expanding service economy (such as Frankfurt-Main) as well as metropolitan regions with a strong base in technology- and research-intensive manufacturing industries (such as Munich, Stuttgart, and Hanover; see Krätke 2007). These urban regions form an essential part of the "regional motors" of the European economy, and they are strongly connected to the worldwide network of global city regions. At the same time, comparable to other European countries the German urban system is home to cities experiencing quite different urban fortunes, comprising large cities with considerable problems of industrial restructuring and related labor market pressures (such as, for example, Cologne and Berlin). In the European and German context, such cities often put particular emphasis on unleashing the presumed new growth potential offered by "creative industries." While the empirical focus is on Germany, the arguments and conclusions presented have broader implications that may enrich the debate on creativity and cities at the European and wider international scale. The analyses concentrate on the case study regions Hanover and Berlin, which have been chosen for their different spatial structures at the intra-metropolitan scale and their contrasting sectoral structures or "lead sectors" of creativity and innovation: in the metropolitan region Hanover-Braunschweig-Göttingen, the creative capacities are investigated at the scale of a polycentric metropolitan region which contains several core cities, whereas in the monocentric Berlin metropolis, the unfolding of creative capacities will be examined at the local level of inner-city districts. The case study region Hanover-Braunschweig-Göttingen is an example of an urban region whose creative and innovative capacities are concentrated in the medium high-tech industries (particularly the automotive industry). By focusing on this example we can prove that creative capacities are unfolding in rather "traditional" industrial sectors which differ from the high-tech industries mostly privileged in urban and regional innovation research. In the case study metropolis of Berlin, on the other hand, the cultural economy represents the "lead sector" of creativity and innovation. The investigation of the creative capacities of cultural products industries also emphasizes the point that there is no reason to assume a "superior" creativity in the culture industries as compared to other industries (such as the automotive sector in the Hanover case study). In sum, we have chosen contrasting case studies in order to underline the diversity of urban "worlds of creativity."

This book aims to make a contribution to critical urban theory in two ways: first, by positioning the issues of creativity and innovation in the framework of the dynamics of a capitalist economic order. This political economy perspective is relevant for understanding the general role of creative and innovative capacities in contemporary urban development. According to Brenner (2009), critical urban theory requires sustained engagement with contemporary patterns of capitalist urbanization which become increasingly generalized on a world scale. Second, critical urban theory will be advanced by a reasoned critique of the latest urban growth ideologies. Currently, the theoretical notions surrounding "creative industries" and "creative cities" exert a great deal of influence over urban economic planning and development. Yet a critique of these concepts should not be reduced to assessing their functional role in shaping urban growth strategies. It is also necessary to employ sound empirical research on urban economic development in order to convincingly refute them. Against this background, the more detailed analyses of the functioning of creativity in specific sectors presented in Chapters 3 and 4 draw on the classical distinction between the localization and urbanization economies of the city, confirming the significance of dynamic agglomeration advantages for urban economies that are pursuing an economic development path that is based on knowledge-intensive activities. The function of urbanization economies hinges on uniquely urban qualities of place and the opportunities offered for cross-fertilization amongst a diversity of branches and actors. The creative capital of cities and metropolitan regions is therefore founded on processes of interactive knowledge creation within specific industry clusters as well as on urbanization economies in technological and artistic fields of innovation. These types of agglomeration economies offer socially produced locational advantages, particularly for knowledge-intensive industries and the cultural economy sector. Ultimately, the book offers a transdisciplinary approach to the analysis of creativity and knowledge generation in an urban context by combining perspectives in economic geography, regional research, and sociocultural urban studies.

1
Creativity and Innovation under the Command of Capital

The Capitalist Imperative of Creativity and Innovation

Contemporary urban and regional research has been shaped by an extensive debate on creativity and innovation, which has been accompanied by the emergence of new urban growth ideologies (such as the "creative class city") and affirmative accounts of today's capitalist societies (such as the notion of a "knowledge-based society"). Particularly in the academic disciplines of economic geography and urban and regional studies, the analysis of urban and regional innovation systems and of the interorganizational networks that foster collaborative knowledge creation, as well as the role of creative milieus as a major ingredient in innovative capacity, has seen many advances in the last decades, resulting in diverse models of the socioeconomic organization and spatiality of innovation (see Fagerberg, Mowery, and Nelson 2005).

An initial working definition of creativity and innovation might start from the point that creativity and innovation are a result of human labor (which includes the labor of knowledge generation) and are embedded in a social division of labor. Everyone can be creative in one sense or another, but we restrict the term here to creative work that is economically valued and geared toward the creation of innovations in terms of new products, new production processes, and new organizational forms. In the contemporary era, this kind of creative work has become the task of a specialized and skilled workforce of scientists, engineers, designers, and artists, etc. Thus, creative work and innovation activities are embedded in the functioning of the economy of historically specific social formations. Moreover, as we will explore in some detail, they are differentiated according to specific sectoral and spatial contexts. Creativity and innovation are closely interrelated or

The Creative Capital of Cities: Interactive Knowledge Creation and the Urbanization Economies of Innovation, First Edition. Stefan Krätke.
© 2011 Stefan Krätke. Published 2011 by Blackwell Publishing Ltd.

"symbiotic," since the creative capacity of workers functions as a prime source of innovative capacity that is at the heart of successful innovation activities. Hence creativity functions as an essential "input" to the process of innovation. It denotes the capability of individuals and of interacting groups of workers (both at the intra-firm level and the level of interorganizational cooperation) to create new knowledge that entails the variation of existing forms or the creation of novel forms which are applied to generate new technologies, products, and organizational forms.

The creation of new knowledge essentially requires a recombination or novel combination of complementary "pieces of knowledge" in terms of either specific competencies residing within a particular field of activity or different knowledge bases of particular economic sectors, scientific disciplines, etc. Hence interactive knowledge generation through the collaboration of creative workers is of key importance in the innovation process. Interactive knowledge creation, on the other hand, entails a shared learning process that strengthens or expands the individual actors' creative capabilities. Innovation is the result of non-linear processes of searching and experimentation, whose course and "success" cannot be known in advance. Hence the generation of new knowledge should not be conceived of as a deterministic process. The process of innovation as a whole comprises research, development, and design activities, the "output" of this creative work being new designs, patents, contents of cultural products etc., and its economic utilization in the form of new products and technologies. Due to the diversity of socioeconomic fields and sectors, where innovation activities are to be found, creative capabilities rely on a specific knowledge base. Yet in the process of creative work, different knowledge bases might be combined in order to generate novel forms. The workforce employed in research, development, and design activities must have specific knowledge and skills, but the unfolding of creative capabilities is based on both specifically skilled human resources and broader *social resources* in terms of the organized interaction amongst creative workers in the innovation process. Thus creativity and innovation are embedded in spatially differentiated socioeconomic and institutional environments; specific forms of collaborative organization and "milieus" of interaction are constitutive factors of creative capabilities at the local and regional level. With regard to interregional competition, creativity and innovative capacity function as a socially produced regional advantage that contributes to uneven development in the urban and regional system.

Existing scholarship in economic geography and regional research has for the most part concentrated on the spatial distribution, functioning, and determining factors of creativity and innovation in urban and regional settings, and on the impact of innovative capacities on urban and regional economic development. However, the current debate on the role of creativity and innovation is characterized by a major shortcoming: there is a common tendency in mainstream writing on this topic to decontextualize the issues of creativity and innovation from their embeddedness in a capitalist society and the imperatives of capital accumulation (see Florida 2004; Fagerberg, Mowery, and Nelson 2005). This book has a different starting point. The geography of uneven development at the global, national, and regional scale is essentially based in the dynamics of a capitalist mode of production. More generally, the contemporary world is characterized by the dominance and global proliferation of the capitalist mode of production, which can be further differentiated according to the variation of regimes of accumulation and modes of regulation and governance into a variety of capitalist development models (see Whitley 1999). These are, however, still characterized by shared basic ingredients such as the primary class division between the owners and "managers" of capital and a workforce dependent on wage labor, and by the overarching imperative of capital accumulation. The decontextualization of creativity and innovation from these basic features of the historical social formation in which such capacities are developing has fostered the emergence and spread of new urban and regional growth ideologies that entail a glorification of capitalism as a socioeconomic formation essentially based on knowledge creation and superior innovative capacities. The most advanced decontextualization is presented in Florida's theory of the "creative class" (see Chapter 2), which denotes "the rise of human creativity as the defining feature of economic life" and claims that "we can read economic history as a succession of new and better ways to harness creativity" (Florida 2004: 21, 56). In such conceptualizations, the primary motives and the partially destructive powers of innovation activities that develop under the command of capital (such as in the sphere of "financial innovations," or in the guise of sectoral and regional "switching crises" resulting from basic technological innovations) are widely neglected. Decontextualization leads urban and regional research to deal "immanently" with the unfolding of creativity and innovation – that is, to neglect the broader socioeconomic framework of a capitalist society that shapes the basic economic motives and social organization of such activities. Despite the many relevant and detailed findings of contemporary urban and regional innovation research, decontextualized approaches give rise to overly affirmative positive general characterizations of the current phase of capitalist development.

In the context of a capitalist society and economy, the unfolding of creativity and innovation activity takes place "under the command of capital." Technological and artistic innovation is dominated by private sector activities, even though national or regional innovation systems often involve cooperative links between private sector firms and public sector research establishments. Private sector dominance leads to the privileging of those fields and modes of innovation activity that promise entrepreneurial and commercial success. Likewise, the issue of creativity is mostly considered with reference to those forms which can be harnessed for economic growth. Creativity and innovation are thus embedded in the basic imperatives of capitalist economies which subordinate creative work and innovation activity to the continued race for competitive advantage and the appropriation of surplus profits. This basic condition represents a determining force that is also relevant to research on the uneven geography of creative and innovative capacities and to research into the specific regional and local conditions that support the generation and successful utilization of creative and innovative capacities.

The work of David Harvey represents the most advanced and detailed Marxist approach to the urbanization of capital and the forces shaping the geography of uneven development under capitalism. In Harvey's theory of capitalist urbanization (Harvey 1989), the embedding of urban and regional processes (including creative and innovative work) in the imperatives of a capitalist economy is the explicit starting point of analysis. At the most general level, capitalism has been characterized as a historically distinct mode of production based on continued "revolution" in production methods, technologies, organizational forms, and spatial arrangements of the economy. Competition is a major driving force of this dynamic. According to Harvey (1989: 136), "the entrepreneurial search for excess profits is fundamental within the social relations of capitalism. Excess profits can be had by virtue of superior technology and organization or by occupying superior locations … The coercive laws of competition force capitalists to search out superior technologies and locations."

Within the framework of capitalist competition, the imperative of innovation activity (that draws on creative work) is the continued striving for surplus profits. These represent excess profits above the prevalent "average" rate of profits. For individual capitalist firms, the command of superior technologies and production methods, the invention of new products as well as incremental product innovations, and the introduction of new organizational forms (including spatial arrangements of production and distribution) offer various approaches to the realization of surplus profits. In this sense, Marx's theory of capital (Marx 1981) contains a concept of "endogenous growth" that emphasizes the role of technological change (innovation) in the process of capital accumulation – and this long before the contemporary rediscovery of technological change and innovation as a major economic growth factor in Romer's "new growth theory" (see Romer 1990). However, as Luxemburg (1951) has shown, the accumulation of capital does not solely rely on innovation and technological change – it can also be based on the geographic expansion of capital accumulation and the incorporation (subsumption) of new sectors of social activity into the domain of private capital accumulation. We will return to a more detailed account of the role of innovation and interregional competition in Harvey's theory of capitalist urbanization in the chapter's third subsection.

In contributions to the theory of global value chains (see Gereffi and Korzeniewicz 1994; Kaplinsky 2004), surplus profits have also been interpreted as representing "economic rents" which take on different forms. Economic rents arise from the possession of or control over unique (scarce) resources. As Schumpeter (1952) has shown, scarcity or unique resources can be constructed through purposive action, and those who create these unique resources can then achieve an entrepreneurial surplus. This essentially happens when capitalist firms innovate: the creation of "new combinations" (new technologies, processes, and organizational forms) provides a competitive advantage that entails the realization of economic rents or surplus profits. These economic returns to innovation then act as an inducement to the replication of these innovations by other firms which also seek to raise returns and acquire surplus profits. In the diffusion of innovations, economic rents or surplus profits are whittled away, which leads to a renewed search for "new combinations" that promise an entrepreneurial surplus. In this way, the process of competition in the search for surplus profit or economic rent and its subsequent bidding away by competitors fuels the innovation process.

Drawing on Kaplinsky (2004), we can distinguish a variety of forms of economic rent relevant to processes of innovation, some of which are endogenously "constructed" by individual capitalist firms, while others are collectively constructed by groups of firms through a process of inter-firm networking in particular value chains. The endogenously constructed forms of rent include "technology rents" (command over superior technologies), "human resource rents" in terms of employing a workforce with superior skills, "organizational rents" stemming from superior forms of internal organization (which also includes the particular spatial organization of a multi-regional firm's production network), and "marketing rents," which result from superior marketing capabilities and the construction of valuable brands. Collectively constructed forms of rent can be denoted as "relational rents" that are based on superior transactional relationships with suppliers and customers and access to specific knowledge resources that reside in inter-firm cooperation and networks. Relational rents may accrue to an ensemble of collaborating firms, and they are particularly related to spatial organization and the firms' positioning within specific urban and regional settings (the main focus of Chapters 3 and 5 will be on these socially produced conditions for reaping relational rents). These collectively created conditions are also at the heart of urban and regional competitive advantage. Kaplinsky (2004) has mentioned further sources of economic rent, such as "resource rents" that accrue to firms from superior access to scarce natural resources, and economic benefits provided by parties external to particular value chains such as "infrastructural rents" that stem from access to high-quality public infrastructures. Infrastructures such as transport systems, the spatial arrangement of the built environment, the public education system, and so on also represent socially produced conditions of production that affect the competitive advantage of individual cities and regions. Furthermore, government policies at different spatial scales actively support the construction of competitive advantage through the upgrading of relevant infrastructures, economic promotion activities, and technology- and innovation-related programs. In general, innovative capacities at the level of individual firms, as well as at the level of groups of interacting firms, have become increasingly important against a background of the rising technological intensity of production, the increasing significance of product differentiation, and the growth of competitive pressures in the context of globalization.

This analysis builds on the assumption that the basic dynamic of a capitalist economy stems from competition and rent seeking (or the race for surplus profits). However, "regulation theory" (see Aglietta 1979, 2000; Boyer 1990; Dunford 1990) underlines the point that different historical phases of capitalism can be distinguished by distinct "regimes of accumulation" and "modes of regulation." In addition, taking into account the economic-institutional varieties of capitalism that are associated with the uneven geography of capitalism, we have to be aware that there are competing modes of capitalist development. Different regimes of accumulation tend to privilege different basic technologies and lead sectors of the economy. Whereas the "Fordist" mode of development was shaped by a focus on mass production technologies and the rise of "medium high-tech" manufacturing industries such as the automotive industry, the contemporary mode of capitalist development – frequently labeled as "Post-Fordism" (Amin 1994) – is shaped by a wider variety of lead sectors. On the one hand, we have seen the spread of flexible production models and the rise of new high-tech industries that are specifically innovation-driven and based on comparatively high R&D inputs. On the other hand, the capitalist economy is increasingly based on a finance-dominated regime of accumulation, wherein the "secondary circuits" (Harvey 1989) of capital, that is, the trade in financial assets and derivatives as well as the real estate business, are becoming the driving forces of capitalism at the expense of investment and innovation in the real economy sector. Capitalist economies are today characterized by different mixes of the aforementioned lead sectors, and this variation produces competing development models. The German economy, for example, is strongly based on high-tech and medium high-tech industries (aside from the rise of financial industries and advanced producer services), whereas the British economy has to a large extent been converted into an economy that primarily depends on the financial industry, complemented by a strong growth of business service industries with a global market reach.

Interestingly, the current phase of capitalist development in highly industrialized countries – generally characterized by an increasing share of unproductive and speculative financial deals and a comparatively weakened position of manufacturing industries (of all technological levels) – has been accompanied by a rise of analytical accounts that describe capitalist economies and societies as developing on a path toward a "knowledge-based" and "creative" economy. Against a background of a finance-dominated mode of capitalist development, whose primary characteristic is the unfolding of unproductive and specifically destructive economic activities, these analyses lead to new affirmative ideologies of contemporary socioeconomic developments. Such uncritical accounts widely ignore the prevalent "casino capitalism" and the destructive consequences of a "dealer economy." Some accounts of the current development phase, such as the "knowledge-based" and "creative" economy, draw selectively on particular types of successful cities and regions that form only part of the geography of uneven development: certainly, there are local and regional economies that focus on knowledge-intensive industries and encompass a "creative" economy with continued innovation efforts in the real economy sectors. These local and regional economies might well achieve competitive advantages in the framework of interurban and interregional competition (which is an essential aspect of urban and regional development in capitalism; see below). They might also represent specific regional systems of accumulation (Leborgne and Lipietz 1991; Peck and Tickell 1994; Krätke 1999). But, as I have shown in this section, they do not represent the currently dominant model of capitalism.

In urban theory, the conceptualization of new pathways of economic and social development such as the "service society" or the "knowledge society," which are related to the rise of new economic lead sectors, have influenced the emergence of various new general conceptualizations of urban development. Yet many of these (except those focusing on globalization) have been decontextualized from the framework of a capitalist society and economy. They have appeared in the guise of a sequence of (partially overlapping) generalizing models of urban economic development that attempt to relate the respective period's prime "motors" of urban economic growth to new leading subsectors of the urban economy. These models have been used to develop new urban growth ideologies such as the "postindustrial city," the "service metropolis," and the "creative city," which in turn have strongly affected urban development strategies. A short review of such generalizing models follows, which will underline the need for a critical perspective on urban development that locates it firmly in the context of contemporary capitalism.

Generalizing Models of Urban Economic Development

For a long time, the coevolution of industrialization and urbanization in Western capitalist countries has shaped understandings of the economic base of cities. Hence the "industrial city" emerged as an influential generalizing conceptualization of urban economic development. The focus on the city's role as a manufacturing center in a "Fordist" phase of capitalist development (see Scott 1988a) could be combined with the notion of a spatial division of labor across the urban system that corresponded to the rise of the multi-regional organization of large firms, leading to a distinction between "headquarter cities" and "branch plant cities" (see Pred 1977; Massey 1984). Critical urban theory considered the combination of an interurban functional division of labor and the hierarchical control relations existing amongst manufacturing establishments to be a crucial determinant of urban economic development in this era (Friedmann and Wolff 1982).

Against the background of secular declines in Fordist production and the rise of a specialized service economy since the 1970s, which had been theoretically articulated by the notion of an emerging "post-industrial society" (Bell 1974), the "postindustrial city" emerged as a new general concept of urban economic development. Declining employment in traditional Fordist manufacturing sectors led to the decline of many cities whose economy was primarily focused on industrial manufacturing. In the realm of the postindustrial city conception, manufacturing-based cities were regarded as the losers of structural change, and cities with an expanding service economy appeared to be the winners (see Smith and Williams 1986; Soja 2000). This simplified concept of structural change has been converted into the new urban growth ideology of the city as a center of service sector activity, particularly of advanced producer services. The new urban growth concept was taken up as a message of hope, and many cities geared their economic and spatial development strategy toward supporting an expansion of the city's service industries (e.g., by new extensions of the city's central business district, by the reconversion of abandoned industrial sites for new office complexes, etc.). In the critical urban theory debate, however, some of the basic propositions about the "postindustrial" economy, namely the notion that it needs a growing share of highly educated workers, have been rejected. Sassen (1996: 581) argued that the new employment regime in service-dominated urban economies predominantly creates low-wage jobs that do not require particularly high levels of education. The debate emphasized the pronounced internal polarization of the service sector's employment conditions. Furthermore, the idea that cities and urban economies are primarily and increasingly relying on service industries (such as particularly the advanced producer services; see Daniels and Moulaert 1991; Bryson and Daniels 2007), which is still influential among urban researchers and the cities' political decision makers, did not take into account that manufacturing activities continued to form a relevant part of most urban regions' economic base. In the binary world of the postindustrial city concept, processes of functional upgrading and structural change within urban regions' manufacturing sectors have been widely ignored. Yet the continued growth of advanced producer services is to a large extent an articulation of organizational restructuring processes within the manufacturing sector itself: organizational restructuring entailed the relocation of the manufacturing firm's internal technology-related service functions (such as R&D, technical testing activities, laboratory services, etc.) to external firms which are subsequently assigned to the service sector (Krätke 2007). These technology-related services are functionally coupled with research-intensive manufacturing sectors. Today, the urban economy of prospering cities (such as Munich) is often based on a comparatively high share of research-intensive manufacturing sectors and technology-related services. This type of sectoral profile differs from those cities and regions that predominantly rely on market-related business services and the financial sector. The "city as a service metropolis" ideology widely ignored the fact that urban economies were characterized by quite diverse sectoral profiles (i.e., the particular mix of manufacturing and service sectors) and development paths (i.e., the main direction of restructuring of the urban economy's sectoral mix), so that, for example, the particular path of London or Paris could not be taken as a general model of future urban economies (Krätke 2007). London's extremely pronounced specialization on the financial sector that is at the heart of a neoliberal "dealer economy" represents a quite unique urban economic profile, which proved to be highly vulnerable after the breakdown of this particular model of capitalist development in 2008.

The emphasis on the city's prominent role as provider of specialized corporate services has also exerted strong influence on the "global city" line of urban research, which represents a particularly relevant concept of urban economic development in the era of intensifying globalization. This approach places cities' external economic relations and their positioning within globally extended corporate networks at the center of analysis. The advanced internationalization and global organization of economic activities in contemporary capitalism requires nodal points in the coordination and control of these global economic processes. Global cities, in which international financial and corporate services are concentrated, are functioning as locational centers for the production of a global control capacity (Sassen 1991, 2000). The notion of a "postindustrial society" is still influential in global city research and has led many scholars to focus on the city's service economy, particularly the so-called FIRE sector (finance, insurance, and real estate). However, whereas traditional concepts of the "service metropolis" have stressed the importance of a city's corporate services for the respective national economic territory, global city research concentrates on the *global* reach of the city's service capacities. The formation of a world city network that is based on the organizational networks of global service providers is the subject of research carried out by the "Globalization and

World Cities Study Group and Network" (GaWC; see Taylor 2004). Taylor (2004) explicitly emphasized that the GaWC analyses investigate *just one process* in global city development, that is, the "servicing of global capital." Yet the impact of globalization processes on urban economies cannot be exclusively related to the role played by global service providers. The expansion and diffusion of industrial urbanism on a global scale, which is led by the formation of global production networks with local anchoring points in metropolitan regions all over the world, is a most distinctive feature of the current phase of globalization (see Soja 2000; Dicken 2007). Cities included in the world city network are characterized by specific profiles of globally connected economic functions, which might well include technology-related R&D, research-intensive manufacturing activities, and global production networks' branch plants. Thus the world city network includes global cities focusing on advanced producer services as well as many other cities with differing profiles of their globally connected activities. This diversity might be interpreted as an articulation of "multiple globalizations" (see Taylor 2004) within the urban system. The "cities in globalization" line of research represents a relevant approach to urban economic analysis that still has great potential for thematic extensions and the deepening of our understanding of urban economic development in an era of intensifying global interurban networking. Since the early 1990s, however, further generalizing models of urban economic development have been presented which are closely related to this period's restructuring phases of urban economies.

The first phase has been shaped by the "new economy" bubble. The rise of information and communication technologies (ICT) and other new industries has been branded by the term "new economy" in order to indicate a superior quality and good prospects as compared to the "old economy" of traditional manufacturing industries (see Hübner 2005). On the level of cities, the related urban growth ideology and development concept emphasized the fact that cities that are able to become prime centers of new economy sectors, particularly the high-tech sectors of the ICT branches and technology-intensive subsectors of the media industries (such as multimedia and the Internet business), will be the winners of economic restructuring. Thus many cities focused their economic development strategy on the promotion of ICT activities and the expansion of the new economy. However, this new economy triggered a speculative bubble in the financial sector around new economy enterprises, which broke down in 2001. After the crash, the new economy hype was substituted by new generalizing concepts of the "lead sectors" of urban economic development.

A second line of debate on a promising strategy of restructuring and urban economic regeneration has been closely related to the cultural economy of cities. The spread of urban regeneration concepts, which drew on cities' cultural economy sectors and further cultural assets, has fostered an increasing interest in the cultural economy of cities. Economic geography and urban research highlighted the strong impact of the cultural economy sector (including the media industry and activities such as film and television, the music industry, publishing, the performing arts, etc.) on urban economies (Scott 2000), and detected its particularly strong embedding in inner urban areas (Krätke 2000, 2002a) as well as its selective clustering in particular centers of the urban system. However, the cultural focus of urban regeneration concepts was accompanied by rather exaggerated expectations concerning the cultural economy's possible contribution to the compensation of shrinking employment opportunities in traditional Fordist industries. In recent times, economic development concepts that concentrate on the city's cultural economy have continued to shape urban development strategies. Yet the cultural economy sectors have increasingly been equipped with the new fashionable branding of "creative industries" (see Garnham 2005; Hartley 2005). These include all of the cultural economy subsectors, with a minor extension to further creative activities such as the software and games industries. The new branding has artificially substituted the former analysis of the cultural economy of cities.

After the termination of the new economy hype in 2001, and parallel to the rise of culturally focused strategies of urban economic regeneration, the "knowledge-based city" became the most influential and still relevant concept of urban economic development and restructuring. This concept is based on the notion that the leading industrial countries' development paths are increasingly shaped by activities of an emerging "knowledge economy" that bets on the generation and economic exploitation of new knowledge in terms of continued innovation activities (Dunning 2000; Cooke 2002). The leading sectors of this model of development are the diverse knowledge-intensive branches of economic activity (including the above-mentioned knowledge-intensive producer services, the cultural economy, as well as research-intensive manufacturing activities). The knowledge-based economy represents an approach to capturing broad trends in contemporary economic restructuring which are of particular relevance to urban economies, since the knowledge-intensive subsectors of the economy are selectively concentrating in large cities and metropolitan regions (Krätke 2007). The debate on urban development prospects in the era of the knowledge economy (see Raspe and van Oort 2006) is strongly related to the debate on urban regions' innovation capacities and the role of cities as major innovation centers for diverse economic subsectors. The debate leads to a reinforced interest in the urban regions' innovation systems and highlights the relevance of knowledge networks and local knowledge spillovers (Tödtling, Lehner, and Trippl 2006; Krätke and Brandt 2009). The "knowledge-based city" concept might be criticized with regard to its prevalent fixation on high-tech industries and advanced producer services, which underestimates the quality and development of the knowledge base of traditional manufacturing sectors, and with regard to its uncritical representation of tendencies that are essentially embedded in capitalist economies' imperatives of accumulation and competition. The "knowledge economy" is not an alternative economic development model; it rather reflects a tendency in the core countries of capitalist economies to increasingly concentrate on knowledge-intensive sectors and activities within a globally extended functional spatial division of labor (see Dicken 2007). The rise of a finance-dominated regime of accumulation in particular is compatible with the notion of a knowledge-based economy, since the financial sector (as a driver of the financialization of capitalist economies) is regularly included among the knowledge-intensive economic subsectors. Nonetheless, the generalizing concept of a "knowledge economy" still represents a relevant perspective on urban economic development and restructuring that focuses on the urban regions' innovation capacities and the expansion of knowledge-intensive subsectors of the urban economy. Even scholars who predominantly contribute to the advancement of critical urban and regional theory have been influenced by this perspective: Allen Scott (2008) argues that the contemporary global resurgence of cities is based on the emergence of a "cognitive-cultural capitalism," the core sectors of which are technology-intensive manufacturing, business services, and cultural products industries (including design- and fashion-oriented forms of production). The underlying empirical generalization of sectoral restructuring trends in highly developed industrial countries might be appropriate, yet the term "cognitive-cultural capitalism" suggests that contemporary capitalism has reached a kind of "superior" stage of development and doesn't reflect the contradictory tendencies and destructive powers of today's global capitalism (see Harvey 2003, 2006; Zeller 2004).

In recent times, the "knowledge-based city" approach has been overtaken by the fashionable concept of the "creative city" as the locational center of a "creative class" (Florida 2004). The "creative city" approach starts from the assumption of a transformation from the industrial to a "knowledge society," in which creativity is becoming an increasingly important resource. This concept exploits the "cultural inflection" of contemporary urban analysis (Peck 2005) and deals with specific attraction factors of cities for members of the creative class, emphasizing particularly sociocultural attraction factors. According to this approach, the creative class is selectively concentrating itself in those cities that offer the best "qualities of place" in terms of specific cultural amenities. The concept combines with a booming debate on "creative industries" and has been transformed into a new urban growth ideology that is characterized by an affirmative concept of class and capitalist development (see Chapter 2). The theory of the creative class doesn't entail any critical account of the socioeconomic embedding of creative work in a capitalist society and economy. Furthermore, it doesn't touch the important question of how creative work is generating successful innovation in the institutional setting of capitalist industries and urban economies. The embedding of innovative capacities in urban and regional economies' specific socioeconomic configurations has been taken up more seriously in the framework of the "knowledge-based city" approach (see above). The macro-level analysis of urban regions' creative capacities (as presented by Florida 2005) predominantly deals with particular "human resource" factors of urban economies and their uneven distribution within the urban and regional system. A more detailed critique of Florida's creative city approach will be presented in Chapter 2 (see below).

Altogether, the rise of new economic subsectors that are strongly based on knowledge-intensive work and continued innovation activity has led to a resurgence of urban economies as strategic activity nodes in the core countries of global capitalism. However, the new urban growth sectors in total cannot compensate for the ongoing loss of traditional "regular" jobs in Fordist industries (due to "offshoring" etc.) and the decline of "regular" low-rank service sector jobs (due to rationalization and the exploitation of informal immigrant labor). Thus many large cities today are facing severe labor market pressures with regard to the large population group of less skilled workers, and are confronted with related problems of social polarization, even though they might achieve a "high rank" or positive development in the new economic growth sectors of knowledge-intensive industries. The urban population of these centers still contains large social groups which tend to be excluded from the gains of the "new islands" of urban growth. The capitalist city has never ceased to create economic and sociospatial polarization, whose driving forces are the imperatives of capital accumulation and competition, with their specific articulation in a system of competing urban regions.

The Role of Innovation and Interurban Competition in Harvey's Theory of Capitalist Urbanization

Returning to this chapter's starting point – the capitalist imperative of creativity and innovation – we will deal with essential arguments on the role of technological innovation and interregional competition in David Harvey's theory of the urban process under capitalism. Harvey proceeded from a detailed account of Marx's theory of capital (Marx 1981) with regard to its spatial implications (Harvey 1982). His work aimed at the integration of the production of spatial configurations as an active element in the development of capitalism. Harvey explicitly conceptualizes urbanization in the context of a predominantly capitalist mode of production (Harvey 1989: 17) and emphasizes the urban system's functioning as a "rational landscape for capital accumulation." He chose the urban as a distinct focus of analysis, without neglecting the relevance of other spatial scales (such as the regional, national, and global) at which the production of spatial configurations takes place. According to Brenner (2009), critical urban theory requires sustained engagement with contemporary patterns of capitalist urbanization, which become increasingly generalized on a world scale. By employing a political economy approach, Harvey presented various insights concerning the urban process under capitalism on which the analysis of creativity and innovation under the command of capital can draw. This section concentrates on a discussion of Harvey's ideas in order to arrive at a basic contextualization of the role of creativity and innovation in urban development under capitalism. Of particular interest is Harvey's approach regarding the spatial configurations of capitalism as an expression of capital flows which can switch their sectoral and geographical directions and imply the unfolding of various crises. Furthermore, the conceptualization of the urban region as a competitive economic and geopolitical unit within the geographical division of labor is relevant for understanding the general role of creative and innovative capacities in urban development.

In his account of the urban process under capitalism, Harvey (1989) emphasized the interplay of three different circuits of capital as a macroeconomic background that directs particular capital flows into the built environment and the infrastructures of technological innovation. In this way, the circuits of capital exert a profound impact on urban development. Harvey distinguishes a primary, secondary, and tertiary circuit of capital: the *primary circuit* is related to the capitalist production process, wherein the creation of surplus value can be focused on diverse forms of "absolutely" extended exploitation (representing "absolute surplus value" in terms of Marx's analysis of capital; see Marx 1981) or on productivity gains derived from innovation of the productive forces through the application of advanced technology, the reorganization of work processes, and the division of labor ("relative surplus value"). The driving force of this continued innovation activity at the level of the capitalist firm is competition and the search for surplus profits arising from the command of superior technology and organizational forms (see above). Harvey's conceptualization of a secondary and tertiary circuit of capital refers to the combined outcome of individual capitals' accumulation processes in the primary circuit, which are leading at the aggregate level to a tendency of periodic "overaccumulation" (Harvey 1989). Overaccumulation means that too much capital has been accumulated in relation to the opportunities to employ that capital profitably. The tendency may become manifest in the overproduction of commodities, in the creation of production capacities that exceed aggregate market potential, in falling rates of profit, in disposable money capital seeking for profitable investment opportunities.

In his account of the "industrial city" form of capitalist urbanization, Harvey emphasized that:

> interurban competition ... increased the pressures toward product innovation and technological change. The industrial city had to consolidate its function as an innovation center if it was to survive. But innovation ... also lay at the root of the overaccumulation problem ... Surpluses could be and were in part absorbed ... within the industrial city through an increasing flow of investments into long-term physical and social infrastructures. (1989: 33)

According to Harvey, the *secondary circuit* of capital denotes capital flows into the built environment for production and consumption. This circuit has a profound impact on urban development in terms of the extension and restructuring of urban infrastructures, and is closely related to the real estate sector. Investment in housing, commercial outlets, office buildings, and so on are included in the secondary circuit. The discontinuous flow of capital into the secondary circuit is detected as a source of "building cycles" (with temporary peaks of investment in the built environment). The switch of capital flows into the secondary circuit represents a feasible – but only temporary – solution to the overaccumulation problem.

The concept privileges investment in the built environment and the real estate sector as the focus of a secondary circuit. The switching of capital flows into large-scale "gentrification" projects and the proliferation of gentrification as a *global* urban development strategy (Smith 2002) can be regarded as a specific manifestation of investment activity in the built environment of cities that has become dominant in present times. However, it can be argued that there are further possible ways of dealing with the overaccumulation problem: according to Rosa Luxemburg (1951), the geographic expansion of capital investments in order to include new spaces in the process of capital accumulation represents a particularly relevant approach, as well as the switching of capital flows into sectors that have not yet been incorporated into the domain of private capital accumulation (as it is articulated by the continued struggle for privatization of ever more sectors and resources). Most important to the dynamic of a secondary circuit of capital flows, however, is the financial sector. The particular sphere of financial investments and the creation of "fictitious capital" has expanded greatly in contemporary capitalism (see Huffschmidt 2002; Chesnais 2004). Harvey's initial concept of a secondary circuit underestimated the continuous "unbounding" of the financial sector in modern capitalism. Part of this development is the incorporation of the real estate sector in the sphere of financial investment and the creation of fictitious capital (Krätke 1992, 1995). Harvey rather emphasized that "a general condition for the flow of capital into the secondary circuit is ... the existence of a functioning capital market and, perhaps, a state willing to finance and guarantee long-term, large-scale projects with respect to the creation of the built environment" (Harvey 1989: 65). This point apparently assigns a service function to the financial sector (i.e., mobilizing and offering financial means for large-scale investment in the urban built environment) and underestimates the sector's specific dynamic. In his more recent works, however, Harvey emphasizes the unbounding of the financial sector and its role in the proliferation of strategies of "accumulation by disposession" (Harvey 2003, 2006).

Accumulation by dispossession denotes the proliferation of accumulation practices that Marx had treated as "primitive" or "original" during the rise of capitalism. Today, such practices include the commodification and privatization of hitherto public assets and the conversion of various forms of property rights (common, collective, state, etc.) into exclusive private property rights; the neocolonial or imperialist appropriation of natural resources; the slave trade which shapes the contemporary sex industry; and, as the most devastating form of all, "financialization" in terms of the worldwide proliferation of speculative financial "products" that serve as a means of primitive accumulation. According to Harvey,

> the strong wave of financialization that set in after 1980 has been marked by its speculative and predatory style ... Deregulation allowed the financial system to become one of the main centers of redistributive activity through speculation, predation, fraud and thievery ... We have ... to look at the speculative raiding carried out by hedge funds and other major institutions of finance capital for these formed the real cutting edge of accumulation by dispossession on the global stage. (2006: 45–6)

With regard to the determinants of the 2008 world economic crisis, a detailed analysis of the proliferation of fraud and thievery in the contemporary financial business sector has been presented by Leo Müller, lecturer of "economic crime investigation," who comes to the conclusion that the financial sector is increasingly driven by criminal activities (Müller 2010).

Today, the secondary circuit of capital in the financial sector has become a dominating sphere of capital accumulation which increasingly decouples from the business of credit provision to the real economic sector. An increasing share of surplus capital desperately seeking profitable investment opportunities circulates within the sphere of speculative financial investments, derivative financial "products," and the business of dealing with financial assets. The term "casino-capitalism" is an accurate catchword reflecting the emergence of a finance-dominated regime of accumulation in contemporary capitalism (Aglietta 2000; Chesnais 2004; Windolf 2005). It is important to note that most large industrial corporations of the diverse manufacturing sectors are actively participating in financial sector deals and financial investment activities (outside the respective firms' real economy activity). In some cases, the share of financial business activity has overtaken the share of real sector manufacturing activity (the Siemens corporation, for example, has frequently been characterized as a "large bank equipped with an electrical engineering department"). Against this background, the industrial corporations can easily switch capital flows to the financial sector circuits. In a finance-dominated regime of accumulation, in which the secondary circuits of capital have become privileged fields of investment, and in which investment in financial assets is "overtaking" real sector investment activity, the capitalist imperative to enhance capital accumulation through technological and organizational innovation in the sphere of manufacturing processes is increasingly subject to competing strategic choices: investment in real sector innovation and technological change is no longer functioning as the major pathway to increased capital accumulation, since financial sector deals and speculative financial investment activities might appear as an equally relevant or even superior strategy. The main conclusion that can be drawn from the increasingly dominant role of the secondary circuit of capital is the point that capitalism today cannot be accurately characterized as an economic development model that is primarily based on continuous *technological* innovation. While technological innovation and the related processes of knowledge creation remain significant sources of competitive advantage and surplus profits, there are different and competing investment options that comply with the imperatives of capital accumulation. On the level of the urban system, some centers are specializing in their sectoral mix on the secondary circuits of capital (e.g., financial centers with a particularly strong share of the FIRE sector) and on the command and control of geographically extended value chains ("headquarter cities"), which offers the chance to channel the gains from manufacturing activities at distant locations into the respective command and control center. Thus on the level of cities and regions, too, there are different pathways to "economic success" in terms of enhanced capital accumulation.

Harvey's general concept of capital circulation also includes a *tertiary circuit* of capital, which comprises investment in science and technology, and a wide range of social expenditures. The tertiary circuit is for the most part mediated through the state, which channels tax income into sectors that are relevant for the reproduction of labor power or generating preconditions for enhanced surplus production. However, the ongoing political struggle on the issue of privatization of public services underlines the fact that there is growing pressure to transfer more and more tertiary circuit activities and subsectors to the domain of private capital accumulation – that is, the primary and secondary circuits of capital. This process of redirecting capital flows also includes intermediate forms such as public–private partnerships and the direct involvement of private capital in the public sector's infrastructural investment projects.

Switching capital flows into the tertiary circuit is suitable for expanding forms of investment that are indirectly productive in terms of expanding the basis for the production of surplus value. Investment in science and technology in particular helps to generate new scientific and technological knowledge that can be applied to expand capital accumulation. In the realm of the tertiary circuit, the development of science and technology is assigned to public higher education and research establishments. However, these establishments are for the most part engaged with basic scientific research (on which the more application-oriented research activities can draw), and they represent only one significant subsector of the national innovation system. Thus the tertiary circuit as conceptualized by Harvey is not the unique source of research and development which enables the expansion of capital accumulation. The national innovation system of capitalist countries basically comprises public higher education and research establishments, agencies for the transfer of knowledge and technology, as well as private research establishments in the form of private sector firms' R&D departments, or specialized private research establishments and related services that conduct knowledge creation and application-oriented technological research as a private business. A large share of investment in science and technology and related institutional arrangements is directly subject to the command of private capital. Thus research and development activities are to a large extent situated in close connection to the primary circuit of capital and can be conceived as an investment option competing with the strategy of switching capital into the secondary circuit. However, there is no reason to believe that all capitalist firms would privilege an innovation-oriented approach in their accumulation strategy. The rise of the secondary circuit of investment in financial assets and speculative deals can function as a threat to the flow of investment in productive innovation and related R&D activity. On the other hand, state-mediated investment in science and technology creates a "public innovation infrastructure" that functions as a basic component of national and regional innovation systems. The creative and innovative capacities of private sector R&D establishments can be enhanced through inter-firm cooperation and cooperation with public sector research establishments in a national and regional innovation system (see Chapter 3).

Harvey's basic conceptualization of capital circuits entails the sectoral and geographical switching of capital flows which imply the unfolding of imbalances and various crises. We can distinguish partial crises affecting a particular sector or geographical region that can potentially be resolved within that sector or region by reorganization, upgrading, and institutional reforms. Second, there are global crises that affect all sectors and regions of the capitalist production system. The current world economic crisis – which was triggered within the secondary circuit of capital by new financial sector accumulation strategies, and spread out to the real economy sectors – is a striking example. Interestingly, the large-scale "bail out" of financial sector firms entails the channeling of future tax income from the tertiary to the secondary circuit. Third, there are sectoral and geographical "switching crises" which stem from the massive relocation of capital from one sphere or geographical location to another. Switching crises involve a major redirection of capital flows. This dynamic can be related to Schumpeter's theory of economic development (Schumpeter 1952), which emphasizes the role of technological change. The process of technological change predominantly includes a sequence of incremental innovations at the level of capitalist firms. However, with regard to "long waves" of technological development, the capitalist economy periodically creates "basic innovations" in terms of new technologies that are becoming essential drivers of technological and organizational change in all subsectors of the economy (such as, at the present time, the new information technologies) and lead to the emergence of new industries. The reallocation of capital into emerging new industries involves a restructuring of the economy's sectoral mix, which can lead to the downgrading and decline of more traditional industrial subsectors. At the level of the urban and regional system, basic innovations and the rise of new industries can trigger geographical switching crises. Besides strategies of accumulation that are not directly related to basic technological innovations and that focus on the spatial extension of production networks, offshoring of jobs, and improvements of the functional spatial division of labor (see Henderson *et al.* 2002; Dicken 2007) – thereby contributing to the decline of regional centers of traditional industries – the rise of new industries implies the shifting of capital flows to the emerging centers of these new industries. This dynamic can be regarded as a specific articulation of capital's sustained search for "the command over and the creation of favourable locations" (Harvey 1989: 29). The active creation of new favorable locations that are essentially based on collective economies of scale through the agglomeration and clustering of activities in specific urban and regional centers is the main subject of Storper and Walker's "theory of geographical industrialization." Storper and Walker (1989) presented a political economy approach to regional development theory that starts from the capitalist imperative of technological change and emphasizes the dynamic of localization and clustering of new industries in cities and regions outside the long-established regional centers of foregoing phases of industrial and technological development. A major finding of this theory of the capitalist dynamic of geographical industrialization is the point that (new) "industries produce regions" through the active creation of locational advantages inherent to the processes of regional clustering (such as sector-related infrastructures, inter-firm networks, a specific knowledge base, and a specialized skilled labor pool). Harvey, too, referred to the role of specific regional economic mechanisms in the creation of favorable locations by saying that capitalist firms seek "to manage their own positive externality effects and to capture the benefits of the urban synergism which they consciously help to promote" (Harvey 1989: 137). Hence the search for surplus profits through technological innovation is not independent of the creation of locational advantages.

Throughout the historical development of capitalism, the city functioned as a centerpiece of accumulation and surplus production. Yet within the urban system, the pathways of accumulation and technological innovation varied from one city to another, and interurban competition further increased the pressures toward innovation and technological change. As competitive economic units within the geographical division of labor, cities rely on "systemic competitiveness" which is based on the sectoral mix and the socially produced collective assets that enhance innovative capacities of the urban economy. Thus in the field of technological change, it is not only individual firms that are competing, but more specifically urban and regional "innovation systems" comprising a diversity of actors and their relational fabric. The individual firms' competitive capacities are to a certain degree dependent on their interaction with the local and regional environment. In Harvey's theory, interurban competition is one important determinant in capitalism's evolution and fundamental to its uneven geographical development. At the urban scale, the search for profitable production possibilities and excess profits under conditions of heightened competition between firms and urban regions triggers shifts in the fortunes of individual cities in terms of the rise or decline of particular urban economies.

It is important to note that there are different pathways to urban competitiveness in capitalist societies. Besides an innovation-oriented path that focuses on the development of innovative capabilities (in diverse subsectors of an urban economy), the space economy of capitalism offers – at least for a number of major urban regions – the option to rely on economic command and control relations for attaining superior competitiveness in the urban system. This pathway is based on the concentration of capital and large firms' headquarters that are able to exploit spatially dispersed external production sites and attract inward flows of value-added from other urban regions. The command and control functions are regularly supplemented by a local concentration of advanced producer services (see Sassen 1991). Based on the interaction between these functions, metropolitan complexes of "strategic business activities" have developed which concentrate on the gains from controlling and managing supra-regional and global production networks in the spheres of manufacturing and producer services. The economic strength and competitive power of urban regions thus may stem from quite different sources, including different functional and sectoral structures as well as different development paths. We have to keep in mind that the unfolding of creativity and innovation activity represents a particular strategic asset in the framework of increasing interurban competition. According to Harvey (1989), in the present phase of capitalist development interurban competition takes on three forms of competition: for command and control functions, competition within the spatial division of labor, and competition within the spatial division of consumption.

The competition for command and control functions, as mentioned before, represents a strategic option that is particularly widespread among the established metropolitan centers of the urban system. This pathway might be supplemented, however, by efforts to enhance the respective urban regions' position within the spatial division of consumption. The extension of high-rank cultural amenities and the fostering of gentrification projects (in a broad sense) – which include many different forms of "upgrading" of the urban built environment according to the preferences of affluent citizens and functional elites of capitalist society – would be functional to the competition for command and control functions.

The urban regions' competition within the spatial division of labor can focus either on the "upgrading" of the urban economy's sectoral mix or on the strengthening of innovative capacities within the established industrial sectors. Strategies for upgrading the sectoral mix concentrate on expanding the urban region's share of firms and employment in prominent growth sectors of the respective period. In contemporary times, the high-tech manu-facturing sectors play a prominent role. More recently, the perspective has widened to include a larger variety of "knowledge-intensive industries" (including the so-called "creative industries") among the most promising growth sectors. By contrast, strategies for strengthening the innovative capacities of the urban economy can be geared toward any established industrial sector of the respective city. The focus of this approach would be the institutionalization and improvement of an urban or regional innovation system that links the relevant industries' firms, the urban region's research establishments, and further supportive institutions in order to strengthen the innovation-related environment for private sector firms' enhanced surplus production and market success.

On the level of capitalist firms, the capacity to develop and apply superior technologies and products as well as organizational forms yields surplus profits (based on "relative surplus value") and opens up comparatively good economic development prospects. However, the impact of a firm's innovation activities on employment is ambivalent: product innovation can result in job growth due to increased turnover and market share.

Organizational innovation can either be a component of intra-firm rationalization strategies or a component of the firm's spatial strategies, such as the supra-regional or global expansion of a firm's organizational network. Process innovation regularly implies shrinking employment figures related to a shift to superior processing technologies that entail the rationalization of intra-firm work processes. With regard to urban labor markets, the loss of jobs resulting from rationalization measures at the intra-firm level represents the downside of technological change. Nevertheless, according to Harvey, "a shift to superior technology and organization helps particular industries within an urban region survive in the face of sharpening competition" (Harvey 1989: 45). Therefore, the role of creativity and innovation in urban economic development might be generally characterized by saying that creative work which leads to technological innovation is functional to the interurban competition within the spatial division of labor. On the other hand, creative work that results in artistic innovation (in terms of the variation or creation of novel forms of cultural products) might *additionally* be functional to the interurban competition within the spatial division of consumption (see below). Cities that develop strong technological innovation capacities might attain a comparatively privileged position within the spatial division of labor as centers of technological innovation – in contrast to cities which predominantly perform "executive" manufacturing functions, or in contrast to declining cities with abandoned industrial activity.

According to Harvey (1989: 21), the spatial division of consumption is as important to the urban process as is the spatial division of labor. The economic development, internal organization, and specific urban qualities of cities such as Paris, Milan, New York, and other cities could not be understood without considering their role as places of consumption. The notion of the urban regions' competition within the spatial division of consumption refers to the qualities of the living environment (in a broad sense) that a city offers, particularly with regard to the more affluent strata of the population and the functional elites of capitalist society. These people possess a greater mobility (in terms of their ability to voluntarily relocate their place of residence) as compared to the working class and the urban poor. Interurban competition for circulating "consumer funds" is directed toward attracting affluent new citizens to the city, as well as cultural tourists, conference tourists, and so on. The competitive strategy in this realm is based on the extension of attractive shopping malls, cultural facilities, entertainment quarters, the insertion of signature architecture, the upgrading of built environments particularly in the inner city areas (as a precondition or supply-side component of gentrification projects), and the provision of high-quality "green" environments and leisure facilities. With regard to the role of the cultural economy sector, the positioning of an urban region as a center of cultural economy activities functions as a relevant ingredient of urban competitiveness within the spatial division of consumption (besides its role in the urban economy's industrial mix and its contribution to employment opportunities). A vital and expanding cultural economy sector, in combination with the development of diverse cultural facilities, contributes to a city's appearance as attractive, exciting, and creative in the realms of lifestyle, culture, and fashion. Hence cities that qualify as centers of cultural production activity might improve their competitive position by appropriating additional shares of circulating revenues (e.g., in the sphere of cultural tourism) and attracting affluent new inhabitants.

The close interrelation between the cultural economy's potential contribution to the development of the urban economy in terms of employment, new business formation, etc., and its specific role in strengthening the city's "consumerist attractivity" is at the heart of the contemporary rise of urban growth strategies that focus on the so-called "creative industries." Furthermore, there might be an interplay between the role of cities as centers for cultural innovation and conspicuous consumption and their role as workshops for advanced industrial production and technological innovation. However, we have to keep in mind that the formation of urban innovation centers needs a whole range of specific inputs beyond a mere "amenity based" local attraction and concentration of high-skilled or technologically creative workers (see Chapters 2 and 3).

Those urban regions that achieve a superior competitive position will survive, at least temporarily, better than those that do not (see Harvey 1989). With regard to a city's industrial sectors, a superior competitive position (temporarily) fuels growth in distinct subsectors of the urban economy and thus benefits the private sector firms located in the city as well as employment in the city's competitive sectors. Hence particular fractions of the local workforce might be facing expanding job opportunities and a temporary relief from the threat of local decline and shrinking of particular industries (related to sectoral or geographic switching crises; see above). The quality of workplaces in these growth sectors, however, might be polarized and partially downgraded (due to flexibilization and precarization of employment relations; see Peck 1996). In sum, Harvey's contribution to critical urban theory stresses the point that interurban competition in its diverse forms is fundamental to uneven development in the urban system of capitalism. Creative work that leads to technological innovation is functional to the interurban competition within the spatial division of labor, whereas creative work that results in artistic innovation additionally enhances a city's positioning with regard to the interurban competition within the spatial division of consumption.

Conclusion

This chapter has offered a basic contextualization of the issues of creativity and innovation in terms of outlining the capitalist imperative of innovation. The prevalent trend to decontextualize the issues of creativity and innovation from basic features of the historical social formation in which these capacities are developing has fostered the emergence and spread of new urban and regional growth ideologies that entail a glorification of capitalism as a socioeconomic formation essentially based on knowledge creation and superior innovative capacities. In such conceptions, the primary motives and the partially destructive powers of certain innovation activities that are developing under the command of capital are widely neglected. The chapter drew on Harvey's theory of capitalist urbanization, wherein the capitalist imperative of accumulation subordinates creative work and innovation activity to the continued race for competitive advantage and the appropriation of surplus profits. We presented a short review of generalizing models of urban economic development that intended to grasp the respective period's prime "motors" of urban economic growth. The rise of new economic subsectors that are strongly based on knowledge-intensive work and continued innovation activity has contributed to a resurgence of urban economies as strategic activity nodes in global capitalism. We proceeded to a discussion of Harvey's approach to urban theory, in which the spatial configurations of capitalism are basically regarded as an expression of capital flows that can switch their sectoral and geographical directions and imply the unfolding of various crises. I have suggested some modifications of the conceptualization of a secondary and tertiary circuit of capital and emphasized the advanced "decoupling" of the secondary from the primary circuit which has led to the rise of a finance-dominated regime of accumulation. In this model of capitalist development, the capitalist imperative to enhance capital accumulation through technological and organizational innovation in the sphere of manufacturing processes is increasingly subject to competing strategic choices – investment in real sector innovation and technological change is no longer functioning as the major pathway to increased capital accumulation, since financial sector deals and speculative financial investment activities can take on the role of an equally relevant or even superior strategy. While technological innovation and the related processes of knowledge creation remain significant sources of competitive advantage and surplus profits, the capitalist economy today can privilege different pathways and investment options that comply with the imperatives of capital accumulation. On the level of cities and regions, too, there are different pathways to "economic success" in terms of enhanced capital accumulation. Besides an innovation-oriented path that focuses on the development of innovative capabilities, the space economy of capitalism offers the option to rely on economic command and control relations for attaining superior competitiveness in the urban system. With regard to Harvey's conceptualization of the urban region as a competitive economic and geopolitical unit within the geographical division of labor, three basic strategic options of interurban competition were examined in order to contextualize the role of creative and innovative capacities in urban development. The unfolding of creativity and innovation activity represents a *particular* strategic option in the framework of increasing interurban competition.

Altogether, Harvey's theory emphasizes the embedding of creativity and innovation in the dynamic of capitalist development. However, the theory does not offer an account of the specific economic-geographical mechanisms that are at work in the formation of urban centers of creative and innovative activity. We need to proceed from the basic contextualization toward a more detailed account of creativity and innovation that employs relevant concepts of economic geography in order to investigate the development of creative and innovative capacities in their *specific* sectoral and regional/local contexts. This extended and detailed analysis represents the book's distinctive contribution to the "critical urban theory" literature discussed above. Yet Harvey's conceptualization of capitalist urbanization provides a comprehensive framework for our reasoning throughout the following chapters.

On a most general level of abstraction, creative work is characterized by a novel "composition" of ingredients such as specific knowledge and know-how. Since this kind of work is always embedded in different sectoral and spatial contexts, a variety of different "worlds of creativity" have emerged, which may coexist in the same local space and even interact with each other. Particularly within the urban space, we can detect different "worlds of creativity" and local innovation systems that are related to specific subsectors of economic activity. This level of analysis will be the subject of Chapters 3, 4, and 5. The next chapter will focus on the deconstruction of the new "creative city" growth ideology.

2

Creative Cities as a New Urban Growth Ideology
The Impact of Creative Occupations on Regional Economic Success

Introduction

According to Richard Florida's new "class theory," we are facing "a large-scale resorting of people among cities and regions..., with some regions becoming centers of the Creative Class, while others are composed of larger shares of Working Class or Service Class people ... The second trend is that the centers of the Creative Class are more likely to be economic winners" (Florida 2004: 235). Hence we can expect successful economic development in those cities and regions where the "creative class" is concentrated. Consequently, urban growth policy should be aimed at attracting members of the creative class (see Florida 2005). Politicians and social scientists in Germany and other European countries now widely subscribe to this concept. Florida's "creative class" theory has gained notoriety in part for its convincing simplicity. It identifies factors for success in regional economic development in an era of intense international competition, and is politically relevant as an easily understood orientating concept for political decision makers in cities and regions. Even German Chancellor Angela Merkel has referred to Florida's findings:

> Ladies and gentlemen, the American scientist Richard Florida has conducted research into the conditions for successful development in the world's regions. He has identified three factors: technology, talent and tolerance. He explains that it is only possible to obtain sustainable economic growth in the fields of development that are key to the future when all three factors are combined – technology, talent and tolerance. What a good message for us. What a good maxim for our actions. Our lives are based on technology, talent and tolerance.

The Creative Capital of Cities: Interactive Knowledge Creation and the Urbanization Economies of Innovation, First Edition. Stefan Krätke.
© 2011 Stefan Krätke. Published 2011 by Blackwell Publishing Ltd.

We are dependent on innovation, on scientific and technological development, on economic and social progress. (Speech at the University of Jewish Studies in Heidelberg on 12 July 2007; author's translation)

Florida's theory is founded on the assumption that we are undergoing a transformation from an industrial society to a knowledge-based society in which creativity is an increasingly important resource. Creativity is understood as the ability to generate new knowledge or to convert existing knowledge into economically successful applications. Focusing on the United States, Florida has demonstrated that the "creative class" is unequally distributed within the country's regional system, and that cities where the "creative class" is concentrated enjoy particularly strong growth in high-technology sectors (Florida 2004, 2005, 2008; Stolarick and Florida 2006; Florida, Mellander, and Stolarik 2008). Based on the assumption that new jobs in innovative and knowledge-intensive economic sectors are created primarily in cities where creative forces are concentrated ("jobs follow people"), Florida explores the specific factors that make cities attractive to members of the creative class. In particular, he emphasizes attractive sociocultural factors such as tolerance, openness, and cultural diversity: "Essentially my theory says that regional economic growth is driven by the location choices of creative people – the holders of creative capital – who prefer places that are diverse, tolerant and open to new ideas" (Florida 2004: 223). Florida ultimately recommends that political decision makers should ensure the availability of high-quality living and leisure amenities for the creative class, as the presence of the creative class encourages creative economic activities which are of great importance for future regional development (see Fritsch and Stützer 2007: 15). The creative class theory serves as the basis for a concept of "creative cities" that isolates a particular set of regional success factors which can be used for the extension and consolidation of entrepreneurial forms of urban governance.

This chapter provides a critique of Florida's creative class theory by combining a theoretical discussion with empirical research on success factors for regional economic development. In particular, the critique of Florida offered by Peck (2005) is further developed. Peck focuses on the urban policy dimension of the newfound cult of urban creativity (see below), emphasizing that the contemporary spread of creativity strategies perfectly works with "the grain of extant neoliberal development agendas, framed around interurban competition, gentrification, middle-class consumption and place-marketing" (Peck 2005: 740). Furthermore, the urban growth ideology of the "creative class" is characterized by its indifference to social polarization – a polarization that is both a prerequisite for the lifestyle of the urban elite and reinforced by inner-city redevelopment processes (Peck 2005). At the same time, social polarization is developing *within* the "creative" workforce in terms of a rapidly expanding freelance workforce with precarious life/ work conditions (see Chapters 4 and 5). Florida's affinity with neoliberal conceptions becomes particularly apparent in his glorification of flexibilized work relations: with reference to increasing flexibility of the creative workforce, Florida (2004: 135) informs us that "the old employment contract was group oriented and emphasized job security. The new one is tailored to the needs and desires of the individual." In the paradise of a new "horizontal" labor market, creative people enjoy "the freedom to move from job to job and to pursue interesting projects and activities" (Florida 2004: 135) in a work-life in which "the lights never go off; the computer never shuts down; the phone is never off" (Florida 2004: 123). With regard to the creative economy's freelancer workforce, Florida's theses can be read as a strikingly affirmative account of 24/7 work in a framework of continuous job-hopping. The overall message is: "We have come to terms with the new labor market ... We simply accept it as the way things are and go about our busy lives" (Florida 2004: 115).

In this chapter, Florida's theory is first evaluated with regard to its positive affirmation of current trends in capitalist development. Secondly, Florida's empirical research concepts are discussed in order to present an alternative approach to the assessment of regional success factors. This includes a discussion of how different groups of "creative workers" should be categorized in order to assess their impact on regional development. The following section presents selected findings of empirical tests of Florida's key claims with regard to Germany's urban and regional system. The final section concentrates on the interrelation between sociocultural "qualities of place" and the selective concentration of creative workers within the regional system, that is, the indirect and direct impact of sociocultural "attraction factors" on the regional concentration of a creative workforce. This section also considers the role of the "creative class" concept in the framework of neoliberalized urban politics.

Critique of Florida's Conception of the Creative Class

Florida's theory of the creative class is characterized by a highly affirmative conception of contemporary class society. Based on a rather nebulous definition of creativity, Florida presents a concept of social classes that is predominantly based on an arbitrary categorization. The creative class concept also promotes the self-glorification of leading occupational groups in a neoliberal model of society (see Butterwegge, Lösch, and Ptak 2008). With regard to its urban and regional policy implications, Florida's theory lends itself not just to the positive encouragement of openness, tolerance, and other sociocultural "attraction factors," but also to the restructuring of the urban space in favor of certain functional elites within a neoliberal social order, that is, gentrification projects and real-estate development for the *socially selective* enhancement of a city's attractiveness (Brenner and Theodore 2002; Harvey 2005).

Based on a superficial concept of "class" at odds with definitions used in political economy, social classes are delimited by occupational groups, social-status groups, income groups, and so on. By contrast, the political economy tradition defines classes on the basis of the specific income form that each category of people (class) obtains and offers a deeper analysis of the role of social classes in economic development (see Anderson 1974; Milios 2000). With regard to "classes" that are defined by occupational groups, Florida draws a distinction between (1) the working class, which is composed of people employed in industrial manufacturing, construction, transportation, etc.; (2) the service class, which is composed of people with less skilled service sector occupations, for example in health care, food services, cleaning, etc.; and (3) the agricultural class, which consists of farmers, fishermen, forest wardens, etc. According to Florida, a new fourth class, the "creative class," is particularly decisive for economic development in the current era. This idea strongly resembles Bell's (1974) notion of a professional class which comprises the leading social group in a "post-industrial society."

Florida's conception of the creative class ignores the difficulties associated with arriving at an accurate definition of creative activities (Howkins 2001). These definitional problems are particularly complicated by the fact that the vast majority of occupational groups in contemporary industrial society involve a certain degree of creativity. Technologically advanced manufacturing processes and the complex forms of economic organization that prevail in modern society would face severe disruption if a large share of the employees in industrial manufacturing occupations did not possess a highly developed "tacit/implicit knowledge" and creative problem-solving abilities. Furthermore, as Wilson and Keil (2008) have pointed out, creativity is also the working poor's major resource for survival in the diverse urban worlds of capitalism. Florida (2005) has responded to the criticism that his categorization of creative activities is arbitrary by allowing that all employees are creative or possess creative potential to some extent. This acknowledgment, however, has not led him to reconceptualize his "creative class" concept. The theory of the "creative class" is characterized by an apparent indifference to social polarization and the fact that the most creative places – the large metropolises of the urban system – tend to exhibit the most extensive forms of socioeconomic inequality (Peck 2005). If the members of the new "creative class," having a share of approximately 30% of the population (in the United States), are the "drivers" of economic development, the remaining uncreative two-thirds are merely passengers. In Florida's theory, the members of the working class and the service class are for the most part "portrayed as servants of the creative class, or the stranded inhabitants of hopeless cities" that are lacking creative potential (Peck 2005: 759). In Florida's own words (2004: xv), "the rise of creative work also brings with it a great deal of work in the service sector. Those of us who work long days and nights at the computer rely on those office cleaners, delivery people and many others in the service economy." Hence "members of the Creative Class ... require a growing pool of low-end service workers to take care of them and do their chores" (Florida 2004: 71). The "creative class" is lauded for its achievements in terms of economic growth and portrayed as a new elite, while the rest of society is rather defined by its creative deficits.

According to Florida, the creative class is composed of three different occupational groups. The first group consists of the "highly creative" occupations ("supercreative core"), including natural scientists and engineers, information scientists, economists, social scientists, physicians, architects, academics, and related occupational types. A second group, which Florida sometimes assigns to the supercreative core, but sometimes regards as a separate group, consists of the so-called "bohemians." This group encompasses diverse occupations in the sphere of the arts (i.e., writers, visual and performing artists, photographers, musicians, designers, etc.) as well as artistically creative occupations in the media and entertainment industry. The occupational groups which are defined as "bohemians" in Florida's approach are, in other research contexts, usually viewed as "cultural economy" occupations. A third creative-class group identified by Florida is the "creative professionals." This very heterogeneous group includes for the most part highly skilled employees who apply their professional knowledge in continuously changing contexts and interactive relations, including technicians, consultants, organizational experts, mediators, and brokers. This group additionally includes social and health care professionals, legal and business consultants, finance and real estate professionals, as well as politicians and government officials. Florida states that the "creative professionals" have the function of "supporting" economic growth, whereas the "supercreative core" is the actual wellspring of innovation and comprises the driving force of economic and technological development (see Fritsch and Stützer 2007: 17).

Florida's definition of the "creative class" is also highly questionable in terms of its various subgroupings. Based on the perspectives offered by innovation theory and regional innovation system analysis, it appears expedient to characterize the occupational groups which are engaged in research and development activities as "scientifically and technologically creative employees," and to regard particular regional concentrations of these employees as a factor explaining the respective regions' innovation capacities and economic development. If this categorization is to be used, however, the group of "scientifically and technologically creative employees" should also contain skilled technicians and health care professionals, which in Florida's theory are assigned to the third subgroup of creative professionals. In addition, the delimitation of a distinct group of "artistically creative occupations" (similar to Florida's "bohemians") seems reasonable for the purpose of research on the cultural economy of cities and regions as well as on the role of artistically creative workers and local cultural districts in urban and regional development. However, it does not seem justified to mix these groups together with Florida's third group of "creative professionals" in order to create an aggregate "creative class" category. It is here that Florida's approach becomes a strong affirmation of contemporary class society, an affirmation that promotes the self-glorification of "leading" occupational groups in contemporary capitalism. This might explain the great success of Florida's theory among the business elites. By denoting the functional elites of capitalist society as members of the "creative class," the new class category indeed captures essential fractions of the "dominant class ... – whose members occupy the power centers of industry, media and government" (Florida 2004: xxix). This subgroup of the "creative class" might particularly welcome Florida's statement that "the members of the Creative Class today need to see that their economic function makes them the natural – indeed the only possible – leaders of twenty-first-century society" (Florida 2004: 315). For the benefit of positive image construction, the subgroup of "creative professionals" in corporate management and financial business can also appreciate being placed alongside diverse groups of scientifically, technologically and artistically skilled people in the new "creative class" category. Florida (2004: 208) even claims that the rise of the creative class entails a chance for business people to become "celebrities in the truest sense of the term." The affirmative character of Florida's "creative class" construct in relation to the dominant classes in contemporary capitalism is further explained in the following three sections:

1. In contemporary capitalism, the "creative professionals" in finance and real estate do not abet knowledge-based economic development, as is commonly supposed. They cannot simply be characterized as "creative applicators of knowledge" that are "supporting" economic development. Rather, these professions represent a "dealer class" in a finance-dominated and increasingly speculative model of capitalist development (see Chapter 1). The financial sector no longer has a mere "supporting" function within the economy, but has become the dominant and driving force in a new model of capitalist development whose influence has spread to all economic spheres and subsectors. The deregulation of financial markets and loosening of supervision of banks exerted a decisive influence on the proliferation of this model of development. The social actors of the contemporary finance-dominated regime of accumulation have created "financial innovations"

that have destabilized global economic development. The development potential and innovation capacity of the manufacturing sectors have also been damaged by the current financial crisis. The "dealer economy" of neoliberal capitalism (see Butterwegge, Lösch, and Ptak 2008) represents *a threat* to economic development. The appropriateness of assigning financial and real estate professionals to the "creative class" is cast into doubt when one surveys the financial crises of the last two decades and the destructive role that financial markets have played in numerous instances (see Huffschmid 2002; Zeller 2004; Huffschmid, Köppen, and Rhode 2007). The current global economic crisis was triggered by the excesses of the dealer economy and has caused worldwide damage of extraordinary dimensions (see IMF 2009). In April 2009, the International Monetary Fund (IMF 2009) estimated that worldwide losses from the financial crisis would amount to nearly $4.1 trillion between 2007 and 2010. Harvey's warning (1989: 277) concerning the destructive powers of financialization turns out to be quite relevant to the current situation: "There are abundant cracks in the shaky edifice of modern capitalism.... The world's financial system – the central power in the present regime of accumulation – is in turmoil and weighed down with an excess of debt that puts such huge claims on future labor that it is hard to see any way to work out of it."

The neoliberal model of deregulated "casino capitalism" has proven to be extremely harmful to economic development all over the world. The current crisis is also leaving a mark on the real economy sectors in terms of rising unemployment (furthermore, causing millions of people in developing countries to fall below the poverty line). Credit has dried up in the crisis, and this is impairing growth and R&D activities in all sectors of the economy. In 2009, the European Patent Authority recorded a considerable decrease of patent applications due to shrinking R&D expenditure by private sector firms (*Tagesspiegel*, May 4, 2010). Investment in innovation activities is threatened by a shortage of sufficient sources of finance, particularly of venture capital (Ketzler and Schäfer 2009). Furthermore – as is usually the case in such crises – advocates of neoliberal capitalism have been calling for government bailouts of the banking sector. This amounts to the socialization of the private sector's losses. In light of current economic developments, a categorization of financial and real estate professionals as members of the "creative class" appears exceedingly naive.

One might even contest the common inclusion of the financial industry under the category of "knowledge-intensive services." According to Anderson (2008), many investment bankers in the City of London (as a leading center of "financial innovation") might have some expertise in the realms of gambling and drug use, but often lack a professional education in finance and certainly don't know anything about business ethics. A large share of "banksters" in the City of London – the outstanding elite of the dealer

class – were educated at elite universities, where they were inculcated with
the extraordinary arrogance that is essential for successful deals in the City
of London's milieu. Apparently, it is not knowledge or creativity, but rather
a specific sort of "cultural capital" (greed, ruthlessness, and arrogance) that
characterizes the best-rewarded functionaries of the dealer class.

2.   In a finance-dominated model of capitalist development, legal and
business consultants as well as the "manager class" perform decisive functions
in order to bring the economy and private sector firms in line with the
imperatives of maximized "shareholder value." Under the pressure of
financial investors, management practices characteristic of the "dealer
economy" have spread to firms in the basic manufacturing and service
sectors at the expense of far-sighted and innovation-oriented models of
business development (see Dörre and Holst 2009). With regard to the
consulting branch, the "creative" activity posited by Florida is highly questionable when one views the standardized products offered by prominent
consulting firms (such as McKinsey) and compares them to creative efforts
required in other areas of the economy, such as the invention of new
technologies. Today, the business consulting industry sends out its newly
minted MBA graduates to preach standard neoliberal management doctrine
to firms and public authorities. Creative activities in terms of real economic
innovation as defined by Schumpeter (1952) – that is, the initiation of
technological and organizational innovations on the basis of technological
and scientific research and development, or on the basis of interorganizational knowledge networking and cooperative inter-firm relations – are
today advocated by a rather "old-fashioned" subgroup of professional
consultants and firm managers who are still attached to the former industrial
model of capitalist development. However, this does not justify the
all-inclusive categorization of managers and consultants as members of a
"creative class." It is worthwhile to remember that Schumpeter's analysis
(1952) of capitalist development starts from the realistic assumption that only
a minority of entrepreneurs and firm managers can be described as "creative
innovators"; the vast majority are instead mere imitators of familiar routines,
business models, and product configurations.

However, the reigning practices and logic of the global financial business
has had wide-reaching influence on the development of social values in large
parts of contemporary society. The "dealer class" is constantly striving for
financial gains based on advantageous short-term business transactions and
not based on the traditional economic performance of the "real economy."
In this way, a logic of action prevails in most major markets of the global
economy which disregards old-fashioned principles of performance at the
expense of rapid gains. This trend has had a powerful influence on social
values. The dealer class has established an economic "culture of chance"
which undermines the principle of good performance. The fast and effortless

acquisition of wealth and fame is the new religion. This model has deeply influenced the younger generation and the working class, whose daily lives are imbued with the modern magic of games of chance, and with the hope of suddenly being "discovered" by the media, fashion, or culture industries (Neckel 2000).

3.   Considerable doubt is also justified with regard to Florida's inclusion of the "political class" – members of legislative bodies, politicians, and public administrators – in the category of the "creative class." The idealization of the representatives of the political class as "creative applicators" of existing knowledge is fostering a depoliticization of the questionable knowledge base and actions of political office holders and functionary cliques in an era of neoliberal class struggle. In general, we have to be aware that the political system may contain "systemic" hindrances to the development of creativity in the arena of politics (see Roth 2001). However, this point will not be discussed here from the perspective of political science. With regard to Germany, the majority of the political class supports a neoliberal economic and social model (see Müller 2005). For more than two decades, the political class has carried out "reform measures" that have led to increasing social polarization and, with regard to the intentional promotion of the dealer economy, have undermined the country's innovative capacity and economic development potential. Former German Chancellor Gerhard Schröder, who initiated a war against the unemployed with his "Hartz 4" legislation, opened up Germany to the international financial service sector (see Herr 2009). The country's real economy sector has been severely damaged as a result. Private equity firms and hedge funds have acquired a large number of formerly stable, innovative mid-sized firms in Germany and have encumbered them with extraordinarily high levels of debt. Due to the weakened equity position of these firms, many of them will not survive the current crisis. As an economic actor, the government has adopted the business strategies of the neoliberal dealer economy and has actively participated in the dealer economy's speculative financial business. Many of Germany's regional state banks (Landesbanken) have purchased high volumes of securitized real estate debt from the United States (Müller 2010). Thus far, these purchases have generated losses of €21 billion – which the country's taxpayers have been forced to absorb. In an attempt to address the crisis, the German government passed a €480 billion economic rescue package. Today, the political class appears to demonstrate a "creative" potential mostly with regard to the socialization of the tremendous losses which have been caused by a finance-dominated model of economic development.

Our critique of Florida's poorly defined "creative class" concept arrives at the conclusion that a more differentiated categorization is necessary. The "creative" professionals active in finance, real estate, management, and consulting sectors do not represent a relevant driver of regional economic success when compared to other occupational groups, such as the "scientifically and technologically creative" workforce. This thesis can be tested empirically by analyzing the impact that diverse occupational groups have on *various* dimensions of regional "economic success," which should not be viewed solely in terms of growth in high-technology sectors. One appropriate measure of "successful" economic development is the growth in a region's employment figures. To account for structural change, another appropriate measure is employment growth in knowledge-intensive economic activities. There are of course further relevant dimensions of urban and regional economic success.

In her critique of Florida's approach, Markusen (2006a) too emphasized that the "creative class" rubric lumps together many disparate occupations which play different roles in urban development. Markusen called for a disaggregation of the "creative class" in terms of a differentiated account of particular occupational groups, and presented an analysis focused on a group of artists, underscoring the point that artists as a group make relevant positive contributions to urban economies and the cultural vitality of cities, but do not concentrate in cities that are necessarily high-tech centers or rapidly growing. Hence Markusen rejects Florida's claim of a causal link between the presence of the creative class and urban economic growth.

In order to analyze the impact of creative occupational groups on regional innovative capacities and economic development, Florida's "creative class" aggregate can be subdivided into five groups. Only the first two have specific relevance for regional innovative capacities:

1. Scientifically and technologically creative workers (occupational groups in the fields of R&D, scientific education, as well as skilled technicians and health care professionals).
2. Artistically creative workers (occupational groups of the cultural economy).
3. The dealer class (finance and real estate professionals).
4. The economic management class (executives, business consultants).
5. The political class (members of legislative bodies, politicians, public administrators).

The rough categorization in groups 3–5 might be understood as generalized groupings analogous to Florida's way of constructing "classes." A rough categorization cannot, of course, take the place of a deeper theoretical analysis of changing class structures in the current era of capitalist development. In contrast to Florida's approach, this book argues that groups 3–5 have no specific impact on prospects for *regional* growth within the scope of innovation-driven development paths. Regional economic development is dependent on the performance of all working people. A focus on the impact that particular subgroups of the "creative" workforce have on regional innovative capacities appears appropriate, as this represents an extremely important topic in contemporary regional research. This does not imply, however, that other subgroups in a region's workforce (such as the traditional working class, or individuals in "low-end" service sector occupations) have no significant influence on regional economic performance.

An Assessment of Regional Economic Success Factors and the Impact of Creative Workers on Regional Development

As empirical evidence for his theory of the "creative class," Florida points to the existence of a significant correlation between regional concentrations of the "creative class" and growth in high-technology sectors (Florida 2005). A clear flaw in this claim is that correlation does not imply causality. Moreover, as Florida's "creative class" aggregate is ill defined, its regional concentration represents nothing more than a co-location of quite heterogeneous social and functional groups. Co-location doesn't necessarily mean that there exists a relationship of interdependence between the locational preferences of occupational groups that are co-located in particular urban regions. A co-location of heterogeneous social and functional groups, diverse economic subsectors, heterogeneous sociocultural milieus, etc. is a defining property of urban regions and particularly of large cities. As a consequence, there is little reason to assume that a concentration of, say, financial and real estate professionals in a particular city might *cause* a corresponding concentration of scientifically and technologically creative workers. In large cities, many statistical correlations between diverse "populations" of the respective territory are detectable – for example, a correlation between the number of hot-dog stands, high-technology firms, drug dealers, financial products dealers, etc. The claim that a causal relationship exists must always be theoretically justified.

It might be reasonable to assume that a concentration of artistically creative workers has a direct impact on the concentration of one particular subgroup of Florida's "creative professionals," however – the "bobos," or bourgeois-bohemians (Brooks 2000). This group represents a new lifestyle variant beyond the standard "new urban professionals" of the yuppie and DINK (double income no kids) variety, and has been identified in urban sociology as a key group that triggers the gentrification of attractive inner-city districts (see Blasius 1993). The bourgeois-bohemian combines a conventional attitude toward economic success with an "alternative style" and might be distinguished from other bourgeois elites by a model of consumption, which – in contrast to the conspicuous consumption of luxury goods – prefers expensive objects with a degree of practical usefulness, such as SUVs for inner-city driving, granite-walled showers instead of golden fittings, professional high-performance stoves instead of designer kitchens, and so on. A local concentration of bohemians might attract bobos, as both favor "cool clubs" and other "trendy" locations. In any event, the identification of a causal relationship between local concentrations of bohemians and bobos is not very relevant to explaining urban economic development, and won't be pursued further here.

Florida's line of argumentation with regard to regional science emphasizes that regional economic prosperity above all depends on a combination of "technology, talent and tolerance" (Florida 2005: 37): "The key to understanding the new geography of creativity and its effects on economic outcomes lies in what I call the *3 T's* of economic development: *Technology, Talent,* and *Tolerance.* Creativity and the members of the Creative Class take root in places that possess all three of these critical factors." This is the main thesis of the "three T's" (see also Knudsen *et al.* 2008), whose catchword character is most attractive to members of the political class. According to Florida, the interrelation of the three T's is as follows. In those cities and regions that have a concentration of the "creative class" (i.e., "talent"), high-technology sectors exhibit particularly strong growth (thesis no. 1). In a reductionist fashion, Florida regards "technology" – in particular, "high technology" – as the key indicator of regional economic success. In this way, he fails to recognize that cities and regions might also achieve successful economic development on the basis of quite different profiles of their economy's sectoral mix (see Krätke 2007). Furthermore, Florida neglects the relevant point that a regional concentration of creative forces in the area of research and development could have a *directly* positive impact on a region's innovative capacity. However, the presence of a scientifically and techno-logically creative workforce has to be combined with further constitutive factors of a regional innovation system. The assumption that a regional concentration of "talent" might be a prerequisite for achieving a particularly high regional innovation output is theoretically plausible and open to empi-rical testing, yet the successful innovation activities might be located in quite different subsectors of a region's economy. The foregoing points underline that Florida's conception does not conform with the state of scholarship in regional innovation research and that his way of relating "talent" and "technology" might be regarded as a remarkable exercise in simplification. Yet the Florida approach still survives, despite these shortcomings, due to its "ideological fit" and affinity to neoliberalized urban politics (see below).

The second main thesis in Florida's line of argument is that the creative class (or "talent") is selectively concentrated in those cities and regions which offer the best "qualities of place" (thesis no. 2). According to Florida, qualities of place are to be understood first and foremost in terms of cultural amenities of a specific character that are particularly attractive to members of the creative class (in contrast to traditional notions of urban cultural amenities), such as a "vibrant music scene," or "cool" clubs, pubs, and restaurants, etc. Second, qualities of place are to be understood in terms of particular sociocultural qualities such as "openness and tolerance" and "cultural diversity." This conceptualization of qualities of place within urban settings might contribute to a better understanding of the relation between economic activity and its sociospatial environment. Since a direct measure of sociocultural qualities of place for the purpose of comparative empirical research is not really possible, Florida has presented quite interesting concepts for the indirect measurement of such qualities, such as the "gay index" as an indicator of a city's "openness and tolerance" vis-à-vis different social milieus. The relevance of sociocultural qualities of place and particularly of openness, tolerance, and diversity for the economic development of urban regions has been emphasized in many contributions to urban and regional research (Landry 2000; Krätke 2002a, 2002b; Helbrecht 2005; Cooke and Lazzeretti 2008a). Empirical analysis could prove the assumption that a regional concentration of "artistically creative" people (or, in Florida's terms, "bohemians") exerts a power of attraction on the "scientifically and technologically creative" workforce. However, one has to keep in mind that the meaningfulness of analyzing this relation might be restricted, as the co-location of both groups in urban areas might not be the product of a direct causal link. The assumption that people with technologically creative occupations would prefer to live in places that are characterized by a concentration of "bohemians" is a critical point. However, a regional concentration of "artistically creative" people could also be used as an indirect indicator of qualities of place in terms of a "vibrant cultural scene." This implies the thesis that a vibrant cultural life functions as an attraction factor for people with scientific and technologically creative occupations.

The "openness" and "tolerance" of a city or region's population are additional sociocultural qualities of place. As these criteria are even more difficult to operationalize, we are in need of plausible auxiliary indicators. A basic problem concerns the heterogeneity of social milieus and attitudes of the population in large cities. Statements about openness and tolerance which are ascribed in a broad manner to a city or region's population should always be understood as rough generalizations. Even in a city which is generally perceived as a highly "tolerant" place for living, a more differentiated analysis might reveal xenophobic or racist attitudes among certain groups of the urban population or in particular urban districts. General statements about the sociocultural attitudes of an urban population are thus only tenable if the assessment's "fuzziness" is kept in mind. On the whole, it seems relevant to analyze the relation between regional economic success and the sociocultural qualities of cities and regions in order to test the hypothesis that "good" sociocultural qualities of place positively affect regional economic development.

Altogether, it should be emphasized that, in Florida's approach, the artistically creative workforce and the cultural economy are removed from their traditional niche function among the so-called "soft" location factors and elevated to a central position among the key factors for regional success. However, Florida's "creative class" concept does not touch the unfolding of creativity in a deeper sense. Rather, it deals with the regional distribution of human resources in particular occupational groups and its impact on regional economic development. In Florida's approach, the artistically creative workforce – which in other debates are defined as actors of the cultural economy – are categorized as "bohemians," and represent a particular subgroup of the "creative class." Florida scarcely claims that the bohemians exert a direct economic impact. They are rather viewed as a locational factor that attracts other members of the supercreative core and creative professionals. Most scholarship on the cultural economy within the subfield of regional science, however, emphasizes that the cultural economy or the so-called "creative industries" by themselves can be characterized as a relevant economic growth sector which strengthens the economic development of cities and regions (for the United States see Scott 2000, 2008; Power and Scott 2004; Markusen 2006a, 2008; for the United Kingdom see Pratt 1997, 2009; Hutton 2008; Evans 2009; for Germany see Krätke 2002a, 2002b, 2003, 2004a; Mossig 2006; Söndermann and Fesel 2007; for Switzerland see Klaus 2006; for Italy see Cooke and Lazzeretti 2008a).

An alternative approach to the empirical analysis of the creative workforce's impact on regional economic development should first of all depart from Florida's concept of reducing the success factors for regional economic development to the growth of high-technology sectors. The "wealth of regions" stems from different economic profiles and development paths. In headquarter cities and financial centers, the wealth of regions is to a large extent reliant on inflows of wealth created by productive activities in other regions. For a city and region's population, the overall growth of regional employment figures can be viewed as a key indicator of regional economic success. The egalitarian distribution of income and income growth across the various strata of a region's workforce would represent further relevant indicators of economic success, provided we dispense with the neoliberal perspective that income polarization is not harmful to urban and regional economies. In the long run, regional economic success is also dependent on a region's capacity to "upgrade" its sectoral structure and economic performance (Goodall 1972; Jacobs 1984). Within the framework of a development path aimed at an increasingly knowledge-intensive economy – with a key emphasis on research-intensive manufacturing activities (encompassing the "high-tech" and "medium-high-tech" branches) and a variety of knowledge-intensive services (such as knowledge-intensive technology-related services) – successful regional economic development could be related to the growth of employment in research-intensive industries and knowledge-intensive technology-related services (Dunning 2000; Acs, de Groot, and Nijkamp 2002; Cooke 2002; Lo and Schamp 2003; Raspe and van Oort 2006; Fromhold-Eisebith 2009). In addition, successful regional economic development can be related to a region's innovative capacity, which can be measured (with some reservations) by the number of patent applications filed by a region's firms. It would be problematic to identify the "emerging" regions of a knowledge-intensive economy solely by means of regional GDP (gross domestic product) growth, as GDP figures also include the returns generated by the finance and real estate sector's "dealer economy" as well as profit inflows appropriated from other regions (due to the "external economic control relations" of a region's firms; see Gräber *et al.* 1987; Krätke 1995). In this way, we can identify the economically successful regions of an emerging knowledge-intensive economy primarily by the growth of employment in research-intensive economic subsectors and by innovation activity (as measured by patent applications). GDP growth might be taken into account as an additional indicator of regional economic development, if the above-mentioned reservations are kept in mind. However, most important in this regard is the realization that regional economic success has many dimensions.

The impact of creative workers on regional economic development can thus be analyzed based on an alternative model founded on the hypothesis that cities and regions with a comparatively high concentration of employees in scientifically and technologically creative occupations exhibit successful regional economic development based on the above-named factors. The analysis should also include additional influencing factors such as the relative concentration of large firms (with headquarter functions, external control relations, and in many cases large R&D centers). This analysis differs from the superficial correlations that are dominant in Florida's analysis of regional success factors. Occupational groups 3–5 in the first section's discussion of Florida's theory (i.e., the dealer class, economic management class, and political class) should not be viewed as constitutive success factors of an innovation-based regional economic development path. As recent history shows, elements of these occupational groups can exert a rather destructive influence on productive sectors and innovation-based regional development. However, the regional economic impacts of the neoliberal dealer economy cannot be comprehensively grasped in the framework of comparative empirical analyses of a country's regional system.

The Impact of Creative Occupational Groups
on Regional Economic Development in Germany

With empirical analysis at the macro level of a country's regional system we can easily show that a regional concentration of employment in the sciences and technology has a positive impact on regional economic development. The analysis conducted here is based on regional data maintained by the Federal Institute for Employment on the workforce in 439 districts and various subsectors of the economy (see the Appendix: "Grouping of Occupations," "Grouping of Economic Subsectors"). These data are supplemented by the author's own evaluation of a database of large commercial firms to determine the regional distribution of large firms and their headquarters. In addition, the analysis also makes use of regional data on "artistically creative" occupations supplied by the German Social Security Fund for Artists (Künstlersozialkasse), regional economic data supplied by the statistical offices of the German states, data taken from a German patent directory (Schmiedl and Niedermeyer 2006), and regional data on the spread of xenophobic or racist attitudes in the German states (supplied by the Institute of Sociology at the University of Bielefeld).

The alternative approach to Florida's analysis provided here is founded on a comparative empirical analysis of Germany's regional system. This analysis verifies the central hypothesis that a regional concentration of scientifically and technologically creative occupational groups has a positive impact on regional economic development. This thesis can be proven without resorting to Florida's theories and their implicit endorsement of contemporary class society.

In Germany's regional system, the scientifically and technologically creative workforce is predominantly concentrated in the core cities of metropolitan regions such as Munich, Hamburg, Berlin, Stuttgart, Frankfurt am Main, and the Rhine–Ruhr Valley (see Figure 2.1). Other relevant centers with a large number of employees in these creative occupations include Karlsruhe, Nuremberg, Braunschweig, Dresden, and Leipzig. A detailed investigation of the regional system, however, reveals that cities and regions with a comparatively high share of creative occupational groups are characterized by different "occupational profiles" (see Appendix, Table A.1). Some regions are home to a high share of creative workers and at the same time to a comparatively low share of other "high-ranked" occupational groups, such as financial services and real estate. Other regions combine a high share of creative workers with a high share of other "high-ranked" occupational groups. An extreme case is the city of Frankfurt am Main, where the proportion of financial professionals even exceeds that of the scientifically and technologically creative workforce (see Appendix, Table A.1). Theoretical considerations concerning the interrelationship

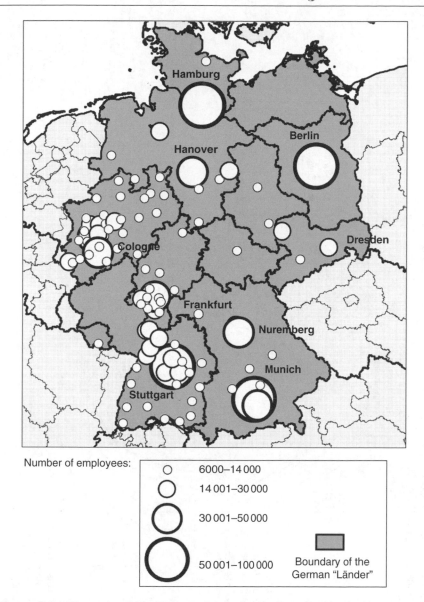

Figure 2.1 The regional distribution of the scientifically and technologically creative workforce in Germany, 2005.

between a "creative" workforce and regional economic success must take into account the variation of occupational profiles within the urban and regional system. Furthermore, it is necessary to be aware that regions with a comparatively high share of "knowledge-intensive" subsectors are

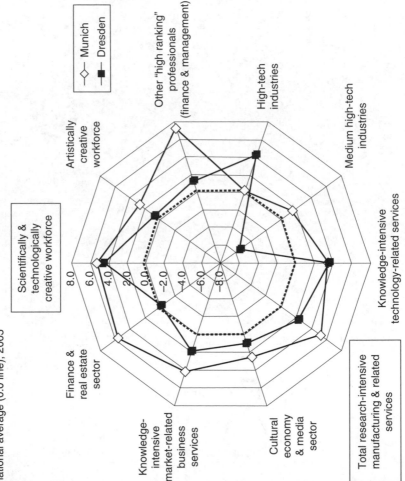

Occupational concentration in selected cities: Percentage-point deviation from the national average (0.0 line), 2005

Figure 2.2 Comparison of the regional economic profiles of two large "high-technology" centers in Germany.

characterized by different "sectoral profiles" (see Appendix, Table A.2). On the one hand, a high share of so-called knowledge-intensive subsectors can be based on a comparatively high share of research-intensive manufacturing sectors and technology-related services. This stands in contrast, on the other hand, to cities and regions which are specialized in knowledge-intensive business services and the financial sector (the city of Frankfurt am Main is good example of this profile; see Appendix, Table A.2).

A certain degree of correspondence is also evident between the occupational and sectoral profiles of a given region. A regional economic profile can be developed by comparing employment in various occupational groups and subsectors to the national average. A comparison of Munich (in southern Germany) with Dresden (in eastern Germany) – which, in the German regional system, are two large cities on a path of economic development based on high technology – is illuminating. The regional economic profiles of both cities reveal a clear correspondence between an above-average proportion of research-intensive manufacturing and technology-related services and the size of the scientifically and technologically creative workforce as a share of total employment (see Figure 2.2). In the city of Munich – which has a strong position among Germany's "media cities" – the relative share of the media and cultural economy exceeds the national average, a fact that is reflected by an "oversized" artistically creative workforce. The most striking difference between Munich and Dresden relates to the size of their financial and business-service sectors. In Dresden, these subsectors and the associated occupational groups are underrepresented. In Munich, however, the financial, real estate, and business-service sectors are all larger than the German average (see Figure 2.2). This, in turn, is reflected in an above-average share of workers in the "high-ranked" fields of financial services, management, and consulting. Munich's regional economic profile is clearly related to its function as a center of business and finance and as a "headquarter city." In this way, Munich combines the profile of a center of research-intensive manufacturing and related services with the profile of a headquarter city. The examples of Dresden and Munich highlight the fact that the creative workforce of a region is "embedded" in a particular regional economic profile. However, the correspondence between occupational and sectoral profiles only becomes clear if an analysis of the impact exerted by creative occupations on regional development goes beyond an all-embracing and undifferentiated "creative class" concept.

Florida's new urban growth ideology claims that the creative class is the key to regional economic success. Yet which are the relevant dimensions of regional economic success? Existing studies emphasize that the "wealth of regions" stems from different economic profiles and development paths. In headquarter cities and financial centers, inflows of wealth from productive activities in other regions might play a significant role in "economic success." However, within the framework of a regional development path that focuses on a knowledge-intensive and innovation-driven economy, regional economic success is becoming ever more dependent on the expansion of research-intensive sectors and innovation capacities.

We will distinguish four key components of "regional economic success":

1. Regional GDP growth (including the impact of wealth appropriation through external control capacities).
2. Total regional employment growth.
3. Employment growth in research-intensive manufacturing subsectors and technology-related services.
4. "Innovation output" in terms of successful patent applications.

At the macro level of quantitative empirical analysis of a country's regional system, factors influencing regional economic success can be roughly represented by the following quantitative indicators: (a) the number of large firms with external control capacities; (b) the share of large firms (representing "leading firms" among regional firms); (c) the number of manufacturing plants (indicating the concentration or clustering of industrial activity); and (d) the number of scientifically and technologically creative workers.

Although a central assumption of this analysis is that cities and regions with a comparatively strong concentration of workers in scientifically and technologically creative occupations should rank well in the above measures of regional economic success, a deeper analysis would start from the thesis that cities and regions with a strong "regional innovation system" can expect the most successful (and sustainable) economic development (Braczyk, Cooke, and Heidenreich 1998; Cooke 2002; Fornahl and Brenner 2003; Asheim and Gertler 2005). From this perspective, a concentration of scientific and technologically creative workers represents a "human resources" factor in the regional innovation system. This system is comprised of: (1) the internal innovation capacity of the region's firms; (2) the region's innovation infrastructure in terms of universities and research establishments; and (3) the region's knowledge network in terms of the density of innovation-related cooperative ties between businesses, universities, and research institutions (Grotz and Schätzl 2001; Graf 2006; Krätke and Brandt 2009).

In order to investigate the relationship between "knowledge-intensive manufacturing activities" and the size of the scientifically and technologically creative workforce, it is first necessary to note that there is a growing trend in the manufacturing sector to outsource technology-related service functions which were previously performed inside the firm (such as technical testing, laboratory services, etc.; Krätke 2007). In this way, it seems reasonable to create a composite group by combining the research-intensive manufacturing subsectors with technology-related services which are functionally coupled with manufacturing (for more details, see the Appendix).

Our empirical analysis reveals that there is a strong and significant relationship on a regional level between the relative share of "knowledge-intensive manufacturing activities" and the proportional size of the scientifically and technologically creative workforce (as the independent variable – see Figure 2.3; the independent variable accounts for 44% of regional variance and is highly significant at the 0.01 level). A concentration of scientifically and technologically creative workers thus appears to have a significant positive effect on a region's economic development potential. By contrast, there is no significant relation between the share of "knowledge-intensive manufacturing activities" and the share of skilled professionals in the fields of financial services, management, and consulting (see Figure 2.4; the independent variable accounts for no more than 5% of regional variance, and its influence is not significant even at a level of 0.05). Thus, the regional distribution of the "dealer class" (or, to use Florida's term, "creative professionals") does not appear to have a significant impact on regional success in developing future-oriented economic structures.

Further evidence of the strong influence exerted by the scientifically and technologically creative workforce on regional economic development can be found by conducting a comparative analysis of regional economic profiles. A profile for each region can be developed by measuring the share of employment in various subsectors and occupational groups against the German average. In the German regional system, Ulm (in southern Germany) and Jena (in eastern Germany) are two examples of successful "high-technology" cities in a smaller size class than the large cities analyzed above. Jena and Ulm's regional economic profiles reveal a strong correspondence between the size of the research-intensive manufacturing and technology-related service sectors and the size of the scientifically and technologically creative workforce as a share of total employment (see Figure 2.5). In addition, the proportional size of the culture and media sectors in these cities is essentially on par with the national average. This is also true for the size of the workforce in artistically creative occupations. Therefore, while it is assumed that artistically creative workers have a positive impact on regional economic success, this dynamic is only relevant in cities with a significantly large cultural and media sector (see above). Furthermore, our analysis reveals that in selected cities with a developed "high-technology" profile, the "high-ranked" fields of financial services, management, and consulting do not play a decisive role in shaping regional success.

So far, the analysis has demonstrated that the "high-ranked" professions of financial services, real estate, management, and consulting do not represent a relevant driver of regional economic success when compared to the productive impact of the scientifically and technologically creative workforce.

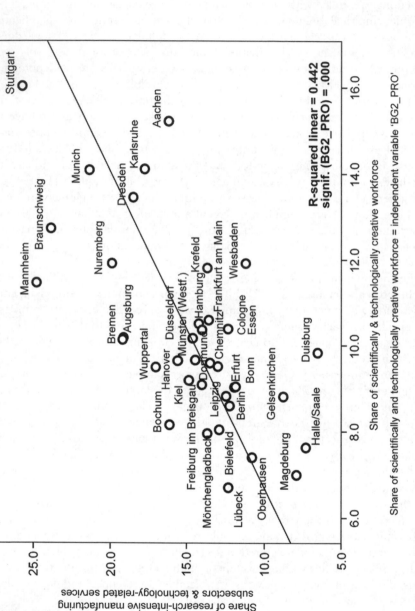

Figure 2.3 Relationship between the proportional size of the research-intensive manufacturing and technology-related services sector and the scientifically and technologically creative workforce on a regional basis in Germany, 2005 (cities > 200 000 inhabitants).

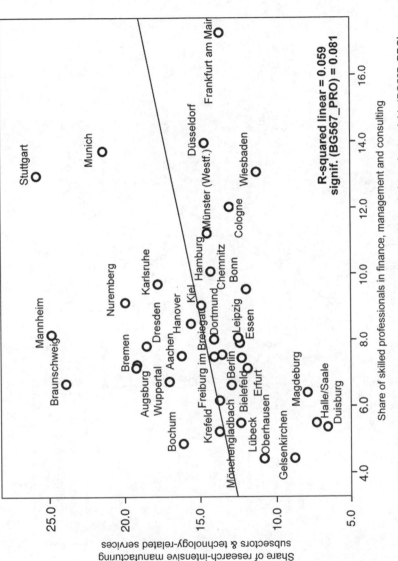

Figure 2.4 Relationship between the proportional size of the research-intensive manufacturing and technology-related service sector and the share of the workforce in the fields of financial services, management, and consulting on a regional basis in Germany, 2005 (cities > 200 000 inhabitants).

Occupational concentration in selected cities: Percentage-point deviation from the national average (0,0 line), 2005

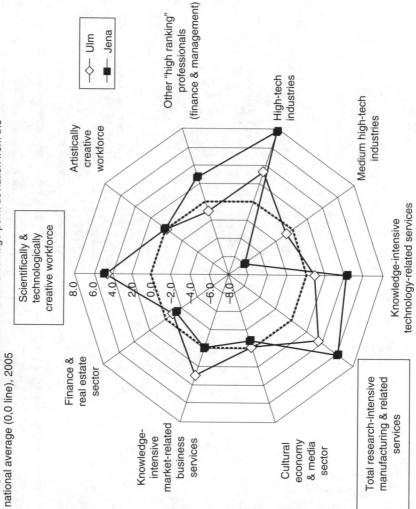

Figure 2.5 Comparison of the regional economic profiles of two successful "high-technology" cities in Germany.

However, a deeper analysis must take into account that a range of "creative" occupations are often geographically clumped in a regional system, particularly in metropolitan areas: the correlation coefficient between the proportional size of the workforce in the group of "high-ranked" professions (financial services, real estate, management and consulting) and in scientifically and technologically creative occupations on a regional basis is 0.46 at a 0.01 level of significance. With regard to artistically creative occupations, the correlation coefficient reaches 0.53 (at a 0.01 level of significance).

Because of the strong correlation between the size of the workforce in financial services, real estate, management, and consulting and the size of the workforce in scientifically and technologically creative occupations, we cannot determine their respective impact on regional economic success by directly including both groups in a single regression analysis (due to problems of collinearity). However, we can first determine the impact of scientifically and technologically creative occupations (and other relevant variables) on various dimensions of regional economic success. In a second step, we can then insert the comprehensive aggregate of a "creative class" (according to Florida's definition) in the empirical model and compare the results of both tests. If the comprehensive aggregate – which contains subgroups of the "dealer class," whose positive impact on regional economic success is not plausible in theoretical terms – achieves the same or a lower degree of explanatory power (in statistical terms), then the outcome will support the central hypothesis of this research: namely, that the impact of scientifically and technologically creative occupations is most important and that the other subgroups have no decisive influence (that is, aside from the artistically creative occupations).

In this section an analytical procedure is presented for evaluating the interrelationships between regional GDP growth, employment growth in scientifically and technologically creative occupations, and the particular impact of headquarter cities' wealth appropriation through external control capacities. In Germany's regional system, we can distinguish between two different groups of headquarter cities. The first group includes cities with a high concentration of large financial and service sector firms that have strong external control capacities (particularly Frankfurt am Main, Düsseldorf, and Hamburg; see Krätke 2004b, 2005b). These cities are characterized by a comparatively low proportion of scientifically and technologically creative workers, yet also have extraordinarily high per capita GDP (see Figure 2.6). This constellation indicates a particularly high level of wealth appropriation through external control capacities. In Germany, these cities could be regarded as the "flagships" of the contemporary dealer economy. The second group of headquarter cities includes cities with a strong commercial base in high-tech and medium high-tech manufacturing, including Munich and Stuttgart. These cities combine a comparatively high per capita GDP with a comparatively large scientifically

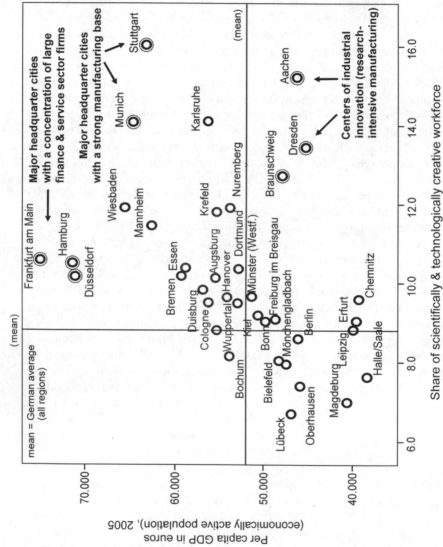

Figure 2.6 Relationship between regional per capita GDP and the share of the workforce in scientifically and technologically creative occupations in Germany, 2005 (cities > 200 000 inhabitants).

and technologically creative workforce. Furthermore, the German regional system contains a number of relevant cities with a high proportion of scientifically and technologically creative workers coupled with an average or comparatively low per capita GDP, such as Braunschweig, Dresden, Aachen, Karlsruhe, and Nuremberg (see Figure 2.6). In such cities, a large creative workforce is a reflection of manufacturing-related innovative activity as well as a well-developed industrial base in knowledge-intensive manufacturing subsectors. However, within the framework of the contemporary finance-dominated model of capitalist development (see above), such a regional economic profile does not yield the highest economic returns (in terms of per capita GDP) as compared to the dominating urban centers of the dealer economy, whose GDP is boosted (in addition to their performance in real economy activities) by the appropriation of wealth from other cities and regions through external control relations.

Factors influencing regional GDP growth

This section presents an analysis of the impact that the creative workforce and large firms with external control capacities have on regional GDP growth. The analysis is based on two hypotheses: (1) the number of workers in scientifically and technologically creative occupations is an indicator of a region's innovative capacity, and, in turn, of its productive capacity and GDP growth; and (2) the number of large firms with external control capacities is an approximate indicator of the concentration of firms receiving economic returns from external subsidiaries and branch offices (see Gräber *et al.* 1987). Within the context of the "financialization" of the world economy, "economic performance" – particularly in headquarter cities, financial centers, and metropolitan regions – is increasingly a function of the appropriation of wealth created in other regions. In this way, we can expect that a high concentration of large firms with external control capacities will have a positive impact on regional GDP growth. This impact might be particularly strong when compared to the impact of productive activities.

In order to test these hypotheses, an ordinary least squares regression analysis is performed for 434 administrative districts in Germany. GDP growth in the period 1996–2005 represents the dependent variable. The independent variables are (1) the number of large firms with turnover greater than €50 million and external control capacities in 2002 (variable label: "large firms") (this information was obtained from a database of large commercial firms; see Krätke 2005b); and (2) employment growth in scientifically and technologically creative occupations in 1995–2005 (variable label: "techno-creative"). In a variant of the test, the last variable is substituted with employment growth in the aggregate category of the "creative class," as defined by Florida (variable label: "creative class").

Table 2.1 Relationship between GDP growth and employment growth in scientifically and technologically creative occupations (OLS regression)

Number of observations	F(2, 431)	Prob > F	R-squared	Adj R-squared	Dependent variable
434	964.12	0.0000	0.8173	0.8165	GDP growth

Variable	Coef.	Std. Err.	t	P > |t|	tol	VIF	Beta
Large firms	111427.7	3129.139	35.61	0.000	0.958	1.044	.7489957
Techno-creative	282.2728	15.80496	17.86	0.000	0.958	1.044	.3756529
const	291137.9	27597.12	10.55	0.000			

Table 2.2 Relationship between GDP growth and employment growth in the "creative class" aggregate (OLS regression)

Number of observations	F(2, 431)	Prob > F	R-squared	Adj R-squared	Dependent variable
434	823.11	0.0000	0.7925	0.7915	GDP growth

Variable	Coef.	Std. Err.	t	P > |t|	tol	VIF	Beta
Large firms	97700.44	3662.939	26.67	0.000	0.794	1.259	.6567238
Creative class	142.9428	9.439349	15.14	0.000	0.794	1.259	.3728518
const	333313.8	29559.38	11.28	0.000			

The results of this analysis are presented in Tables 2.1 and 2.2. The first regression analysis has an explanatory power (in terms of the adjusted R-squared measure) of 81% and reveals that both independent variables have a highly significant impact on regional GDP growth (see Table 2.1). The standardized regression coefficients (Beta), however, indicate that a concentration of large firms with external control capacities (variable: "large firms") has a much stronger influence on regional GDP growth than employment growth in the scientifically and technologically creative workforce (variable: "techno-creative"). This suggests that the power of value appropriation (concentrated in the leading headquarters cities of the regional system) still has a stronger impact on regional economic performance in terms of GDP than the development of the regions' creative workforce. This finding corresponds to the overall characteristic of the contemporary model of capitalist development.

The second regression analysis using Florida's notion of the "creative class" has an explanatory power of 79% and again reveals that both independent variables have a highly significant impact on regional GDP growth (see Table 2.2). The standardized regression coefficients (Beta) indicate that a concentration of large firms with external control capacities (variable: "large firms") has a stronger influence on regional GDP growth than employment growth in a comprehensive aggregate of creative occupations that includes financial services, real estate, management, and consulting (variable: "creative class"). However, the most important conclusion that can be drawn from this analysis is that the aggregate "creative class" variable did not produce a higher explanatory power (in statistical terms) than the first regression analysis, which accounted solely for the scientifically and technologically creative workforce. Thus, Florida's comprehensive "creative class" aggregate obviously hides the fact that the impact of scientifically and technologically creative occupations on GDP growth is most important. The dealer class, by contrast (in Florida's terms, the creative professionals), has no decisive influence on regional economic performance, aside perhaps from its indirect influence in organizing a "space of financial flows" within the regional system to ensure the accumulation of wealth in the prominent headquarter cities.

Factors influencing total regional employment growth

In a second test of the factors that influence regional economic success, it is possible to demonstrate the impact of the creative workforce on total regional employment growth. As displayed in Figure 2.7, there is a positive linear relationship between the change in total regional employment and employment in the particular sector of the scientifically and technologically creative workforce. This analysis aims to test three hypotheses. (1) An increase in the number of scientifically and technologically creative workers is an

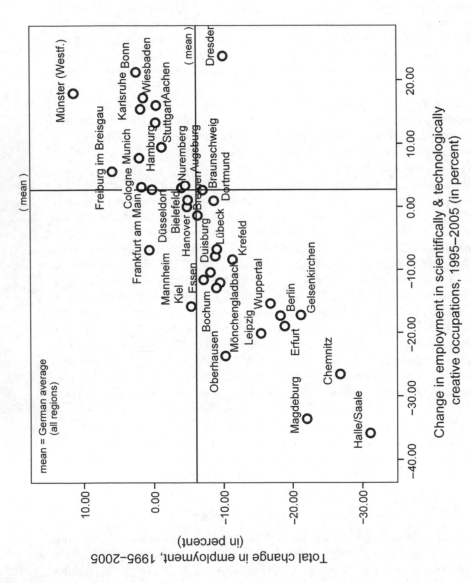

Figure 2.7 Relationship between the total change in regional employment and employment growth in scientifically and technologically creative occupations in Germany, 1995–2005 (cities > 200000 inhabitants).

indicator that a region's "innovative capacity" is growing. As the innovative capacity of a region influences its productive capacity, we can expect that this indicator will have a positive impact on total employment. (2) The ratio of large firms to total firms in a region is an approximate indicator of the concentration of "lead firms" which have a particularly high number of employees and a potential for large-scale changes in workforce size. We can expect that this indicator will have a significant impact on the total change in employment within a region. (3) An increasing number of manufacturing plants is a positive indicator of industrial development and contributes directly to employment growth within a region. We can expect this indicator to have a positive effect on the total change in employment in a region.

These hypotheses are tested for 434 administrative districts in Germany using an OLS regression. The absolute change in the regional economy's total employment from 1995 to 2005 is the dependent variable ("total job growth"). The independent variables are (1) the share of large firms with a turnover of more than €50 million among all regional firms in 2002 (variable: "large firms share"), (2) the growth in the number of manufacturing plants in 1995–2004 (variable: "manufact plants"), and (3) absolute employment growth in scientifically and technologically creative occupations in 1995–2005 (variable: "techno-creative"). As a second variant of the test, the last-mentioned variable is substituted by employment growth in the aggregate category of the "creative class," as defined by Florida (variable: "creative class").

The results of the OLS regression are presented in Tables 2.3 and 2.4. The first variant has an explanatory power (in terms of the adjusted R-squared measure) of 68% and reveals that all of the independent variables have a highly significant impact on the total change in regional employment (see Table 2.3). The standardized regression coefficients (Beta) indicate that employment growth in the scientifically and technologically creative workforce (variable: "techno-creative") has a much stronger effect on the total change in regional employment than the concentration of large firms (variable: "large firms share"). In this analysis, the increase in the number of manufacturing plants – a rough indicator of industrial health – is the second most influential factor (variable: "manufact plants").

The second variant has an explanatory power of 70%. As before, all of the independent variables have a highly significant impact on the total change in regional employment (see Table 2.4). The standardized regression coefficients (Beta) indicate that employment growth in the aggregate category of creative occupations (which includes "creative professionals" in the fields of financial services, real estate, management, and consulting; variable: "creative class") has a stronger influence on the change in regional employment than the other variables in the analysis. The most important finding of this analysis, however, is that the variant using the "creative class" aggregate does not have a significantly higher explanatory power than the

Table 2.3 Relationship between total change in regional employment and employment growth in scientifically and technologically creative occupations (OLS regression)

Number of observations	F(3, 426)	Prob > F	R-squared	Adj R-squared	Dependent variable		
430	310.54	0.0000	0.6862	0.6840	Total job growth		

Variable	Coef.	Std. Err.	t	$P > |t|$	tol	VIF	Beta
Large firms share	1320.539	223.3334	5.91	0.000	0.907	1.103	.1685050
Manufact plants	203.6555	17.42079	11.69	0.000	0.915	1.092	.3316158
Techno-creative	5.52259	.2302678	23.98	0.000	0.925	1.081	.6767634
const	−9000.999	786.2882	−11.45	0.000			

Table 2.4 Relationship between total change in regional employment and employment growth in the "creative class" aggregate (OLS regression)

Number of observations	F(3, 426)	Prob > F	R-squared	Adj R-squared	Dependent variable		
430	338.62	0.0000	0.7045	0.7025	Total job growth		

Variable	Coef.	Std. Err.	t	$P > |t|$	tol	VIF	Beta
Large firms share	1009.479	219.5416	4.60	0.000	0.884	1.132	.1288127
Manufact plants	262.0726	16.57911	15.81	0.000	0.952	1.051	.4267374
Creative class	2.856837	.1131648	25.24	0.000	0.925	1.082	.6914114
const	−8273.494	767.8001	−10.78	0.000			

variant that only includes scientifically and technologically creative occupations. In this way, it again appears that Florida's "creative class" concept belies the true sources of employment growth: the size of the scientifically and technologically creative workforce has the most significant impact on employment, whereas no decisive influence is exercised by the category of the "dealer class" (in Florida's terms, "creative professionals").

Factors influencing employment growth in the research-intensive manufacturing sector

Another test demonstrates the positive relationship between employment growth in the scientifically and technologically creative workforce and employment in the research-intensive manufacturing sector. This sector, which is of strategic importance for industrial development in Germany and Western Europe (see Krätke 2007), is comprised of numerous high-tech and medium high-tech subsectors (see Appendix). The analysis aims to test three assumptions. (1) An increasing number of scientifically and technologically creative workers is an indicator of the development of a region's "innovation capacity" and contributes in particular to the development of the research-intensive manufacturing sector. We can therefore expect this indicator to exert a positive impact on employment growth in high-tech and medium high-tech industries. (2) The ratio of large firms to total firms in a region provides an indication of the concentration of "leading firms" which have a particularly high number of employees and a potential for large-scale changes in workforce size. We can expect this ratio to exert a significant impact on the development of employment in the high-tech and medium high-tech industries. (3) An increasing number of manufacturing plants is a positive indicator of industrial development. We can expect this indicator to have a positive impact on employment growth in high-tech and medium high-tech industries.

In the OLS regression model used for the analysis, the absolute change in employment in high-tech and medium high-tech industries in 1995–2005 is the dependent variable ("job growth hmh-tech"). The independent variables are: (1) the share of large firms with turnover of more than than €50 million among all regional firms in 2002 (variable: "large firms share"); (2) the increase in the number of manufacturing plants in 1995–2005 (variable: "manufact plants"); and (3) absolute employment growth in scientifically and technologically creative occupations in 1995–2005 (variable: "techno-creative"). In a second variant of the analysis, this variable is again substituted for the variable representing Florida's "creative class" category (variable: "creative class").

The results of the analysis are presented in Tables 2.5 and 2.6. The first variant has an adjusted R-squared measure (explanatory power) of 43% and reveals that both manufacturing plant growth (variable: "manufact plants") and the growth of the scientifically and technologically creative workforce (variable: "techno-creative") have a highly significant impact on growth in

Table 2.5 Relationship between employment growth in high-tech and medium high-tech manufacturing sectors and employment growth in scientifically and technologically creative occupations (OLS regression)

Number of observations	F(3, 426)	Prob > F	R-squared	Adj R-squared	Dependent variable		
430	110.45	0.0000	0.4375	0.4336	Job growth hmh-tech		

Variable	Coef.	Std. Err.	t	P > |t|	tol	VIF	Beta
Large firms share	43.37772	58.17749	0.75	0.456	0.907	1.103	.0284491
Manufact plants	57.61278	4.538048	12.70	0.000	0.915	1.092	.4821684
Techno-creative	.6092429	.0599839	10.16	0.000	0.925	1.081	.3837298
const	−639.1618	204.8251	−3.12	0.002			

Table 2.6 Relationship between employment growth in high-tech and medium high-tech manufacturing sectors and employment growth in the "creative class" aggregate (OLS regression)

Number of observations	F(3, 426)	Prob > F	R-squared	Adj R-squared	Dependent variable		
430	78.33	0.0000	0.3555	0.3510	Job growth hmh-tech		

Variable	Coef.	Std. Err.	t	P > |t|	tol	VIF	Beta
Large firms share	73.2423	63.08678	1.16	0.246	0.884	1.132	.0480357
Manufact plants	65.21587	4.764121	13.69	0.000	0.952	1.051	.5457997
Creative class	.1946568	.0325187	5.99	0.000	0.925	1.082	.2421372
const	−723.1504	220.6326	−3.28	0.001			

the high-tech and medium high-tech manufacturing sectors. By contrast, the share of large firms has no significant impact (see Table 2.5). The standardized regression coefficients indicate that industrial plant growth has a stronger influence on employment growth in the high-tech and medium high-tech sectors than employment growth in scientifically and technologically creative occupations.

The second variant has an adjusted R-squared measure of 35% and again reveals that manufacturing plant growth has a highly significant impact (variable: "manufact plants"). The creative occupations aggregate variable is also shown to have a significant influence on employment growth (variable: "creative class"; see Table 2.6). As before, the analysis with the aggregate "creative class" variable does not have a significantly higher explanatory power than the variant that only included scientifically and technologically creative occupations. The analysis thus indicates that Florida's "creative class" concept obscures the true sources of employment growth: the scientifically and technologically creative workforce has a relatively strong impact on employment in high-tech and medium high-tech manufacturing sectors; no significant impact, however, can be observed for the "dealer class" (i.e., Florida's "creative professionals").

Factors influencing regional "innovation output"

Within the context of a regional economic development path that draws on knowledge-intensive activities, a strong innovative capacity is becoming the most important factor for regional economic success. In the following analysis we test the impact exerted by the creative workforce of a region on "innovation output," as measured in terms of successful patent applications. Patents may be used as a rough indicator of innovative strength. This indicator, however, only relates to one dimension of a region's capacity for innovation (see above) and is not suitable for comparisons between different subsectors. In the German urban and regional system, successful patent applications are concentrated in prominent metropolitan regions and large cities, including Berlin, Munich, Stuttgart, Hamburg, Dresden, and the metropolitan region of Hanover-Braunschweig-Göttingen (see Figure 2.8).

According to Figure 2.9, there is a positive linear relation between regional "innovation output" (i.e., patent applications per 100 000 economically active persons) and the share of employment in scientifically and technologically creative occupations. The analysis, which takes a range of likely influencing factors into account, is based on three assumptions. (1) The number of scientifically and technologically creative workers is an (indirect) indicator of a region's innovative capacity. We can expect this indicator to have a positive impact on a region's innovation output, as measured in terms of the number of successful patent applications. (2) The share of large firms in a region is an approximate indicator of the presence of firms with

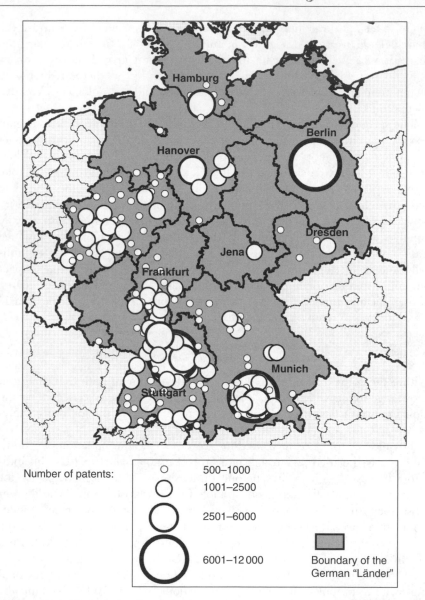

Figure 2.8 The regional distribution of "innovation output" (patent applications) in Germany, 2000–2005.

large R&D departments (which enhance a region's innovative capacity). We can expect this indicator to have a positive impact on a region's innovation output. (3) The number of manufacturing plants is a rough indicator of the regional concentration and diversity of industrial firms, and, indirectly, of

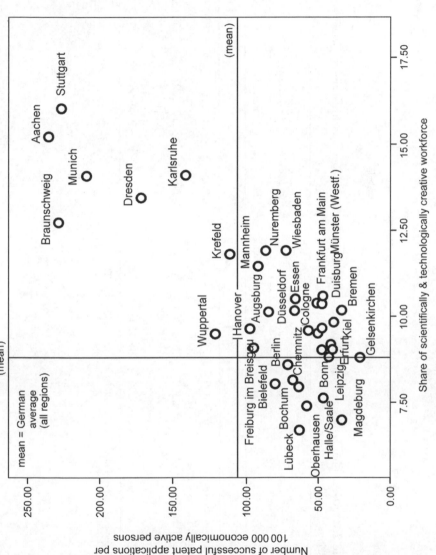

Figure 2.9 Relationship between regional "innovation output" (patent applications) and the share of employment in scientifically and technologically creative occupations in Germany, 2005 (cities > 200 000 inhabitants).

Table 2.7 Relationship between regional "innovation output" (patent applications) and the share of scientifically and technologically creative workers (negative binomial regression)

Number of observations	LR chi2(3)	Prob > chi2	Pseudo R2	Log likelihood	Dependent variable
430	440.60	0.0000	0.0939	−2124.7229	Patents

Variable	Coef.	Std. Err.	z	P>|z|	95% Conf. Interval	
Large firms share	.0856839	.0277952	3.08	0.002	.0312064	.1401614
Manufact plants share	.005714	.000538	10.62	0.000	.0046595	.0067685
Techno-creative share	.2042362	.0161363	12.66	0.000	.1726097	.2358627
const	1.583326	.1232028	12.85	0.000	1.341853	1.8248
/lnalpha	−.4839833	.067484			−.6162496	−.3517171
alpha	.6163235	.041592			.5399657	.7034791

Likelihood-ratio test of alpha = 0; chibar2(01) = 1.5e+04; Prob>=chibar2 = 0.000

the potential for regional inter-firm knowledge networking (which strengthens a region's innovative capacity). We can expect this indicator to have a
positive impact on a region's innovation output.

Since the data on patent applications are count data, which are
characterized by overdispersion, a negative binomial regression model
(which controls for overdispersion in count data) is used in order to test the
above hypotheses. In the regression analysis, the number of successful patent
applications (counts of patents) of the regional firms in 2005 is the dependent
variable ("patents"). The independent variables are: (1) the share of large
firms with a turnover of more than €50 million of all regional firms in 2002
(variable: "large firms share"); (2) the total number of manufacturing plants
in 2004 (variable: "manufact plants share"); and (3) the share of the workforce
in scientifically and technologically creative occupations of all employees in
2005 (variable: "techno-creative share").

The results of the regression analysis are presented in Table 2.7. In contrast
to an OLS regression, a negative binomial regression does not provide an
indicator of a model's explanatory power (in statistical terms), nor does it offer
standardized regression coefficients by which the respective "strength" of each
variable's impact can be compared. However, our analysis does reveal that all
three independent variables have a positive and significant impact on
innovation output. Thus, alongside the share of large firms and number of
manufacturing plants, the share of scientifically and technologically creative
workers has a significant influence on regional economic success.

The foregoing analyses at the macro level of a country's regional system
demonstrate the impact exerted by the creative workforce on four dimensions
of "regional economic success." While the "wealth of regions" stems from
different economic profiles and development paths, the tabular representation
of results (see Table 2.8) highlights that the share of scientifically and
technologically creative workers has a significant positive effect on each
dimension of regional economic success. The three OLS regression models,
however, make clear that creative workers do not always have the strongest
impact on regional economic success when compared to other variables in
the analysis. The presence of large firms and the regional clustering of
manufacturing plants also have a decisive influence. In sum, a large or
increasing share of scientifically and technologically creative workers has a
positive impact on regional GDP growth, total employment growth,
employment growth in research-intensive manufacturing subsectors and
technology-related services, and innovation output (as measured in terms of
successful patent applications). Furthermore, the use of an aggregate variable
that encompasses all members of the creative class (as per Florida's definition)
in lieu of a variable that only includes scientifically and technologically
creative workers does not significantly augment the explanatory power of
the tested models. Consequently, we can conclude that the "creative class"
category obscures the particularly relevant and strong (as well as theoretically

Table 2.8 Results of empirical tests on the impact of the creative workforce on four dimensions of "regional economic success"

Dependent variable: >> Independent variables:	GDP growth, 1996–2005	Total employment growth, 1995–2005	Employment growth in research-intensive industries, 1995–2005	Innovation output (number of patent applications), 2005
Growth of scientifically & technologically creative workforce (abs.), 1995–2005	0.375 0.000	0.676 0.000	0.383 0.000	
Size of scientifically & technologically creative workforce (as a share of all employees), 2005				0.204 0.000
Number of large firms with turnover > €50 million & external control capacities, 2002	0.748 0.000			
Number of large firms with turnover > €50 million (as a share of all regional firms), 2002		0.168 0.000	0.028 0.456	0.085 0.002
Growth in the number of manufacturing plants (abs.), 1995–2004		0.331 0.000	0.482 0.000	
Number of manufacturing plants (abs.), 2004				0.005 0.000
Type of regression model and R2 (the model's "explanatory power")	OLS 0.81	OLS 0.68	OLS 0.43	Neg. binomial
Test variant (substituting the first variable above): Growth of the comprehensive "creative class" aggregate (abs.), 1995–2005	0.372 0.000	0.691 0.000	0.242 0.000	
R2 of the variant	0.79	0.70	0.35	

Table fields indicate (a) regression coefficient (in case of OLS regression the standardized "beta" coefficient) in row 1; (b) significance level of the regression coefficient in row 2.

plausible) impact of the scientifically and technologically creative workforce. Our results indicate that the regional distribution of the "dealer class" has no significant influence on regional economic success.

Relationship between "Qualities of Place" and the Regional Concentration of Scientifically and Technologically Creative Workers

This section considers the theoretically plausible interrelationship between urban sociocultural "attraction factors" and the selective concentration of creative workers within the regional system. A short analysis at the level of Germany's regional system is conducted to assess the impact of sociocultural "qualities of place" (like openness and cultural diversity) on innovation-based economic development. The ability of places to attract creative and highly skilled workers is of importance for urban and regional development prospects particularly in the framework of an innovation-oriented development path. However, it is still open to debate whether qualities of place or employment opportunities are decisive for attracting creative and highly skilled workers. Moreover, the relevant qualities of place can be conceptualized in different ways: Florida has emphasized the sociocultural qualities of place, whereas other approaches are predominantly dealing with "amenities" in terms of cultural or entertainment facilities (see Glaeser, Kolko, and Saiz 2001). The latter concept is based on a rather narrow definition of qualities of place and is seemingly more convenient for "practical" purposes, since urban policy makers might be convinced to foster investments in cultural or entertainment facilities in order to attract highly skilled workers. We will focus on the more "ambitious" conceptualization of sociocultural qualities of place presented by Florida (2004, 2005).

Throughout history, immigration has fueled the creative capital of cities by contributing different skills, values, and approaches that encourage the evolution of new ideas and practices. The idea that social and cultural diversity positively affects a city's creative and innovative capacity is widely shared by scholars of urban development (see Siebel 2008). In development studies it has been repeatedly emphasized that "open" regions that attract foreign talent and open themselves to inflows of foreign technology and knowledge are more innovative and productive (see Ernst and Kim 2002). In regional science, the interrelation between local culture and regional innovation networks has been a particular subject of research (see Pilon and DeBresson 2003). For the formation, functioning, and evolution of regional innovation networks, the complementary aspects of cultural cohesion and cultural diversity seem to be especially relevant. Cultural cohesion – that is, common values and accepted practices, as well as the exchange of experiences between local and regional actors – lowers the transaction and coordination costs of cooperation. Cultural cohesion denotes the *facilitating* function of local and regional culture. By contrast, cultural diversity – as measured in terms of an inflow of new practices and knowledge, as well as other stimulating factors – can lead to an acceleration of local learning processes and a widening of the pool of local and regional knowledge resources. This aspect of cultural diversity relates to the *stimulating* function of the cultural encounter. As Pilon and DeBresson (2003: 30) note: "By assuming that local culture is most often a product of cultural diversity, we believe that rich, munificent open local cultures, apt in managing the coexistence and cross-fertilization of multiple cultures, are more proficient in benefiting from the constant stimulus and challenge of new technological innovations." As cultural diversity is typically most pronounced in large cities and metropolitan regions, it would appear that sociocultural factors of openness and diversity play a strong role in establishing the metropolis as a center of creativity and innovation.

While many scholars have discussed the impact of sociocultural qualities of place on the development of knowledge-intensive activities and innovation capacities in urban regions, an empirical operationalization of sociocultural attraction factors is particularly difficult. In an attempt to operationalize "qualities of place," we could first seek to demonstrate that a regional concentration of "artistically creative" people (i.e., occupational group no. 2 in the first section's discussion, or, to use Florida's term, "bohemians") is correlated with a large scientifically and technologically creative workforce, and infer that the presence of the former attracts the latter. This inference would be spurious, however, as correlation does not imply causation. Yet a regional concentration of "artistically creative" people could be used as an *indirect* indicator of qualities of place in terms of a "vibrant cultural scene" (comparable to the meaning of Florida's "bohemian" and "coolness" indices). The hypothesis, therefore, is that a vibrant cultural life functions as an attraction factor for people with scientifically and technologically creative occupations. However, a macro analysis at the aggregate level of metropolitan regions does not touch the spatial distribution of different groups within the urban area. Markusen (2006a) emphasizes that at the sub-metropolitan level, members of Florida's creative professions such as engineers and scientists, managers and business operations specialists disproportionately live and work in suburbs – that is, outside the high-density inner-city districts where the artists and "bohemians" are concentrating.

Sociocultural qualities of place also include other relevant criteria such as the "openness" and "tolerance" of a city or region's population. As these criteria are even more difficult to operationalize, we are in need of plausible auxiliary indicators. As mentioned, the heterogeneity of social milieus in large cities poses a significant problem. Broad statements about the openness and tolerance of a city or region must be understood as extremely rough generalizations. A more in-depth analysis of a city initially labeled as highly "tolerant," for example, might reveal racist attitudes among certain population groups or in particular districts.

The "openness" of a city or region might be indirectly grasped with reference to the criterion of cultural diversity. This criterion can be operationalized for a comparative regional analysis based on the international composition of a region or city's population. The "tolerance" of a city or region, by contrast, might be indirectly grasped in the context of Germany's regional system by examining the prevalence of xenophobic or racist attitudes among the population, or the share of voters affiliated with right-wing extremist parties (see Berlin-Institut 2007). The University of Bielefeld maintains data on the distribution of xenophobic attitudes in Germany. These data are only differentiated geographically at the state level, however. In this way, for our analysis, it was necessary to extrapolate rough estimates for each city and region. In order to test the hypothesis that "good" sociocultural qualities have a positive effect on regional economic development, however, it seems relevant to analyze the relation between the regional distribution of scientifically and technologically creative workers and the sociocultural qualities of place at a macro level (covering Germany's entire urban and regional system).

In our analysis, the impact of sociocultural qualities of place on the regional distribution of scientifically and technologically creative workers is estimated on the basis of three rough indicators: (1) the regional distribution of artistically creative occupations and the regional distribution of students at universities and technical colleges as (indirect) indicators of an attractive cultural scene; (2) the prevalence of xenophobic attitudes as a rough indicator of a lack of openness and tolerance among the regional population; and (3) the share of foreigners (international immigrants) as an indicator of sociocultural diversity among the regional population.

The group of artistically creative workers includes, first and foremost, full-time employees in the culture and media sectors. In this group, however, "regular" company employees who are subject to social insurance contributions comprise a limited share of the total workforce. Self-employed freelancers represent a comparatively large and steadily growing share of the creative workforce (see Chapter 4). For this reason, we included a second subgroup: self-employed artists (based on membership in the "Social Security Fund for Artists"). In the German urban and regional system, the artistically creative workforce is selectively concentrated in prominent metropolitan regions and large cities (see Krätke 2002a), particularly Berlin, Munich, Hamburg, and Cologne (see Figure 2.10).

There is significant regional variation in the prevalence of xenophobic attitudes in Germany. In a large-scale representative survey conducted by

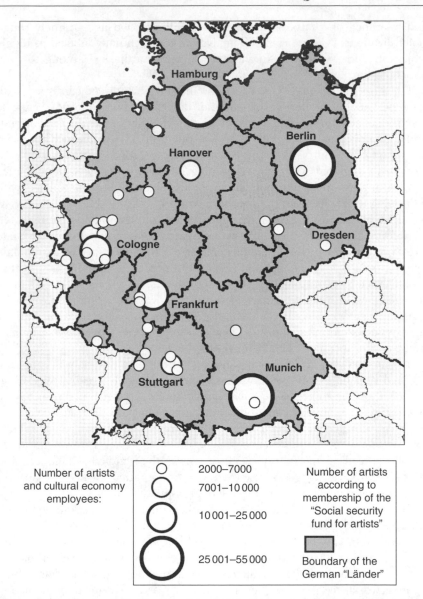

Figure 2.10   Regional distribution of the artistically creative workforce (self-employed artists and employees of the cultural economy) in Germany, 2004/2005.

sociologists at the University of Bielefeld, xenophobic attitudes were measured according to one's agreement with the following two questions: (1) "There are too many foreigners living in Germany"; and (2) "If jobs become scarce, foreigners living in Germany should be sent back to their home countries" (Gostomski, Küpper, and Heitmeyer 2006). In the survey, the share of the population with xenophobic attitudes ranged between 36.9% and 63.7% at the state level. There was also a clear east–west division: the former East German states had the highest share of people with xenophobic attitudes, followed by the West German state of Bavaria. Berlin, by contrast, had the lowest share of the population with xenophobic attitudes among all of the German states. Particularly with regard to the former East German states, it is worth underlining the possibility that xenophobic attitudes might be caused by economic decline, which raises questions about the direction of "causal arrows" between tolerance and growth in Florida's model.

The highest share of foreign migrants can be found in the core cities of Germany's leading metropolitan regions, including Munich, Stuttgart, Frankfurt am Main, the Rhine–Ruhr Valley, as well as in Hamburg and Berlin (see Figure 2.11). Again, there is a clear east–west division in Germany. The former East German states contain the lowest shares of foreigners and, according to this rough measure, the lowest sociocultural diversity. Interestingly, in all of East Germany, a low share of foreigners is correlated with a high share of xenophobic attitudes.

To test the impact of sociocultural "qualities of place" on the regional distribution of scientifically and technologically creative workers, a regression analysis is conducted based on three assumptions. (1) The number of artistically creative workers (freelance and employed artists) and the number of students at universities and technical colleges are (indirect) indicators of an "attractive cultural scene." We can expect both indicators to have a positive impact on the concentration of scientifically and technologically creative workers. (2) The share of the population with xenophobic attitudes is an approximate indicator of a lack of "tolerance and openness" among the region's population. We can expect this indicator to have a negative impact on the concentration of scientifically and technologically creative workers. (3) The share of foreigners in the total population is an approximate indicator of the "diversity and openness" of the regional population. We can expect this indicator to have a positive impact on the concentration of scientifically and technologically creative workers.

Since the dependent variable ("techno-creative abs") – that is, the number of scientifically and technologically creative workers in 2005 – is drawn from count data that exhibit overdispersion, a negative binomial regression model (which controls for overdispersion) is used. The independent variables are: (1) the number of artistically creative workers in 2004/2005 (freelance and employed artists; variable: "artists"); (2) the number of students at universities and technical colleges per 1000 inhabitants in 2003 (variable: "students"); (3) the share of the population with xenophobic attitudes, 2002–2006 (variable: "xenophobia"); and (4) the share of foreigners in the total population in 2005 (variable: "foreigners").

The results of the regression analysis are presented in Table 2.9. As noted before, in contrast to an OLS regression, a negative binomial regression

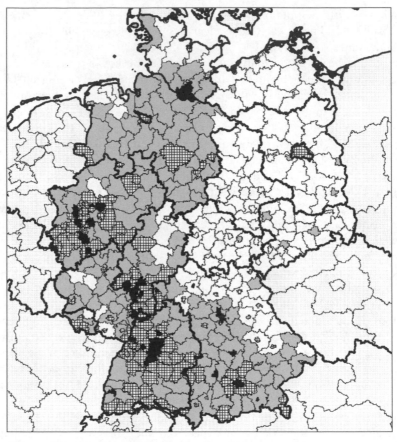

Share of foreign population
(Classification by "Natural Breaks") in %:

☐	0.74–4.15	☐ Administrative districts
▦	4.15–8.25	
▦	8.25–14.00	■ Boundary of the
■	14.00–26.04	German "Länder"

Figure 2.11   Share of foreign migrants in the population, 2006.

does not provide an indicator of a model's explanatory power (in statistical terms), nor does it offer standardized regression coefficients by which the respective "strength" of each variable's impact can be compared. Nevertheless, the analysis reveals that all four independent variables have a significant impact on the regional distribution of scientifically and technologically creative workers. The impact of a high share of the population with

Table 2.9 Relationship between "qualities of place" and the regional distribution of scientifically and technologically creative workers (negative binomial regression)

Number of observations	LR chi2(4)	Prob > chi2	Pseudo R2	Log likelihood	Dependent variable	
439	530.27	0.0000	0.0631	-3937.1471	Techno-creative abs	

Variable	Coef.	Std. Err.	z	P>|z|	95% Conf. Interval	
Artists	.0001285	.0000202	6.35	0.000	.0000888	.0001681
Students	.002927	.0008715	3.36	0.001	.0012189	.0046352
Xenophobia	-.0184213	.0060584	-3.04	0.002	-.0302957	-.006547
Foreigners	.0990988	.009978	9.93	0.000	.0795423	.1186553
const	8.23956	.3514913	23.44	0.000	7.55065	8.928471
/lnalpha	-.9764247	.0637692			-1.10141	-.8514393
alpha	.3766554	.024019			.3324021	.4268002

Likelihood-ratio test of alpha = 0; chibar2(01) = 9.4e+05; Prob>=chibar2 = 0.000

xenophobic attitudes, indicating a lack of "tolerance and openness," was negative (as expected), whereas the other three variables had a significantly positive effect. In this way, we can conclude that sociocultural attraction factors like a "vibrant cultural life," "sociocultural diversity, openness and tolerance" positively affect (or reinforce) the selective regional concentration of scientifically and technologically creative workers.

This conclusion does not imply, however, that sociocultural attraction factors are decisive or major determinants in the selective concentration of scientifically and technologically creative workers within the regional system. Other determinants such as a region's "innovation infrastructure" (public and private research establishments) or the presence of research-intensive economic subsectors and related job opportunities might exercise a much stronger influence. This is in line with a "people follow jobs" thesis that contradicts Florida's "jobs follow people" thesis. The thesis that creative workers will be attracted to cities which offer good qualities of place without having job opportunities for them has been clearly rejected by Scott (2006), who stresses that "any city that lacks a system of employment able to provide these individuals with appropriate and durable means of living is scarcely in a position to induce significant numbers of them to take up permanent residence there, no matter what other encouragements policy makers may offer" (Scott 2006: 11; see also Scott and Storper 2009).

Furthermore, the above analysis has measured the *co-presence* of sociocultural qualities of place and a concentration of technologically creative workers. The impact of qualities of place on the ability to attract creative and highly skilled workers could be more accurately assessed by investigating the *mobility* of these workers and its determining factors. Focusing on Florida's "jobs follow people" hypothesis, a recent European research project based on empirical data from 11 European cities (Martin-Brelot *et al.* 2010) has tested Florida's hypothesis regarding the spatial mobility of the "creative class" and the role of soft factors in their decision about place of residence. The relevance of this research is underlined by the point that although most critiques of Florida's theory point to the weakness of its empirical basis, few of them display new empirical evidence. This is precisely the intention of the study, which in part "imports" the Florida model in order to specifically test the hypotheses which claim a high mobility of the creative class and a significant role of "soft" factors in attracting creative people. The analysis uses Florida's definition of "creative professions" and includes the whole range of supposedly creative occupational groups which have been aggregated to a "creative class" (thus accepting the basic all-encompassing creative class construct which has been criticized and disaggregated in the foregoing sections). The researchers' basic idea was that some of the Florida arguments might be applicable to the United States but don't work in Europe – thus holding on to the credibility of the original claims of the "creative class" theory. Nevertheless, the study represents a first attempt to explore the mobility aspect of Florida's theory with regard to European cities. The results of the analysis claim two points (Martin-Brelot *et al.* 2010). Firstly, the European creative class is not as mobile as Florida suggests the creative class should be. The overwhelming majority of respondents simply stayed in the city where they were born or graduated. Those creative workers who came exclusively from outside the city and its region made up a share of less than 30% of the respondents. The share of those who were born elsewhere in the country but studied in the city was almost as important as the internationally mobile creative professionals. This finding points to the relevance of universities and other higher education establishments in the spatial distribution of creative workers. In conclusion, the author emphasizes that the so-called "personal trajectory factor" (i.e., the attachment of a person to a geographical location resulting from his/her previous life course), which is not taken into account by Florida, is very important.

Secondly, when looking at location factors in order to test the significance of "soft" location factors (in terms of sociocultural "qualities of place") for the mobility of creative people, the project's findings reveal that personal trajectory factors play the most dominant role in the selection of actual place of residence among creative people. This is followed by typical, mostly job-related "hard" factors (indicating employment opportunities). "Soft factors" were indicated by the smallest number of respondents (among the total number of reasons mentioned, the "soft factors" had a share of only 9%). Thus the survey highlights that "soft factors" are rarely considered by creative people as the most important reasons why they live in a particular city. However, if the "creative professions" were disaggregated, the specific group of artists and cultural economy freelancers might be attracted to those cities which offer a "good mix" of hard and soft location factors in terms of combining job opportunities (particularly for freelance work and flexible participation in project networks of the cultural economy) with sociocultural attraction factors that are emerging within an established creative milieu. This might attract artistically creative people particularly to the prime centers of the cultural economy sector, reinforcing the agglomeration of the cultural economy in this group of cities. On the other hand, the relatively low mobility of creative professionals as a whole indicates that urban policies that are directed at restructuring urban space for the presumed needs of a "creative class" are not a promising path to urban economic regeneration.

According to Martin-Brelot *et al.* (2010), the relatively low mobility of creative workers in Europe can be explained partly by cultural constraints (differences in languages, cultural barriers, necessity to obtain local know-how to settle down, etc.) and partly by institutional constraints (differences in educational and health care systems, limits set by national pension schemes, bureaucratic barriers for employing migrants or starting businesses). Furthermore, the study emphasizes the point that for creative people searching for a location, hard factors (mainly job opportunities) are the reasons why they choose *a particular city*, while soft factors might determine why they choose *a particular district* within the urban space.

The urban policy dimension of Florida's theory has been a focus of critical analysis too. According to Peck (2005: 764), the nascent practices of creative city strategies provide "a means to intensify and publicly subsidize urban consumption systems for a circulating class of gentrifiers" and are thus "peculiarly well suited to neoliberalized urban landscapes." The positive response of city leaders to Florida's claim that cities have to compete in the new "race for talent" and have to restructure themselves for the needs of the "creative class" is articulated in the spread of creative city strategies trying to attract "talent" and to adopt the city to the needs of the "creative class" (Peck 2009). The fast proliferation of such strategies can be related to several points: Firstly, Florida's principal method of offering city rankings according to multiple measures of "creative performance" is extremely popular among urban policy makers, since this kind of city league table allows "some city leaders to congratulate themselves on a job well done, even if this had been achieved subconsciously, while the rest have something, or somewhere, to aim at" (Peck 2005: 747). Secondly, creative city strategies involving public subsidies for the local arts scene, street-level spectacles, and improved urban facades entail a new legitimization of rather well-known urban regeneration concepts and might offer "returns" in the form of gentrification and tourist income. According to Peck (2005: 749), "investments in the soft infrastructure of the arts and culture are easy to make, and need not be especially costly, so the creativity script easily translates into certain forms of municipal action." Within the framework of creative city strategies, both familiar "bricks-and-mortar" methods (rehabilitation and new construction of buildings such as theatres and galleries, streetscaping and facade improvements, extension of bike paths, etc.) and "softer" methods, focusing on cultural events, can be applied. Thirdly, the discourse of interurban competition in the "creative age" adds a new dimension to urban place marketing strategies in terms of an "artistically inflected place promotion" that mobilizes previously untapped cultural resources and constitutes "new objects of governance and new stakes in interurban competition" (Peck 2005: 762, 763). Here, we might recall Harvey's argument (1989: 48) on the role of urban image construction and the related promotion of new amusement options and cultural facilities: "The city has to appear as innovative, exciting, and creative in the realms of life-style, high culture, and fashion" in order to succeed in the competition for circulating revenues. In sum, Peck concludes that city leaders "are embracing creativity strategies not as *alternatives* to extant market-, consumption- and property-led development strategies, but as low-cost, feel-good *complements* to them. Creativity plans do not disrupt these established approaches to urban entrepreneurialism and consumption-oriented place promotion, they *extend* them" (Peck 2005: 761).

The urban sociologist Walter Siebel (2008) has pointed out that Florida's "creative class" construct is based on a simple admixture of different middle-class groups with varying levels of education. The notion that this "class" is homogeneous in its social and cultural values, consumption preferences, and composition is not corroborated by sociological research, which has found that the middle class in particular is characterized by a wide dispersion of preferences and lifestyles, from the "staid" and "traditional" to the "avant garde" and "bohemian." In this way, the locational preferences of a great many managers, engineers, professors, medical specialists, and so on might be more readily explained in terms of an attraction to upscale suburban living in cities which offer good positions and a warm climate (see Peck 2005). Of course, some members of these occupational groups prefer to pursue a yuppie or "bobo" (bourgeois-bohemian) lifestyle in inner-city districts. However, one cannot simply assume that such groups in general seek to live in close proximity to the "trendy" inner-city districts occupied by bohemian milieus (see Lloyd 2006; Markusen 2006a). According to Siebel (2008), Florida's urban policy recommendations can be described in terms of the modernization and extension of the classical repertoire of inner-city redevelopment and gentrification policies. In the promotion of "modern" bohemian-style urban cultural amenities, for example, the resulting develop-ment projects are invariably designed to cater to the urban lifestyle needs of affluent professionals.

The phenomenon of gentrification (see Smith and Williams 1986; Smith 1996; Atkinson 2005; Lees, Slater, and Wyly 2008) additionally highlights that there is "class struggle" *within* Florida's "creative class." The classical pioneers of gentrification are to a large extent individuals with low economic and high cultural capital – that is, low-income bohemians, artistically creative people and highly skilled young people at the bottom of the labor market food chain. These pioneers are subsequently dislocated in the gentrification process by the more affluent subgroups of the "creative class," the high-income urban professionals who prefer to live in trendy inner-city districts in order to pursue yuppie or bobo lifestyles and, in particular cases, to take part in a locally concentrated and networked professional milieu. Landry (2000: 125) has presented a very clear description of this dynamic:

Classically artists agglomerate in interesting yet run down areas, often subject to potential redevelopment pressures, but where the process has not yet started. The artist in effect is the explorer and the regenerator kick-starting a gentrification process, bringing life to run-down areas and generating the development of support structures such as cafés, restaurants and some shops. They then attract a more middle-class clientele who would not have risked being the first, either through fear, the dislike of run-down areas or pressure from peer groups.

From the perspective of urban sociology, Siebel (2008) challenges the idea that the creativity of cities is simply dependent on the strong presence of a homogeneous "creative class" by emphasizing that the specific contribution of cities to creativity is the integration of diversity within the framework of a densely populated urban territory. Large cities in particular offer a framework for interaction amongst diverse milieus, and in exactly this sense cities function as "cauldrons" of creativity. This perspective on diversity is also present in urban economic geography: within a large city – that is, a dense spatial agglomeration of heterogeneous economic activities and subsectors – one can witness a variety of local economic clusters and the emergence of a diversity of local productive milieus. At the same time, cities function as "super clusters" composed of various smaller clusters with overlapping and partially interconnected activities that allow for a productive interaction of diverse local productive milieus. The classical notion of "urbanization economies" is a direct expression of this productivity-boosting interplay of diverse economic milieus, an interplay that predominantly takes the form of local knowledge spillovers. Large cities and metropolitan regions represent an economic environment that enables knowledge spillovers between neighboring industries. This kind of knowledge spillover, which is based on a sectoral proximity effect within the urban economic space, has been described by Boschma (2005) in terms of "related variety" (to be distinguished from "unrelated variety," which applies to the mere co-location of different industries). However, the basic idea of urbanization economies was already present in the writings of Jane Jacobs (1969), who argued that the prime economic advantage of cities stems from a diversification of economic activities. This notion of diversity, however, does not run against industrial specialization in local and regional cluster formations (which fosters knowledge spillovers and enhances innovation capacities). Rather, it refers to an aspect of the economic and spatial organization of the urban space that creates a second type of agglomeration economies (see Chapters 3 and 5).

Conclusion

The theoretical discussion in this chapter presented a critical deconstruction of Florida's notion of the "creative class." It emphasized the need to disaggregate Florida's questionable grouping of occupations which have quite diverse economic functions in the framework of contemporary capitalist development. Florida's "creative class" includes financial sector professionals, firm managers, and the political class as particular subgroups of "creative professionals." Our approach argues that these groups cannot be assigned to the creative workforce. A constructive macro-level analysis of creative workers' impact on urban economic development has to be restricted to scientifically and technologically as well as artistically creative workers. Thus the empirical analysis presented here only included those occupational groups that are directly engaged in scientifically/technologically or artistically creative work. The macro-level analysis with regard to the regional system of Germany proves that a regional concentration of scientifically and technologically creative workers has a significantly positive impact on regional economic development. It was possible to test this thesis without resorting to Florida's "creative class" theory, which is ultimately an affirmation of contemporary class relations. However, the findings also indicate that the impact of prominent factors of capitalist economic development such as entrepreneurial control capacities and capital concentration in large firms still has a "greater" influence on the cities' economic performance than a concentration of creative workers. Furthermore, the empirical analysis demonstrated that the regional distribution of the "dealer class" (in Florida's terms the "creative professionals") does not have a significant impact on the regions' success in the development of sustainable economic structures.

The concentration of scientifically and technologically creative workers is an indicator of the development of a region's "innovation capacity" and contributes in particular to the development of research-intensive manufacturing sectors. However, within the context of a knowledge-based development path, regional economic success is not only dependent on the presence of a large scientifically and technologically creative workforce. The development of a highly networked regional innovation system is also crucial (see Chapter 3).

Despite the numerous flaws in Florida's "creative class" theory, we might affirm the thesis put forth by Florida and several scholars of urban and regional research that sociocultural "qualities of place" represent a significant regional development factor. However, this kind of macroanalysis is not suited to confirm the thesis of a particularly high mobility of creative workers. Recent research has demonstrated that the majority of creative workers stay in the city where they were born or where they graduated. For creative people searching for a location, personal trajectory factors and "hard" factors such as the quality of jobs offered or good job opportunities are the main reasons why they choose a particular city, while "soft" factors might determine the choice of a particular district within the urban space. These findings indicate that urban policies directed at restructuring urban space for the presumed needs of a "creative class" are not a promising path to urban economic regeneration.

Yet it would appear that *sociocultural* qualities of place within a city have wide-reaching effects for the entire urban and regional population, as a vibrant cultural scene, diversity, and tolerance enhance the economic prospects of the entire city and region. On the basis of the foregoing analysis, there is clearly no justification for urban restructuring measures that favor certain functional elites in a neoliberal model of society (i.e., Florida's "creative professionals"). The development of a future-oriented regional economic structure that is undergirded by a strong regional innovation system and its networked human resources is not at all dependent on gentrification and real-estate development projects for the socially selective enhancement of an urban area's attractiveness.

This chapter did not aim to present a full account of all contributions to the Florida debate. In the United States and Europe, Florida's "creative class" theory and the related urban growth receptory has enjoyed an extremely positive reception and has led to a fast proliferation of affirmative "Florida studies" (such as, for example, Kalsø Hansen, Vang, and Asheim 2005; Fritsch and Stützer 2007; Boschma and Fritsch 2009). Additionally, urban policy consulting activities by Florida and many other consulting firms have begun to exert considerable influence on many cities' contemporary development agendas (Peck 2005). Even though critical analyses or comments have been presented both in the academic discussion and in the media (e.g., in the *American Prospect* and the *Toronto Star*), criticisms of the creative class thesis have been widely ignored by Florida and his supporters. Both academic and policy-making supporters of Florida appear not to want to engage with the critiques, and the Florida bandwagon is rolling on. In Europe and Germany in particular, the Florida thesis initially has been interpreted as a welcome supporting argument that removes the artists and the cultural economy of cities from a traditional niche function and places them among the key factors for successful urban development. At the time of the publication of Florida's book, *The Rise of the Creative Class* (2004), there was already a growing interest in the cultural economy's relevance for urban and regional development. In recent years, the term "creative industries" has served as a buzzword for the cultural economy (Hartley 2005). Contributions to supporting the role of the cultural economy in urban development could therefore be positively related to Florida's points on the role of creative work and the sociocultural attraction factors of cities.

Four factors might explain the successful spread of the "creative class" theory. Firstly, it has been perceived as containing very "clear" theoretical statements. Secondly, these theoretical statements are widely viewed as empirically grounded – outside the professional scene of academic scholarship, the presentation of city rankings and league tables in particular is usually confused with sound empirical analysis. Thirdly, it delivers a roadmap for practical action to urban decision makers. Despite the extension of place-marketing initiatives to rebrand the city as a creative center, the proposed creative city strategies are recycling "a rather narrow repertoire of newly legitimized regeneration strategies" (Peck 2005: 752), including investment in authentic historical buildings, bike-path networks, walkable streets with plenty of coffee shops, art and live-music spaces, etc. – the typical features of gentrifying mixed-use inner-city districts. Such proposals are welcomed by urban policy makers, since they are in line with supply-side strategies of the politics of the "entrepreneurial city" (see Harvey 1989; Brenner and Theodore 2002). Fourthly, Florida's theory claims a leadership role for the "creative class" in economic and social development, so that the leading groups of today's capitalist society, as well as a relevant part of the middle-classes, can easily identify with the theory's ideological message. The potential for positive identification is further extended to include artists, a group whose role in social and economic development has been neglected for a long time. With reference to the creative class concept, the artistic community can improve its public legitimacy and attain a better bargaining position in the struggle for public support (Markusen 2006a).

In general, Florida's theory offers an urban governance paradigm that is well suited to the neoliberalized politics of the "entrepreneurial city." Recipients in Europe, however, seem to believe that the neoliberal underpinnings of Florida's thesis are essentially an American phenomenon, and will be tempered by the presence of welfare state institutions. Yet by extending the pressure for cities to enhance competitiveness in the "war for talent," the creative class growth ideology may function as a "Trojan horse" of neoliberalism in Europe and beyond.

Florida's theory has given rise to a scholarly debate in which four main lines of critique can be distinguished: (a) critiques that focus on the "creative class" construct and emphasize the need for its disaggregation (see Markusen 2006a; Siebel 2008); (b) critiques concerning the impact of the creative class on urban economic growth (see Peck 2005; Markusen 2006a; Scott and Storper 2009); (c) critiques that concentrate on the role of urban amenities for attracting creative class members to particular places (see Scott 2006; Martin-Brelot *et al.* 2010); and (d) the critique related to the urban governance paradigm of the creative class theory, which emphasizes its role as a complementary extension of neoliberal urban politics (Peck 2005). These different lines of critique have been taken up and referred to in this chapter, extending the critique particularly along the lines (a) and (b). Florida's wider claims concerning the relationship between creativity and urban economic growth will be further examined in Chapter 5 with reference to the case of Berlin. The next chapter will deal with a distinct sector of creative activity and investigate the unfolding of scientific and technological creativity in urban regions, focusing in particular on the role of regional knowledge networks.

3

Innovation and Knowledge Networks in a Metropolitan Region

The Impact of Localization Economies and Networking on Technological Creativity

Introduction

The capacity of scientifically and technologically creative workers to develop new products, processes, and organizational forms manifests itself in a specific regional and sectoral context. This chapter focuses on the relationship between scientific and technological creativity and the collective properties that characterize a regional innovation system. In this regard, the ability of regional knowledge networks to enhance creativity is highlighted as the decisive "relational" component of a regional innovation system. The chapter presents a meso-level analysis of the interactive basis of creative innovation activity within a metropolitan region. The analysis draws on debates concerning the sources of regional innovation capacity and engages in a detailed investigation of regional actors' collaborative knowledge networks in a selected medium high-tech manufacturing sector in the German metropolitan region of Hanover-Braunschweig-Göttingen. The knowledge network that binds economic actors of a particular subsector or "field of competence" in an urban region can be understood as the most important articulation of localization economies. The case study region Hanover-Braunschweig-Göttingen is an example of urban regions whose creative and innovative capacities are concentrated in the medium high-tech industries (particularly the automotive industry). By focusing on this example we can prove that creative capacities are unfolding in the more "traditional" industrial sectors, which differ from the high-tech industries mostly privileged in urban and regional innovation research. Compared to the internationally well-known metropolises of the German urban system such as Frankfurt-Main, Munich, Hamburg, and Berlin, the case of Hanover-Braunschweig-Göttingen is

The Creative Capital of Cities: Interactive Knowledge Creation and the Urbanization Economies of Innovation, First Edition. Stefan Krätke.
© 2011 Stefan Krätke. Published 2011 by Blackwell Publishing Ltd.

characterized by a different sectoral profile and rather represents a "typical" urban region of Germany whose economy is shaped by the strong presence of technology-intensive manufacturing industries. This kind of urban industrial region and regional innovation system – centered around technological excellence in advanced manufacturing sectors – forms the "real economy" backbone of the German economy. However, the same type of metropolitan region with a strong base in technology-intensive manufacturing is also present in other countries of Europe (e.g., the urban regions of Bologna, Barcelona, Nantes and Lyon).

This chapter deals with the "internal" functioning of innovation activity in the real economy and the creation of "regional advantage" in the sphere of technological innovation capabilities. The capitalist imperative of accumulation, the continued race for competitive advantage, and the appropriation of surplus profits is the prime driver of innovation activities at the level of individual firms (see Chapter 1), including those in the particular industrial sectors discussed in the following analysis. However, the chapter does not refer to the intra-firm organization of R&D activity that leads to innovation. The intra-firm perspective will be taken up in Chapter 4, which discusses the cultural economy sector, a sector which is seldom approached in contemporary debates in terms of capitalist firms following the imperatives of profit seeking and organizing cultural production according to this end. Instead, this chapter focuses on the meso-level of regional innovation systems analysis where creativity is embedded in an inter-firm division of labor and the networks of interorganizational collaboration among firms and research establishments in the innovation process, thus tracing the urban and regional basis for innovation and creativity in these sectors. Second, we emphasize that the creative capacity stemming from innovation-oriented knowledge networking unfolds in a context defined by a specific combination of economic sectors and a region's predominant industrial clusters, and is thus shaped by a particular region's distinctive development path.

Weber's theory of agglomeration economies remains the basic theoretical approach for assessing the impact of location-specific economies of scale (Weber 1914). Based on Marshall's notion of externalities (Marshall 1920), the theory of agglomeration economies can be subdivided into two concepts with greater specificity: "localization economies," designating intra-industrial externalities within local and regional clusters of a particular industry's firms, on the one hand, and "urbanization economies," which refer to positive externalities offered by the presence of a diversity of industries within particular urban and regional economic territories, on the other. Localization economies arise from the concentration of a particular industry in a specific location and are associated with the presence of an intra-industry inter-firm division of labor, a skilled labor pool, and knowledge spillovers. Urbanization economies, on the other hand, are related to the size of local markets, an urban labor market with diversified skills, a mixed industrial structure, and the knowledge spillovers arising from the diversity and density of actors and industrial subsectors. Large cities offer an economic environment which enables complementary knowledge spillovers between neighboring industries. The benefits of diversity have been emphasized by Marshall (1920), Jacobs (1969), and many other scholars. The diversity of urban economies is particularly pronounced in metropolitan regions and is based on the local mixture of industries, the existence of different specializations, and the variety of people and activities in a densely populated urban territory. This diversity fosters the formation of dense communication networks, knowledge exchange, and the rapid diffusion of impulses for innovation.

The concept of agglomeration economies underscores the continued relevance of geographic proximity for local and regional economic actors in the innovation process (see Boschma 2005). "In the context of a globalizing economy, centres of geographical agglomeration are centres of innovation … because they offer to the wide collectivity a well consolidated network of contacts, knowledge, structure and institutions" (Amin & Thrift 1994: 13). In geographical terms, centers of innovation are usually anchored in a metropolitan agglomeration and

> seem to have a maximum size constraint: partners in innovation have to be able to travel back and forth easily to each other's organizations within a day to solve any problem that may emerge in the process of collaboration on an innovative project…. The core partners in an innovative network must be localised within the confines of this problem-solving communication space. (Pilon & DeBresson 2003: 18)

Different urban centers of innovation, however, can be interlinked by cooperation and knowledge flows that exceed the boundary of *regional* innovation networks. The positive externalities offered by metropolitan agglomerations do not emerge solely due to the propinquity of a multitude of actors, but depend on actual *interaction* amongst firms and institutions within a metropolitan region, and, in particular, on "local synergies" in the creation of innovations through cooperation and knowledge networking. This basic insight also informs the "innovative milieu" concept (see Aydalot and Keeble 1988; Camagni 1991a, 1999; Ratti, Bramanti, and Gordon 1997; Moulaert and Sekia 2003; see also Meusburger, Funke, and Wunder 2009). An innovative milieu represents a territorialized ensemble of actors and institutions with shared expertise, standards, and rules, as well as a dense network of cooperative relations.

The relationship between scientific and technological creativity and the collective properties of a regional innovation system is analyzed in this chapter based on an exploration of the knowledge network that links actors in a particular subsector of an urban region's economy. The formation of regional knowledge networks can be regarded as an important articulation of localization economies (i.e., intra-industrial external economies within a metropolitan region). However, urbanization economies are also of relevance with a view to the cross-sectoral knowledge networking that takes place between different industries in an urban region's economy. Most large cities and metropolitan regions are characterized by the presence of a diversity of industries ("multi-industry cities"). The concept of urbanization economies implies the presence of technological externalities amongst different industries within a city or urban region (see Firestone 2008). In a more general sense, the logic of urbanization economies might also lead to the notion of "the city as an innovative milieu" (Camagni 1999). Using actor-centered regional network analysis, it is possible to identify the organizations which are positioned at the intersection of various industries' knowledge networks, thereby serving as a "bridge" for knowledge spillovers amongst a regional economy's diverse subsectors.

The academic debate surrounding regional innovation networks has focused in recent years on the topic of knowledge networking. Contemporary innovation research has come to the central finding that innovations arise mainly from the interaction between firms as well as between firms and research establishments (Gertler 1995; Koschatzky 2001; Lo and Schamp 2003; Malerba and Vonortas 2009). In short, the greatest stimulus to innovation arises from the networking of knowledge resources. However, this networking takes place on various spatial scales: irrespective of the knowledge flows within a given locality, regional actors such as research establishments and firms rely to varying degrees on supra-regional networking – both national and international – for knowledge acquisition (Grotz and Braun 1997; Cooke 2002, 2006). The phrase "local buzz and global pipelines" has been coined to describe regional knowledge generation as a product of the interplay between local networks and global knowledge transfer (Bathelt, Malmberg, and Maskell 2004). The subject of knowledge networking is of particular relevance to approaches in regional theory that emphasize the integration of a region's knowledge resources in local and global networks (Cooke 2002, 2006; Lo & Schamp 2003; Matthiesen 2003). By promoting the mobilization of local knowledge resources, regional knowledge networks can become a socially produced locational advantage and, as such, a key factor in a region's economic development potential.

The positive effects that can be attained by interlinking a region's research institutions with each other and with a region's firms are emphasized both in the theory of regional innovation networks and in the theory of regional clustering (Malecki and Oinas 1999; Keeble and Wilkinson 2000; Cooke 2002; Cooke and Schwartz 2007). In the theory of regional innovation networks, the exchange of knowledge among a region's economic actors is considered as the foundation of innovation capacities that are specific to a given region (Braczyk, Cooke, and Heidenreich 1998; Grotz and Schätzl 2001; Diez 2002; Fromhold-Eisebith 2009). The dynamic agglomeration advantages of knowledge generation within regionally networked ensembles of specialized firms and research institutions is also a central topic in the theory of regional clustering (Krätke 2001; Schamp 2002a). In the debate on clusters it is frequently emphasized that local knowledge spillovers are an important driving force in cluster dynamics (Graf 2006). The cooperation of cluster firms and R&D establishments mobilizes specific knowledge resources on the regional level that have become a strategic resource in the competition to innovate. At the same time, a region's innovation capacity also depends on the linkage of regional knowledge networks to partners in the national and global arena, as supra-regional (i.e., national and international) partnerships offer access to important external pools of knowledge and "innovation impulses" (Dunning 2000; Rehfeld 2001; Schamp 2002b; Bathelt, Malmberg, and Maskell 2004; Cappellin and Wink 2009).

However, while the current debate on regional knowledge networking emphasizes the intensity and geographic scale of knowledge networks as a relevant factor in a region's innovative capacity and competitiveness, very few empirical studies that make use of advanced techniques in social network analysis have been conducted to date (e.g., Krätke 2002b; Owen-Smith and Powell 2004; Giuliani 2007; Fritsch and Kauffeld-Monz 2008; Krätke and Brandt 2009; Morrison and Rabellotti 2009). The key challenge in the empirical analysis of regional knowledge networks is to analyze the density and structure of the interlinkages between a region's research establishments and firms and to compare knowledge networks across subsectors and regions.

The analysis of collaborative interorganizational networks as a "relational" component of regional innovation systems can be distinguished from recent network studies which have focused on the geography of interpersonal research networks, collaborative patent generation, and co-patent applications (Breschi and Lissoni 2004; Cooke 2006; Graf 2006; Maggioni and Uberti 2006; Maggioni, Nosvelli, and Uberti 2007; Hoekman, Frenken, and van Oort 2008). These studies fail to discuss intra-regional knowledge networks. Nevertheless, they offer valuable insights into the geography of research networks and collaborative knowledge production. Hoekman, Frenken, and van Oort (2008) analyzed inter-regional research collaboration in 29 European countries in terms of scientific publications and patents with multiple addresses. Using gravity models, they explored the effects of geographical and institutional distance on inter-regional research collaboration and detected the existence of "elite structures" between "excellence regions" as well as capital city regions. Yet the mechanisms of knowledge-related interactions and their relevance for innovation still need to be explored. As Tödtling, Lehner, and Trippl (2006: 1035) explain, "clustering and local knowledge spillovers are frequently stated phenomena, although it is still unclear as to what extent knowledge interactions at the regional level are indeed relevant and what the exact mechanisms of knowledge flows are."

This chapter draws on a detailed network analysis of the cooperative relations between scientific institutions and firms in the metropolitan region of Hanover-Braunschweig-Göttingen (H-B-G). Research took place in 2006 and 2007 within the scope of a research project conducted by Norddeutsche Landesbank's Department of Regional Economics, entitled "Innovation networks in the metropolitan region of Hanover-Braunschweig-Göttingen." The project sought to identify R&D-related cooperative relations between research establishments and private sector firms of this region. The research findings have been documented in Brandt *et al.* (2008), Krätke and Brandt (2009), and Brandt *et al.* (2009). The metropolitan region of Hanover-Braunschweig-Göttingen was established as a new administrative unit in 2005 in order to strengthen regional competitiveness by focusing on innovative capacities. A detailed network analysis should provide information on the R&D-related interactions of the regional actors in various subsectors of the regional economy. Thus the research focused on the actors of a particular administrative region. The territory of this metropolitan region is quite extensive and includes several large urban centers. However, the metropolitan region's administrative delimitation is not congruent with the dynamics of regional innovation networks (see below). Research aimed at testing the central assumption that regional knowledge networks represent a key factor in a region's innovative capacities. The following sections present a more detailed description of the theoretical approach and methodology that was taken to analyze regional knowledge networks. The chapter then discusses the structure of the studied region's internal knowledge networks, and presents an empirical test for evaluating the impact of knowledge networks on the innovative output of firms.

Innovation and Knowledge Networks: Theoretical Approaches

Within the scope of an economic development path that hinges on innovation, knowledge is gaining increasing importance as a factor for success on a national and regional level (Dunning 2000; Murmann, Jones, and Galambos 2006; Tödtling, Lehner, and Trippl 2006). For the purposes of our research, the term "knowledge" can be defined as the outcome of a learning process by which information is incorporated into an actor's reasoning and decision making. In regional research, the debate on knowledge and its impact on regional development has centered around the distinction between codified (explicit) and tacit (implicit) knowledge (Polanyi 1967; Storper 1997; Maskell and Malmberg 1999a). While codified knowledge (e.g., in the form of manuals, blueprints, etc.) can be easily transferred amongst distant regions (given sufficient absorptive capacity), tacit knowledge is a personalized type of knowledge based on an individual's "practical" experience and specific "know-how"; its transfer depends on face-to-face contact. Thus, the interregional transfer of tacit knowledge depends on the migration of its human carrier (Bastian 2006). However, tacit knowledge can also be externalized through a process of transformation into codified knowledge. According to Nonaka and Takeuchi (1995), knowledge is created in a continuous process of transformation between tacit and codified knowledge. The debate on the role of knowledge in regional development has been shaped by the assumed "stickiness" of tacit knowledge (see Markusen 1996) and its function as a regionally specific development resource that fosters processes of local cluster formation (Maskell and Malmberg 1999a, 1999b; Sternberg 1999). In light of the interrelationships between tacit and codified knowledge (Ernst and Kim 2002; Bastian 2006), a narrow focus on tacit knowledge does not appear to offer an appropriate approach for understanding the impact of knowledge resources on regional development.

Furthermore, the geographies of knowledge networks might differ significantly due to sectoral characteristics. The theoretical debate has suggested a distinction between "synthetic" and "analytical" knowledge bases (Coenen, Moodysson, and Asheim 2004; Asheim and Coenen 2005; Asheim and Gertler 2005; Tödtling, Lehner, and Trippl 2006; Moodysson, Coenen, and Asheim 2008). According to Tödtling *et al.* (2006: 1036–1037), a "synthetic" knowledge base is prevalent in the more traditional industries, particularly in medium high-tech industries such as mechanical engineering, and is

> characterized by the application or novel combination of existing knowledge …
> Learning by doing and interacting, practical skills and tacit knowledge are
> highly important, leading to an incremental innovation pattern in industries
> with a synthetical knowledge base. In comparison, the innovation process in
> industries with an analytical knowledge base like biotechnology or information
> and communication technologies (ICTs) is clearly different in nature. There is
> a strong reliance on scientific inputs and codified (or codifiable) knowledge is
> in general far more important than in traditional sectors…. Although the
> codification of knowledge plays a decisive role in sectors with an analytical
> knowledge base, tacit knowledge is of relevance, too.

The process of innovation comprises research, development, and design activities, the "output" of this creative work in terms of new designs, patents, contents of cultural products etc., and its economic utilization in the form of new products and technologies. The term "innovative capacity" designates the ability to generate new knowledge and transform it into new products, processes, and organizational forms. This capacity also includes the ability to make use of knowledge from external sources (i.e., external to the innovating firm and/or external to the innovating firm's region). The creative capacity of workers is a prime source of innovative capacity and functions as an essential "input" in the process of innovation. Creativity denotes the capability of individuals and of interacting groups of workers both at the intra-firm level and the level of interorganizational cooperation to create new knowledge or solutions to problems which are applied to generate new technologies, products, and organizational forms. Creative work entails a recombination or novel combination of differently specialized knowledge, leading to the variation of existing forms or the creation of novel forms. The need to combine different knowledge resources usually calls for a collaboration of creative workers in the innovation process. This interaction includes a learning process, which in turn enhances the actors' creative capabilities. Due to the diversity of socioeconomic fields and sectors of innovation activities, creative capabilities are related to specific "sectoral" knowledge bases. Yet, in the process of creative work, different knowledge bases might be combined in order to generate novel forms.

Contemporary innovation research has largely departed from the "linear" model of innovation that entails the notion of a clear-cut division between different phases of the innovation process (such as basic research, applied research, product development, etc.), which are performed by different organizations such as universities and research establishments, private sector firms' R&D departments, etc. (see Fagerberg, Mowery, and Nelson 2005). By contrast, the new approach to innovation theory emphasizes that many improvements of products and processes are growing out of multiple encounters between the different actors of a networked production system. A major share of innovations arises from the interaction that takes place between firms as well as between firms and scientific institutions (Lundvall 1988, 1992; Lo and Schamp 2003). Consequently, the innovative capacity of regional economies can be strengthened through the formation of interorganizational networks that foster processes of interactive knowledge generation and knowledge diffusion. Interorganizational collaboration within particular subsectors of economic activity entails the interaction of creative workers with "related" knowledge bases (in terms of sectoral proximity) that leads to a variation of existing forms, whereas cross-sectoral collaboration between creative workers with previously "unrelated" knowledge bases may result in the creation of novel forms (Lorenzen and Frederiksen 2008). The creative combination of previously unrelated knowledge bases depends on the knowledge absorption and processing capabilities of the workers involved (see below). However, due to the advanced specialization of scientific, technological, and artistic knowledge within particular fields of activity, an empirical delimitation of related and unrelated knowledge bases is hard to achieve. Likewise, an empirical differentiation between the variation of existing forms and the creation of novel forms might be difficult and would have to be restricted to very specific sectoral contexts.

The networking of knowledge resources takes place at different spatial scales: while geographical clustering and inter-firm networking within a region can promote interorganizational knowledge flows, supra-regional and global contacts might constitute a more important source of external knowledge (Bathelt, Malmberg, and Maskell 2004). In this way, innovative success will be dependent on an appropriate combination of knowledge inputs from local and regional as well as national and global sources of knowledge (Cappellin and Wink 2009). The relative importance of these different scales of knowledge acquisition to particular economic sectors and regional economies is still unclear, however. The geography of knowledge networks might differ considerably between knowledge-intensive and other sectors, as well as between synthetic and analytical knowledge bases.

Existing scholarship on national and regional innovation systems has underscored the varying geographic scales of interactive knowledge generation as well as the variety of involved actors (Lundvall 1992; Braczyk, Cooke, and Heidenreich 1998; Asheim and Gertler 2005). A regional innovation system (in terms of a regionally interacting knowledge generation and exploitation system that is connected to external systems) might be conceptualized as a construct with three pillars: (1) the regional firms' internal innovative capacity; (2) the region's innovation infrastructure, which consists of public and private research establishments, technology transfer agencies, etc.; and (3) the regional knowledge network that interlinks actors on the regional level through formal and informal relations that channel interorganizational knowledge flows. These three components do not represent all relevant drivers of innovation, however, for regional actors can also draw on innovation infrastructures at the national level as well as on national and supra-national knowledge networks (see above). It is important to note as well that regional knowledge networks can be enhanced through political initiatives (much like regional innovation infrastructure) within the context of a broader campaign to pursue an innovation-based economic development path. In regions that are well endowed with public research establishments, educational institutions, innovation centers, etc., knowledge generation and diffusion can be actively stimulated, provided "that these organizations develop dense links to the firms of the region" (Tödtling, Lehner, and Trippl 2006: 1041). This underscores the relevance of research on *regional* knowledge networks. Innovating firms make use of various sources of knowledge aside from networking, including formal R&D cooperation, contracted research, and other forms of collaborative activity. Additional types of knowledge sourcing such as the hiring of specialists, the acquisition of licenses and patents, and participation in conferences and fairs are also relevant (Tödtling *et al.* 2006). Nevertheless, networks for knowledge sourcing are of particular importance, for "they constitute intentional and selective relations to particular partners in the innovation process and they are more interactive and durable than market links" (Tödtling *et al.* 2006: 1050–1051). An analysis of knowledge transfer in 16 regional innovation networks encompassing various German firms and research organizations found that "strong ties" – such as formal R&D cooperation – were more beneficial for the exchange of knowledge than "weak ties" (see Fritsch and Kauffeld-Monz 2008; see also Granovetter 1973).

The theory of regional innovation networks emphasizes that the interlinking of knowledge resources facilitates interorganizational knowledge flows. However, it is extremely difficult to directly measure knowledge flows taking place in cooperative relations. As Krugman points out, "knowledge flows ... are invisible; they leave no paper trail by which they may be measured and tracked" (1991: 53). Practical experience testifies that collaborative research and consulting projects lead to an exchange of knowledge and ideas, which in turn generates new knowledge and creative impulses for all parties involved. However, it is essentially impossible to determine whether one of the parties obtains greater benefits from the knowledge exchange. The acquisition of benefits depends on the knowledge absorption and processing capacities of the actors as well as the specific subject of the collaboration. As Nooteboom notes, "often the absorptive capacity of small firms is small relative to that of large firms, so that in collaboration, with the joint production of knowledge, the advantage can be one-sided, with the large firms expropriating the advantage of joint knowledge production" (2003: 107). The types of actors involved in a collaborative knowledge network might be of great significance with regard to the governance dimension of interorganizational knowledge flows. Nooteboom claims that the term knowledge "transfer" might be misleading, since it suggests that knowledge can be transported like physical goods (2003: 118). Knowledge transfer is not a simple linear flow, but requires an ongoing process of interaction and the capacity to *understand* knowledge from distant sources. Consequently, the notion of knowledge transfer or knowledge flow should be explicitly understood as a rough metaphor for an interaction of considerable complexity.

From a more general perspective, the problems of knowledge transfer can be analyzed based on the notions of "cognitive distance" and "absorptive capacity" (Cohen and Levinthal 1990; Nooteboom 2003; Amin and Cohendet 2004). Since knowledge is always generated in a specific cognitive framework, there will be a greater or lesser cognitive distance between actors that have developed their knowledge in different environments (and have not been in communication with each other's environment). Absorptive capacity can be defined as the ability to surmount cognitive distance and thus to connect different types of knowledge or different knowledge bases (see above). In this way, cognitive distance in combination with a lack of absorptive capacity would constitute a hindrance to knowledge transfer. In the literature on innovation theory, a common perception is that innovations are often produced through explorative activities. The particular power of interorganizational networks to enhance innovative capacity (see Nooteboom 1999) stems from: (1) the relative autonomy of network participants and thus the presence of cognitive distance and diversity; (2) new possibilities that can be achieved by combining network participants; and (3) the specialization – in certain cases – of network participants in specific "stages" of innovative activity, such that some organizations in the network (e.g., research establishments) might concentrate on exploration and others (such as innovative private sector firms) on the practical application of an innovation. Nooteboom (2003: 111–112) concludes that

> for an RIS (Regional Innovation System) to function (that is produce and utilise innovations), it needs to combine exploitation and exploration. For exploitation, it needs organisational units that each have sufficient focus to ensure efficient utilisation of their specialised competencies. For exploration, there should be organisational units with a cognitive distance that is large enough to ensure a variety of cognition but not too large to block mutual understanding and relevance…. The performance of an RIS is enhanced by the ability of firms to communicate and to absorb tacit knowledge. This enhances the ability to cross cognitive distance and enables an individual to deal with larger cognitive distances. This yields a greater variety of knowledge sources, which enhances innovation.

The nature and mechanisms of interorganizational knowledge flows are still unclear. The literature on regional clusters and innovation networks frequently assumes that transaction-based interorganizational linkages contribute to the diffusion of knowledge and spread of "innovation impulses" among the ensemble of interconnected firms and organizations. From this perspective, formal (contractual) network relations offer strategic benefits to the whole ensemble of interconnected actors in terms of knowledge spillovers. However, geographic clustering might also lead to a dense web of informal network relations that function as an equally important mechanism of interorganizational knowledge diffusion. According to Owen-Smith and Powell, there are two ways in which formal networks might be understood to transmit knowledge between organizations: these network "linkages can represent either 'open' channels or more proprietary, 'closed' conduits" (2004: 5). The first concept interprets linkages as channels that direct knowledge flows between network nodes in a rather diffuse manner, facilitating knowledge spillovers to the collective benefit of both loosely connected and centrally positioned organizations. The second concept sees network links as relatively closed conduits ("pipelines"), which are characterized by legal arrangements that ensure that only the parties to a specific partnership benefit from the knowledge exchange (Owen-Smith and Powell 2004). A predominance of organizations committed to proprietary uses of knowledge would prevent the diffusion of knowledge in the network structure to indirectly (or loosely) connected actors. The closed conduits concept also implies that positive benefits are offered first and foremost to tightly connected network participants. Owen-Smith and Powell (2004) argue that the specific institutional characteristics of the organizations that represent nodes in a network are important in assessing whether a network represents a fabric of unfettered channels for knowledge flows or a fabric of proprietary pipelines for knowledge and resource transfer between partnered organizations. In contrast to private sector firms and commercial R&D organizations, public research institutions (such as universities) are generally characterized by an "open science" attitude that allows for knowledge to be more easily transferred outside of institutional boundaries. As a result, we would expect that the knowledge resources within a network primarily composed of public research institutes would be more easily accessible to all network participants (even in cases where commercial applications are concerned), and that this kind of network structure more readily facilitates knowledge spillovers. However, in addition to institutional characteristics, "absorptive capacity" is also crucial to determine whether and how knowledge flows within a cluster or region (Giuliani 2005).

The effects of knowledge networks on innovative output still need to be investigated empirically. A first detailed analysis of these effects conducted by Owen-Smith and Powell (2004) was confined to Boston's biotech sector. In the study, a regression analysis with patent applications as the dependent variable demonstrated that "within a major regional biotechnology community, collaborations among organizations matter for explaining the innovative output of firms" (2004: 15). Even a loose connection to the main component of the local network, simply expressed as network "membership" (notwithstanding any measure of centrality), enabled firms to capture geographically bounded knowledge spillovers. The study also showed that within a wider, supra-regional collaborative network, a central position has a positive effect on a firm's innovation output. However, the effects measured by the authors might be different in sectors that draw on a dissimilar knowledge base.

In sum, the theoretical debate on knowledge generation and transfer in a regional context is of key importance for the issues of creativity and innovation. The debate has advanced concepts that draw on the distinction between types of knowledge, specific sectoral knowledge bases, the characterization of knowledge flows, and so on, emphasizing the role of interactive knowledge creation and interorganizational knowledge networks as a most important context for the unfolding of creativity in the innovation process. The interlinking of knowledge resources appears crucial to innovative capacities. On a general level, the theoretical debate on interactive knowledge generation may advance our understanding of specific agglomeration advantages and the articulation of localization economies in the regional system. Nonetheless, further research needs to be directed toward the varying geographic scales of interorganizational knowledge flows, the structure and functioning of regional knowledge networks, and their impact on innovation "output."

The Application of Network Analysis to Urban Regions' Knowledge Networks

The interdisciplinary methodology of "social network analysis," which is based on the "assumption of the importance of relationships among interacting units" (Wassermann and Faust 1994: 4), can provide appropriate tools for analyzing regional knowledge networks. Its analytical instruments furnish an actor-based method for identifying the essential properties of a region's network structure (see Knoke and Kuklinski 1982; Burt and Minor 1983; Wasserman and Faust 1994; Jansen 1999). The network analysis offers the potential for insights of a much more sophisticated nature than the "non-rigorous" statements common in contemporary regional research on interorganizational connectivity and networking. Such statements are in most cases derived from interviews with regional experts, who by necessity only have a limited overview of the complete network that makes up a regional innovation system. The network analysis provides an overall assessment of the network structure and its properties, but fails to obtain in-depth information of individual cooperation links and attitudes. On the other hand, a network analysis provides a "mapping" of the existing links within a given territory and measures of network properties that allow for a comparative analysis. As there is a low degree of awareness for empirical network analysis in regional research, a short description of the methodological approach used in our case study analysis of regional knowledge networks is presented here.

The core method of data gathering is a survey of firms and institutions at the regional level; network relations are determined based on the targeted questioning of relevant actors. After the composition of a network has been ascertained, an analysis of the network's properties can be performed, so that structural components as well as the "degree of connectivity" and positioning of the individual actors become recognizable. Actors are classified as "focal" actors if they occupy a central position in a network, or as relatively isolated actors if their level of integration is weak or absent.

Our analysis of knowledge networking in the metropolitan region of Hanover-Braunschweig-Göttingen (H-B-G) is based on a survey of 1138 regional economic actors (453 public research establishments, 613 private sector firms, and 72 other establishments) conducted by the Department of Regional Economics at Norddeutsche Landesbank in two phases between January 2006 and May 2007. In the first phase, the region's scientific institutes were surveyed. Besides the various non-university public research establishments that are present in the region, every single research institute of the region's universities has been examined as an independent research establishment with particular competences and specific interorganizational links (this explains the large number of 453 research establishments; for example, the Technical University Braunschweig contains nearly 80 technological/engineering institutes with a different specialization profile). The second phase concentrated on the innovation-oriented private sector firms, starting from those firms which had been named by the public research establishments as cooperation partners and, additionally, from the metropolitan region's economic promotion agencies' listing of firms that are active innovators. In this way, the number of private sector firms was considerably extended and also included those private sector firms which only innovate in cooperation with other firms. Nonetheless, the actors included in the network analysis show a clear bias toward science-based innovation, which reflects the research project's primary focus on investigating the region's innovation networks that are based on the interaction amongst the innovation-oriented regional firms (in terms of R&D-related inter-firm cooperation) and between these firms and the region's public research establishments. The survey participants' detailed responses concerning their specific fields of activity were used to define various subsectors for comparative analysis. Participants were asked to identify outside R&D partners by name as well as indicate the precise nature of cooperative relations. Based on the responses, cooperative relations were grouped into three levels of intensity: the highest level of intensity included formal "collaboration within joint research projects or research assignments" and "long-term strategic cooperation" (first level); medium intensity (second level) was assigned to "selective collaboration for addressing particular topics," and included formal (contractual) as well as informal interaction within the context of a longer-term, but semi-sporadic form of partnership. The lowest level of intensity (third level) was reserved for "partnership in the field of education or training." "Cooperation within the scope of joint research projects or research assignments" was the most frequently cited form of partnership. From a total of 2183 recorded partnerships in the region, 58% fell in this category. The second most common form of cooperation was "selective collaboration for addressing particular topics"; 35% of partnerships fell into this category. Whereas the first type (high-intensity level) of network relations represents "strong ties," the second type might rather be interpreted as representing "weak ties" in terms of Granovetter's approach (Granovetter 1973), so that our analysis contains a mixture of strong and weak ties. The figures show that the vast majority of cooperative ties assumed the most intense form of collaboration. For the purpose of our analysis, therefore, the networks can be characterized as R&D-related cooperative networks. It is assumed that the interlinking of knowledge resources between scientific institutions and firms leads to interorganizational knowledge flows, regardless of whether they are "open" channels or "closed," proprietary conduits.

The large volume of relational data necessitated subdividing the network analysis into different layers of representation. The supra-regional (i.e., national and international) relational data were displayed at the coarser macro level. The myriad interconnections amongst actors at the regional or "meso level" were the focus of analysis. The network actors were subdivided into a total of seven different subsectors. These subsectors were derived from the survey responses concerning primary fields of activity: (a) Life sciences (including medical research, medical engineering, pharmaceuticals, biotechnology); (b) Information and communication technology; (c) Energy industry and environmental engineering; (d) Agriculture and forestry; (e) Planning and construction, civil engineering; (f) Automotive industry; (g) Production technology (including material sciences, production engineering, mechanical and electronic engineering, microsystems engineering, measurement technology, laser technology). These categories permitted a comparison of network properties between subsectors. We will restrict the detailed presentation of network properties (see below) to the automotive industry subsector, which has been selected due to its high share of employment and "profile shaping" role in the metropolitan region H-B-G. As this analysis represented the first comprehensive study of a metropolitan region's knowledge network in Germany, a cross-regional comparison was not possible.

Measuring network properties

The network analysis was aimed at identifying the relative strengths and weaknesses of R&D-related cooperative networks in particular subsectors. In general, the methodology of network analysis provides a wide range of possibilities for measuring the properties of networks and the positioning of particular actors (Wassermann and Faust 1994; Jansen 1999). Owen-Smith and Powell recommend the use of methods of measurement that are readily interpretable, and stress "the benefits of simplicity in network measures" (2004: 19). Most network analysis techniques examine the degree of connectivity of specific actors in relation to other actors. When analyzing knowledge networks in the H-B-G region, the following measures of network properties and underlying hypotheses were applied:

1   *Network density*: measured in terms of the number and intensity of connections (i.e., the sum of valued links) divided by the number of surveyed network actors (i.e., the active nodes). Based on the assumption that the investigated R&D-related collaborative network represents a system of "open channels" of knowledge flows in a regional context, network density influences the processes of knowledge diffusion among the interrelated regional actors. Network density increases if more actors in a particular subsector are interconnected and/or if their interrelations become more intensive. A large number of linkages between actors can yield a large "cognitive variety" (Nooteboom 2003), and this combination of diverse knowledge sources amplifies the potential benefits of knowledge networks. A comparatively high network density implies an extended or "thickened" system of channels for the interorganizational flow of knowledge and can thus be interpreted as a sign of relative strength over other subsectors in the regional economy.

2   *Network cohesion*: measured according to the number of separated network components. Higher values thus indicate network fragmentation, while lower values indicate relatively strong cohesion. If the network structure reveals no separated "islands" or sub-networks without a connection to the major component of interlinked network actors, one can speak of a relatively cohesive network structure. The presence of unattached network components in the network structure indicates that there are breaks in the system of knowledge channels which are a hindrance to the process of knowledge diffusion. The cohesion of a network thus can be measured in terms of the number of separated network components, which includes isolated single actors. This categorization includes actors whose knowledge links are exclusively situated on a supra-regional level (i.e., disconnected from the region's internal network structure). Network cohesion and density are interrelated insofar as a fragmented network structure may also lead to a reduced network density. A highly coherent network structure is thus characterized by a small number of separated network components, and this can be interpreted as a sign of the relative strength of the respective network.

3   *Network centralization*: measured by the sum of valued links of the first five ranks of central actors (ranked according to the sum of valued links). While highly complex measures of network centralization are available (such as centrality in terms of "betweenness"), we chose a measure that should indicate the relative importance of centrally positioned actors within a network. The number of central actors that possess an outstanding degree of connectivity might positively influence interorganizational knowledge flows; these particular actors can obtain access to a variety of specific knowledge resources. They potentially can broker the flow of information and synthesize ideas arising in different parts of the network. The actors with a high degree of connectivity might also be able to react faster to

innovation impulses or speed up the interorganizational diffusion of relevant new knowledge and ideas. Thus network centralization could be of particular relevance in the framework of regional innovation networks. With regard to individual actors, high centrality reveals the position of "focal" actors (Krätke 2002b). Furthermore, centrally positioned actors who span specific "structural holes" in a network (Burt 1992) can obtain additional advantages for themselves; Nooteboom, for example, observes that, "if individuals or communities A and B are connected only by C, then C can take advantage of his bridging position by accessing resources that others cannot access" (2003: 116). Owen-Smith and Powell (2004), however, have advanced the thesis that centrality is particularly important in networks that are characterized by more proprietary, "closed" conduits (as opposed to "open channels"). According to this distinction, the definition of centrality is therefore dependent on the institutional characteristics of the actors that dominate the network structure.

4   *Connectivity to regional firms*: measured in terms of the number of regional firms partnered with public research institutions as a percentage of network actors. This measure is of relevance for assessing the interconnectedness of a region's private sector firms and public research establishments (i.e., one type of "innovation infrastructure"). In the debate on regional innovative capacity, it is often noted that the possession of a highly developed and differentiated ensemble of public research establishments is in itself insufficient; strong ties to the region's private sector firms must also exist if the infrastructure's positive potential is to be fully harnessed. If such ties are lacking, the flow of knowledge and "impulses" for innovation is comparatively weak. Hence, a high degree of connectivity to regional firms can be interpreted as a sign of the relative strength of a subsector's network.

5   *Supra-regional connectivity*: measured in terms of the share of network actors with strong supra-regional ties (i.e., above-average number of national and international partnerships). This criterion quantifies interlinkages between regional actors and supra-regional (national and international) cooperative partners and sources of knowledge. Supra-regional and international ties represent "pipelines" (typically of a more proprietary nature) for reciprocal exchange, through which regional actors gain access to external sources of knowledge and innovation impulses, and through which regional actors' specific knowledge flows outward to partners in other regions or countries. While the cooperative relations investigated within the scope of this research are not the sole source of external knowledge acquisition, a high share of network actors with supra-regional ties can be interpreted as a sign of a subsector's relative strength. Drawing on the debate concerning the positive effects of combining internal and external R&D-related cooperative links (see above), the supra-regional connectivity

indicator is geared to broadly capture the magnitude of the external inflow of knowledge, which is assumed to enhance the innovative capacity of regional actors. Emanating outward from actors with strong supra-regional ties, external knowledge and innovation impulses might be indirectly channeled into the overall network structure via regional ties, even if the supra-regional "pipelines" in question are proprietary in nature.

Geographic Scales and Structural Properties of Knowledge Networks in the Metropolitan Region of Hanover

The relative importance of the different geographic scales of knowledge networks is a subject of ongoing debate. Research on the "geography of innovation" has shown that major metropolitan regions (e.g., London, Paris, Stockholm, Munich, Berlin) have the highest levels of private investment in research and development, greatest concentration of knowledge resources and infrastructure, and the highest innovation output (see Simmie 2003; Krätke 2007). The concentration of universities, research facilities, and firms in large metropolitan regions provides differentiated "pools" of scientific and technological knowledge. As Simmie notes, "One of the key advantages of agglomerations of knowledge infrastructure is that they provide possibilities for 'picking and mixing' knowledge inputs as and when they are needed…. So the ability to call on different specializations … is a crucial advantage to be found in large urban agglomerations" (2003: 612). The combination and mixing of diverse knowledge inputs (within or across particular fields of activity and specialization) requires knowledge networking. Within a metropolitan region, the formation of (formal and informal) collaborative networks for knowledge exchange is abetted by the close geographic proximity of actors and network partners. However, empirical research has demonstrated that extremely strong knowledge network ties exist between leading metropolitan centers of innovation at the international level, indicating that a great deal of knowledge is exchanged internationally between key urban regions (see Simmie 2003; Cooke 2006; Tödtling, Lehner, and Trippl 2006). According to Simmie, this selective transnational knowledge networking between major metropolitan regions is strongly pronounced "because [such regions] are often the repositories of leading edge knowledge in the activities in which they are specialized. These regions are the leading nodes in the internationally distributed system of innovation" (2003: 617).

The subject of our case study – the metropolitan region of Hanover-Braunschweig-Göttingen (H-B-G) (see Figure 3.1) – has a polycentric structure, with three prominent urban centers of varying economic

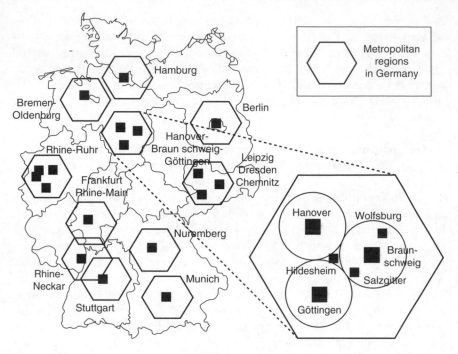

Figure 3.1 The metropolitan region Hanover-Braunschweig-Göttingen and Germany's formally established metropolitan regions.

composition. Hanover, the region's largest urban center, is home to the region's service economy and also features a strong industrial sector. Braunschweig is the industrial subcenter of the region in combination with the nearby Volkswagen headquarters in Wolfsburg. Göttingen, for its part, is a center of science and research (particularly in the life sciences). Compared to other metropolitan regions in the European Union, the sectoral profile of H-B-G's regional economy is characterized by a comparatively strong share of medium high-tech industries (particularly the automotive industry) and knowledge-intensive high-tech services (Krätke 2007). According to regional data maintained by Eurostat, the share of R&D employees in the region's workforce in 2003 was close to that of the Stockholm metropolitan region, and exceeded that of the metropolitan regions of Barcelona, Madrid, and Lyon (Brandt *et al.* 2008). With regard to innovation output (as measured in terms of inventor-based patent output), some subdistricts of the metropolitan region of H-B-G have attained a relatively high rank in the German regional system: in 2000–2005, the subdistricts of Hanover, Braunschweig, and Wolfsburg were ranked in 10th, 18th, and 67th place, respectively, of 439

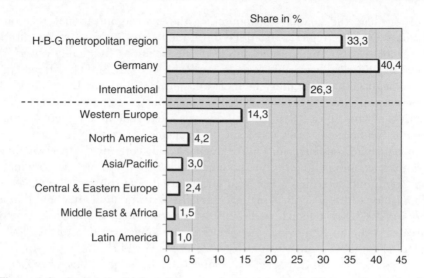

Figure 3.2 Spatial distribution of interorganizational ties for the Hanover-Braunschweig-Göttingen region, 2007.

districts (Kreise) in Germany. Göttingen, by contrast, was ranked 123rd, an upper-mid-level ranking (Schmiedl and Niedermeyer 2006). Although the H-B-G region seems to have relatively strong innovation potential, it ranks below the leading innovation centers in Germany (such as Munich) and the EU (such as Paris).

In the first phase of network analysis, the surveyed actors' ties to scientific institutions and firms at the regional, national, and international level were catalogued in order to ascertain the relative prevalence of cooperative relationships at three geographic scales. The macro analysis revealed the presence of a high percentage of supra-regional (national and international) ties in the network structures of the H-B-G metropolitan region. Some 66% of all surveyed network relations were supra-regional in nature; the remaining third involved connections to actors within the metropolitan region (see Figure 3.2). Some 40% of relations were with partners within the economic territory of Germany outside the H-B-G metropolitan region; in light of Germany's polycentric regional system (see Figure 3.1), one would indeed expect such ties to comprise a high share of all relations. Yet international ties also comprised a significant share (26%) of the total, indicating a potentially strong involvement in "global pipelines" of knowledge transfer. The geographic distribution of international relations was characterized by a strong overrepresentation of ties to Western Europe (14% of all relations), followed by ties to North America (4%) and Asia-Pacific (3%).

Altogether, the spatial distribution of the interorganizational relations reported by the region's scientific institutions and private sector firms corresponds to the geographic profile of interrelations frequently observed for well networked economic regions (see Rehfeld 1999; Bathelt, Malmberg, and Maskell 2004; Tödtling, Lehner, and Trippl 2006). In his analysis of urban regions as national and international nodes for the transfer and sharing of knowledge, Simmie has demonstrated that major metropolitan regions "combine a strong local knowledge capital base with high levels of connectivity to similar regions in the international economy. In this way they are able to combine and decode both codified and tacit knowledge originating from multiple regional, national and international sources" (2003: 607). The debate on regional network structures has repeatedly highlighted that a shortage of supra-regional (national and international) connections could threaten a region's innovative capacities in the long term due to the "lock-in" of the region's internal network relations (Grabher 1993). From this perspective, access to extra-regional sources of knowledge is thus a key factor in a regional economy's innovative capacity. Geographically, the R&D-related network relations of the metropolitan region of H-B-G seem well balanced. The regional actors combine knowledge sources from the region with those of national and international origin.

The region's internal knowledge network structure
in the automotive industry subsector

The second phase of analysis was devoted to assessing the region's *internal* knowledge network, that is, the density and structure of innovation-related cooperative ties within the region's economy. This knowledge network is composed of "inner-regional channels" through which knowledge can flow between organizations. At the regional level, the exchange of knowledge and innovation impulses does not merely take the form of "local buzz" (Bathelt, Malmberg, and Maskell 2004; Storper and Venables 2004), but rather stems to a large degree from structured network relations between economic actors. In this section, the results of the analysis of H-B-G's internal knowledge networks are presented for the automotive industry subsector. According to Eurostat's categorization of knowledge-intensive subsectors, the automotive industry represents a prominent medium high-tech industry. A description and graphic representation of the subsector's network properties are presented. The network actors appearing in the charts are identified with an ID code, and the actors with a central network position are emphasized with a thick black border.

With a total of 192 network actors, the automotive industry subsector is a mid-sized network in the comparative analysis. In terms of the number of surveyed actors, the networks range in size from 122 (agriculture and forestry) to 367 (production technology). The "visual" density of the automotive industry's knowledge network strikes one as relatively high (see Figure 3.3). However, this impression is caused by the large number of actors included in the chart. An analytical measure of network density is more reliable, and is obtained by measuring the number and intensity of recorded connections (i.e., valued links) divided by the number of surveyed actors which function as "active" nodes in the network. The automotive industry subsector has the *highest network density* (26.0) of all surveyed subsectors. The density values of the seven investigated subsectors range from 14.5 to 26.0. Of the criteria used to assess a network's strengths and weaknesses, network density is an important indicator of the relative extent of a regional network's interconnectedness. The automotive industry subsector exhibits the greatest structural density of all subsectors with regard to interregional channels for the flow of knowledge between organizations. This can be interpreted as a particular strength of this knowledge network. The automotive industry's high network density is influenced and reinforced by the relatively *strong cohesion* of the network, as measured by the number of separate network components and the number of regionally isolated network actors (lower values indicating stronger cohesion). An analysis of network cohesion allows the detailed identification of weakly integrated or isolated actors. The chart (see Figure 3.3) shows that this network is composed of one large and strongly interlinked "central component," which contains 172 of the 192 network actors, as well as 11 additional smaller network components which are not connected to the central component. Of these smaller components, six are isolated actors and five are small components consisting of only two to four interlinked actors in each case. This comparatively high degree of network cohesion can be interpreted as a particular strength of the automotive industry subsector's regional knowledge network.

The overall degree of network centralization – as measured by the sum of valued links of the first five ranks of central actors – is quite strong in this field of competence. Of all investigated subsectors, network centralization was the second highest in the automotive industry. The chart highlights the 11 most important central actors (see Figure 3.3). Of those actors with a "focal" position in the regional knowledge network, the majority are public research institutes, while three are large private sector firms. One of these firms is Volkswagen AG, based in Wolfsburg, which exhibits an outstanding degree of connectivity to the other actors in the region's automotive industry subsector.

Roughly 40% of all surveyed network actors in this subsector are public research institutes. The network's structural dependence on public research establishments can be investigated by removing these actors, which leads to an overall disintegration of the network into 42 separate network components and isolates. In the chart of the network's structure, it appears that the

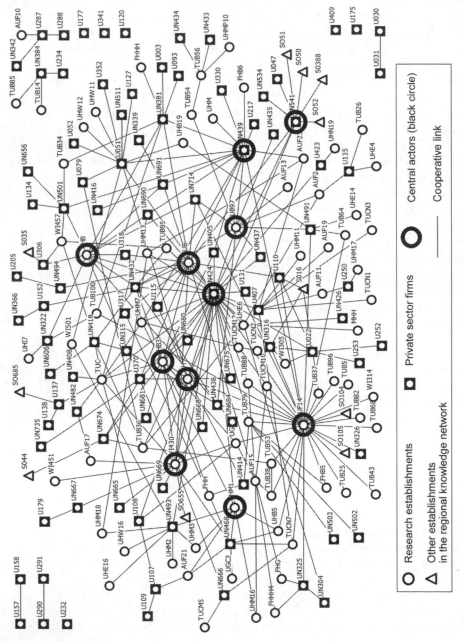

Figure 3.3 The structure of network relations of regional firms and research institutes in the automotive industry cluster of the metropolitan region of Hanover-Braunschweig-Göttingen, 2007.

majority of actors with multiple links are public research institutes. Precise calculations come to the result that the public research institutes' average degree of connectivity significantly exceeds that of the private sector firms. With reference to the discussion above that networks dominated by public organizations tend to adopt an "open science attitude," we can therefore assume that this network predominantly functions as a system of "channels" for interorganizational knowledge flows.

In terms of the degree of connectivity between the region's public research establishments and the corporate economy, the automotive industry subsector's ranking is "medium." Thus in this respect the sector does not exhibit a specific strength. This corresponds to the finding that the public research establishments in the region's automotive industry subsector have a comparatively high share of ties to private sector firms at the national and international level. However, the network structure of this subsector also reveals that there are well-developed cooperative relations between the region's private sector firms and research institutes. Branch-specific knowledge and innovation impulses are generated within this region and transferred between actors via regionally bound "channels."

In the theory of regional clusters and innovation systems, the interplay between a region's internal knowledge sources and its actors' supra-regional knowledge acquisition and transfer has frequently been emphasized (see above). This essential point has to be taken into account in the analysis of regional knowledge networks. In the network analysis presented here, the actors with exceptionally strong supra-regional (national and international) connections were determined by using the average degree value of supra-regional and international connectivity across all actors as a benchmark criterion. The identification of actors with exceptionally strong supra-regional and international connections is relevant for an evaluation of individual actors' network positions – particularly with regard to those actors which are only weakly integrated into the *regional* network structure, but which could have a strategically significant role in the mobilization of external knowledge resources as a result of their strong supra-regional connectivity. On the aggregate level of analysis, each network's supra-regional degree of connectivity was measured in terms of the percentage of actors with exceptionally strong supra-regional connections of all actors in the sector. At 50.6%, the automotive industry's supra-regional connectivity is quite high when compared to other fields (values ranged from 35.0 to 55.1%). Figure 3.4 presents the individual actors with exceptionally strong supra-regional connectivity.

In total there are 40 actors in the regional network which have strong supra-regional ties at both the national and international level. They include the majority of the network's most central actors. Both public research establishments and private sector firms are among the actors with

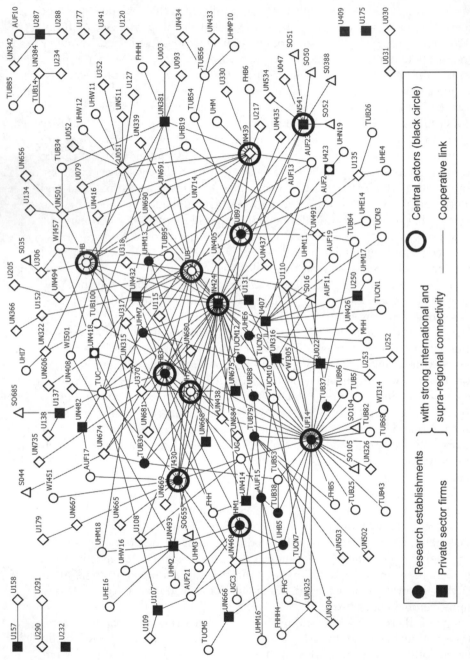

Figure 3.4 Network nodes with strong supra-regional connectivity in the automotive industry cluster of the metropolitan region of Hanover-Braunschweig-Göttingen, 2007.

exceptionally strong supra-regional ties. These actors in particular constitute the intersection between regional "channels" for the flow of interorganizational knowledge and supra-regional (national and international) "pipelines" of knowledge acquisition and transfer. However, five of the small isolated network components contain private sector firms with exceptionally strong supra-regional connections (see Figure 3.4). In these isolated pockets, regional channels of knowledge transfer still have to be developed.

Regarding the size of private sector firms in the region's automotive knowledge network, there appears to be a balanced mixture of small and medium-size enterprises (SMEs) (<250 employees) and large firms (>500 employees). This underscores the point that the regional knowledge network is not focused on SMEs. In a regional cluster of the automotive industry that has been long established (as is the case in the H-B-G metropolitan region), the knowledge network normally includes SMEs as well as large firms, together with public research establishments of different size.

The relevance of cross-sectoral knowledge networking

The opening discussion on regional network analysis emphasized that the detected cooperative links might be interpreted as an expression of localization economies. However, urbanization economies in terms of *cross-sectoral knowledge networking* between different industries of an urban region's economy are also of relevance, as our network analysis identified many actors which are also integrated into the knowledge networks of diverse subsectors of the regional economy. The concept of urbanization economies implies the notion of technological externalities between different industries within a city or urban region (see above). Most large cities and metropolitan regions are characterized by the presence of a diversity of industries ("multi-industry cities"), and this structural property also applies to the investigated case study region.

Using actor-centered regional network analysis, it is possible to identify those organizations which are positioned at the intersection of diverse industries' knowledge networks and thus take on a *bridging function* for knowledge spillovers between the regional economy's diverse subsectors. This includes a combination of related knowledge bases, such as in the case of innovation-related cooperation between actors of the automotive industry and the production technology sector, or a combination of previously unrelated knowledge bases. Figure 3.5 depicts the actors with network ties across sectors in the H-B-G region. Due to their multidisciplinary scope, the region's prominent universities and technical colleges are involved in all subsectors. Furthermore, there are many firms and research establishments

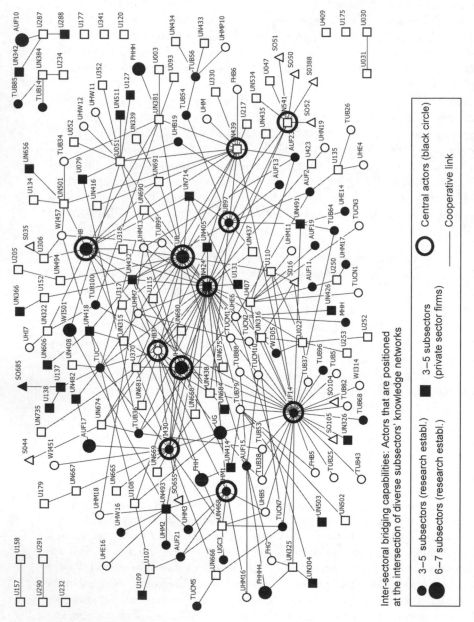

Inter-sectoral bridging capabilities: Actors that are positioned at the intersection of diverse subsectors' knowledge networks

● 3–5 subsectors (research establ.)

● 6–7 subsectors (research establ.)

■ 3–5 subsectors (private sector firms)

○ Central actors (black circle)

— Cooperative link

Figure 3.5 "Bridging function" of actors at the intersection of diverse subsectors in the metropolitan region of Hanover-Braunschweig-Göttingen, 2007.

Table 3.1 Knowledge network properties in selected subsectors of the regional economy (Hanover-Braunschweig-Göttingen, 2007)

Comparative criteria: Subsector	(1) Network size	(2) Network density	(3) Network cohesion	(4) Centrali- zation	(5) Connectivity to regional firms	(6) Supra- regional connectivity
Life sciences	167	16.8	23	289	17.5	55.1
Information and communication technology	209	14.5	29	282	40.7	35.0
Automotive industry	192	26.0	12	452	37.7	50.6
Production technology	367	22.5	22	555	44.3	41.1

Definition of comparative criteria: see pages 107–108 above.

with innovation-related cooperative ties which span 3–5 different subsectors of the regional economy (see Figure 3.5). These actors possess an inter-sectoral bridging capability that harbors a potential for innovation based on new combinations of technological know-how. Actors who are integrated in the knowledge networks of various subsectors presumably have a systemic competence and might be specifically qualified to integrate different technologies in order to generate "ground-breaking" innovations.

A comparative view of network properties in selected subsectors

Table 3.1 presents the most important results of the network analysis in a selection of subsectors and provides a comparative overview of each subsector's relative strengths and weaknesses. The size of a network has no apparent direct impact on its other properties. Of the networks presented in the table, the automotive industry and production technology subsectors have the strongest network density and cohesion. Furthermore, these two subsectors are characterized by comparatively strong supra-regional connectivity at the national and international level; the connectivity between private-sector firms and public research establishments is also comparatively well developed. In addition, both subsectors score highest in overall network centralization due to the centralized position of numerous large firms and prominent research institutes.

Yet certain comparative weaknesses are also evident, particularly in the ICT and the life sciences subsectors (see Table 3.1). The network density in both of these subsectors is quite low, indicating relatively weak cooperative ties at the regional level. However, the life sciences subsector has the highest *supra-regional* connectivity among all investigated subsectors. This corresponds with research findings on the geography of life science knowledge networks in other regions (see Coenen, Moodysson, and Asheim 2004; Owen-Smith and Powell 2004; Tödtling, Lehner, and Trippl 2006). Compared to the ICT and production-technology subsectors, the life sciences subsector in the H-B-G metropolitan region is characterized by a low degree of connectivity to regional private sector firms. However, regional connectivity to private sector firms is dependent on the presence of partnering firms that leverage the knowledge resources of regional research institutions. When asked to identify their private sector partners, the public research institutes in the life sciences subsector of the H-B-G region predominantly cited large global enterprises based in southern Germany, and not locally.

To summarize, the analysis of knowledge networks in the case study region of H-B-G reveals considerable differences between economic subsectors. The region's medium high-tech subsectors (such as the automotive and production technology subsectors) exhibit particular strengths in terms of density and cohesion. The region's high-tech subsectors, by contrast (such as the ICT and life sciences subsectors), are characterized by certain weak points, particularly with regard to network density and cohesion. The comparative "strength" of the region's medium high-tech subsectors can be attributed to the fact that these subsectors play a decisive role in the region's economy and have long shaped its economic development path. The H-B-G region cannot be characterized, however, as a regional economy strongly specialized in a particular industry; indeed, the metropolitan region has a diversified economic structure. The particular strength of the region's medium high-tech subsectors is a testament to the long-term regional clustering of a complementary group of industries, such as the automotive and production technology subsectors. This has created specific regional "labour qualities" (Harvey 1989: 133) in terms of a unique mix of knowledge bases, and a favorable environment for the development of a dense network of cooperative ties between actors in these fields of competence. In 2005, the medium high-tech subsectors of the H-B-G metropolitan region accounted for 49.8% of all manufacturing employment, which is far above the average share for this sector in the metropolitan regions of the EU (Krätke 2007). Within Germany, this percentage is only surpassed by the metropolitan region of Stuttgart. By contrast, the high-tech subsectors in the H-B-G region only accounted for 4.8% of employment, which is below the EU-average share for this sector. With regard to the distinction that can be drawn between subsectors with "synthetic" or "analytic" knowledge bases (see above), a comparison of network properties might also support the assumption that innovation networks in medium high-tech subsectors – which draw on a rather synthetic knowledge base – are more reliant on "sticky" (tacit) knowledge and interactive learning *at the regional level* (see Tödtling, Lehner, and Trippl 2006), and thus form regional knowledge networks of comparatively high density.

In view of the polycentric structure of the H-B-G metropolitan region, questions also arise concerning the intraregional spatial configuration of knowledge networks: are knowledge networks geographically well integrated, or do various subregional networks predominate? The H-B-G metropolitan region is a recently formed political amalgamation of the three relatively autonomous subregions of Hanover, Braunschweig, and Göttingen. The network analysis clearly indicates that network actors are geographically dispersed and that interorganizational cooperative links are unequally distributed in accordance with each subregion's specific economic profile. Thus, the automotive and production technology networks are predominantly concentrated in the subregion of Braunschweig-Wolfsburg; the life sciences network is mainly situated in the subregions of Göttingen and Hanover; and the ICT network is strongly overrepresented in Hanover (Brandt *et al.* 2008). According to these findings, the metropolitan region's actors are still challenged by the need to extend cooperative ties in particular fields of competence over all areas of the region's territory. In this way, our findings indicate that the newly constituted metropolitan region of H-B-G is still somewhat of an "artificial" construct. This metropolitan region was in fact established in order to achieve better integration between the subregions of H-B-G and to overcome the competitive attitudes that have undermined cooperative development between these subregions to date. Regional authorities are making use of the findings obtained in this research in order to strengthen intraregional ties and promote awareness that each subregion is part of a wider metropolitan region, as this regional scale is the best spatial framework for strengthening innovative capacities.

Assessment of Network Impacts on Regional Firms' Innovation Output

The strength of a knowledge network can be assessed first and foremost in terms of the regional and supra-regional connectivity of its actors. This connectivity is the decisive *relational* basis of a region or subsector's scientific and technological creativity. In order to test the central hypothesis that "strong" regional network properties increase a region's innovative capacity, the impacts exerted by knowledge networks on the innovation output of firms are analyzed for all firms that provided patent application data – a key indicator of innovation output. Since the data on patent applications (the dependent variable) are *count data*, a negative binomial regression is used.

Table 3.2 Variable labels and definitions (regression analysis of network impacts)

Variable	Definition
Dependent variable:	
Patents	Number of patent applications (counts of patents)
Independent variables:	
R&D size	Number of R&D employees
Firm age	Age in years since firm founding
Supra-regional links (Model 1)	Degree of connectivity to national and international partners outside the H-B-G region (number and intensity of links)
International links (Model 2)	Degree of connectivity to international partners outside Germany (number and intensity of links)
Regional connectivity	Degree of connectivity in the regional network (number and intensity of links to regional partners)

This regression model was also used by Owen-Smith and Powell (2004) in their analysis of network impacts in Boston's biotechnology sector. The negative binomial regression is suitable for correcting overdispersion in count data (our data include a large share of cases with low counts and a small number of cases with particularly high counts).

Model specification (see Table 3.2): Innovation output as the *dependent variable* is measured by the number of successful patent applications filed by 412 private sector firms in the H-B-G region (these data were collected in the context of the network analysis survey; only reporting firms are included). Innovation output is operationalized as the number of patent applications (counts of patents) in the period under investigation.

Independent variables: "R&D size" is a rough indicator of a firm's internal innovative capacity. This variable is based on survey data concerning the number of R&D employees at each firm. "Firm age" might also be relevant to innovative capacity in terms of the length of the firm's R&D experience. In addition, several network measures are derived from the overall analysis described above. In order to test the possible impact of the firms' supra-regional connectivity (which provides access to external knowledge resources), the variable "supra-regional links" is operationalized as the number and intensity of links to national and international partners outside the region. As an additional measure of the regional firms' linkage to external knowledge resources, the variable "international links" is operationalized as the number and intensity of links to *international* partners (i.e., partners outside Germany). Since these two variables of supra-regional connectivity are strongly correlated (r = 0.67 at a 0.01 level of significance), they are included *alternatively* in different variants of the regression analysis (Models 1 and 2). Particularly relevant to the impact of *regional* network properties is the variable "regional connectivity," which measures the number and intensity of a firm's ties to regional partners. This could be interpreted as a simple measure of the centrality of an actor's network position (see above). However, this measure is also the basis of the measurement of overall network density (see above) and indicates how tightly an individual firm is connected to an ensemble of regional partners. Thus the degree of connectivity captures the number and diversity of "channels" through which a firm accesses a region's knowledge resources. If the density of *regional* network relations matters for innovative capacity at the firm level, we can expect a positive impact of "regional connectivity" on the firms' innovation output (Hypothesis 1). Furthermore, it is frequently posited in regional innovation theory that the density of a firm's supra-regional ties – particularly international ones – has a significant impact on innovation capacity (see above). We can therefore expect "supra-regional links" and "international links" to have a positive impact on innovation output (Hypothesis 2).

Results: Tables 3.3 and 3.4 present the findings of the two tested variants (Models 1 and 2). Both variants confirm the relevance of "R&D size" for innovation output. Model 1 shows that "R&D size," "regional connectivity," and "supra-regional links" all have a highly significant impact on a firm's innovation output (see Table 3.3). "Firm age" has apparently no significant impact. These findings support Hypothesis 1: that the degree of a firm's connectivity to regional partners positively affects innovation in terms of the number of successful patent applications. The regression model also supports Hypothesis 2: the assumption that supra-regional connectivity has a relevant impact on innovation output. Table 3.4 presents the findings of the second variant (Model 2). Here, as well, "R&D size" and "regional connectivity" have a highly significant impact on a firms' innovation output. The analysis thus supports Hypothesis 1: that a firm's innovation output is positively affected by its connectivity to regional partners. This test also underscores the particular importance of international links on innovation output.

In sum, the results confirm the central hypothesis of the network analysis approach: namely, that regional connectivity is of decisive importance for innovation capacity. Interorganizational connectivity represents the relational foundation of a region's scientific and technological creativity.

Table 3.3 Negative binomial regression of patent applications: Model 1 (including variable "supra-regional connectivity")

Number of observations	LR chi2(4)	Prob > chi2	Pseudo R2	Log likelihood	Dependent variable
412	206.58	0.0000	0.1065	−866.93512	Patents

Variable	Coef.	Std. Err.	z	P>|z|	95% Conf. Interval	
R&D size	.0059462	.0013845	4.29	0.000	.0032326	.0086598
Firm age	.0044679	.0035202	1.27	0.204	−.0024315	.0113673
Regional connectivity	.0737484	.0166155	4.44	0.000	.0411826	.1063142
Supra-regional links	.0527369	.0111586	4.73	0.000	.0308664	.0746073
const	−.1970054	.2236298	−0.88	0.378	−.6353118	.2413010
/lnalpha	1.778474	.0937855			1.594658	1.962290
alpha	5.920816	.5552865			4.926645	7.115606

Likelihood-ratio test of alpha = 0; chibar2(01) = 7.5e+04; Prob>=chibar2 = 0.000

Table 3.4 Negative binomial regression of patent applications: Model 2 (including variable "international connectivity")

Number of observations	LR chi2(4)	Prob > chi2	Pseudo R2	Log likelihood	Dependent variable
412	191.73	0.0000	0.0988	−874.35632	Patents

Variable	Coef.	Std. Err.	z	P>|z|	95% Conf. Interval	
R&D size	.0056453	.0016428	3.44	0.001	.0024254	.0088651
Firm age	.0053163	.0035163	1.51	0.131	−.0015756	.0122081
Regional connectivity	.0999288	.0164817	6.06	0.000	.0676252	.1322324
International links	.0820848	.0294587	2.79	0.005	.0243468	.1398227
const	−.0213179	.2281971	−0.09	0.926	−.4685761	.4259403
/lnalpha	1.841328	.0926534			1.659731	2.022926
alpha	6.304908	.5841712			5.257896	7.560412

Likelihood-ratio test of alpha = 0; chibar2(01) = 8.1e+04; Prob>=chibar2 = 0.000

Conclusion

This chapter aimed at a presentation of the specific socioeconomic context of technological creativity in a selected metropolitan region, focusing on the analysis of the urban region's knowledge networks and their impact on innovative capacity. The chapter started from a discussion of the literature on urban and regional innovation networks, including the debate on knowledge and its impact on regional development, the distinction between different types of knowledge, and the distinction between "synthetic" and "analytical" knowledge bases that highlights the significance of the specific sectoral characteristics of a local economy in the innovation process. Existing scholarship on national and regional innovation systems has considered the different geographic scales of interactive knowledge generation, as well as the variety of actors involved. Regional and urban innovation networks represent the framework for "collaborative" knowledge generation that drives technological creativity in research-intensive industrial sectors. Yet the mechanisms of interorganizational knowledge flows remain underexplored. According to Owen-Smith and Powell (2004), there are different ways in which networks might be understood to transmit knowledge between organizations: the network linkages can represent either "open" channels or more proprietary, "closed" conduits. Open channels facilitate knowledge spillovers to the collective benefit of both loosely connected and centrally positioned organizations. Although the literature on innovation networks and interactive knowledge generation is helpful for understanding the unfolding of creativity in innovation-oriented subsectors of the economy (beyond the level of individuals' creative skills), it is characterized by a lack of detailed analyses of the structure and functioning of urban innovation networks. This chapter therefore presented a substantive analysis of an urban region's knowledge networking, using the interdisciplinary methodology of "social network analysis."

The theoretical discussion emphasized that the scientific and technological creativity of an urban region is to a large extent dependent on the knowledge networks maintained by regional actors. The network analysis of cooperative ties between public research establishments and private sector firms in the metropolitan region of Hanover-Braunschweig-Göttingen identified various strengths and weaknesses. Knowledge networks in the medium high-tech industries (such as the automotive and production technology subsectors) exhibited particular "strengths" in terms of density and cohesion, areas that were weak points for the region's high-tech industries (such as the ICT and the life sciences subsectors). A comparatively low network density and weak network cohesion signifies in general that a region's interorganizational knowledge flows are impaired; it indicates that existing regional knowledge resources are not being sufficiently mobilized. Weak linkages between a region's scientific establishments and private sector firms can obstruct the intraregional diffusion of knowledge, and weak supra-regional linkages curtail the potential to exploit external knowledge resources for regional growth.

The network analysis presented provides an assessment of the network structure and its properties, but does not produce in-depth information about individual cooperation links. Network links facilitate interorganizational knowledge flows, whether they take the form of "open" channels or "closed," proprietary conduits. However, geographic clustering can also lead to a dense web of informal network relations which might function as an equally important mechanism of interorganizational knowledge diffusion. Innovating firms make use of various forms of knowledge resources, including formal R&D cooperation, contracted research, and selective collaboration among regional actors. The above analysis has clearly shown that regional knowledge networks have a significantly positive impact on the innovative output of firms: the empirical assessment of the impact of networks on innovation output supports the hypothesis that regional connectivity decisively matters for innovative capacity. The analysis also confirmed that the actors' supra-regional (and particularly international) connections positively influence innovative capacity. Based on this study, the general conclusion can be drawn that in the realm of technological innovation the creative capital of cities depends on the properties or "strengths" of their knowledge networks in specific branches of economic activity. This also implies that the creative capital of cities is likely to have a specific "sectoral profile," defined by one or more dominant local sectors with "strong" knowledge network properties.

One consequence of this analysis would be that the economic territory of metropolitan regions could be described as a network of production districts connected by urban infrastructures. Lipietz (1993) suggests that large cities and metropolitan regions can be characterized as a "network of (industrial) districts." However, the analysis in this chapter also suggests a reversal of this term proposed by Lipietz (1993), that is, that the metropolitan region's economic area can also be regarded as a "district of networks." Detailed investigation of knowledge networks in diverse subsectors of the Hanover metropolitan region detected that there are many regional economic actors who perform a "bridging function" between the knowledge networks of different subsectors, as in "multi-industry cities" regional actors draw on cross-sectoral knowledge spillovers. The existence of a metropolitan "district of networks" could be seen, therefore, as a prerequisite for the inter-sectoral spread of innovation impulses.

The analysis here concentrated on knowledge networks as a particular "relational" component of regional innovation systems; other components include the internal innovation capacities of firms and the regional innovation infrastructure. Also, extra-regional triggers of innovation are clearly important, as regional actors can draw on innovation infrastructure at the national scale and on knowledge ties to national and global partners. However, regional knowledge networks are a socially produced form of "creative capital" and a source of innovation which can be harnessed by a region's strategic development initiatives in order to pursue an innovation-driven economic development path. Thus regional knowledge networks are a key component of the creative capital of urban regions.

4

Creativity in the Culture and Media Industries

The Impact of Commercial Imperatives on Artistic Creativity

Introduction

This chapter examines the link between cities and creativity from the perspective of the production of cultural goods. It focuses on the institutional structure of present-day cultural production and its spatial organization at the regional and international level. The culture industry can be regarded as a prototype of the flexible organization of industry due to its reliance on inter-firm networking, flexible work relations, and the cross-marketing of new products in ever shorter cycles. Similar organizational features emerge in other industries, which, like the culture industry, are engaged in fierce competition to produce innovative products. To some extent, the cultural economy can be regarded as a bellwether of the future organizational form that urban economies might take, as it produces new "city industries" whose impacts are felt far beyond that of older "city industries" such as the printing and publishing trades. Urban clusters of cultural production increasingly comprise a considerable share of regional economic activity and exhibit strong networks of inter-firm cooperation. The selective concentration of cultural industries in a limited number of large cities and metropolises within national urban systems – a concentration also evident at the level of the global urban system (cf. Krätke 2003; Krätke and Taylor 2004) – is a major feature of the geographical distribution of the cultural industries.

A second important feature of the contemporary cultural industries' institutional form is the globalization of large cultural enterprises, which enables global media firms with their worldwide network of subsidiaries and branch offices to forge links between clusters of cultural production in different cities. Transnational linkages amongst local culture and media

The Creative Capital of Cities: Interactive Knowledge Creation and the Urbanization Economies of Innovation, First Edition. Stefan Krätke.
© 2011 Stefan Krätke. Published 2011 by Blackwell Publishing Ltd.

industry clusters are at the heart of an emerging network of global cultural economy centers within the worldwide urban system.

The cultural economy as a whole comprises commercial, non-profit, public, and community organizations. However, the commercial or capitalist sector has a lead role in the economic circuits of cultural production and is based on for-profit firms that employ artists or contract with them for services, while the non-profit sector encompasses public cultural establishments (such as museums and opera houses) and small informally organized community arts facilities and artists' centers (Markusen 2008). Thus today's cultural economy is a highly differentiated field of activity incorporating diverse subsectors that range from traditional artistic production to the high-tech branches of the media industry. In addition, parts of the culture industry (such as the multimedia sector) have integrated knowledge-, design-, and technology-intensive production activities. A broad delimitation of the cultural economy also includes architectural firms and the video games industry (KEA 2006).

According to Scott, the culture industries comprise economic activities that are concerned with "image production" (Scott 1996, 1997). The products of these activities are of the utmost cultural importance as they function as agents of information, influence, and persuasion or as vehicles of entertainment and image construction. The culture industries include the diverse branches of the entertainment and media industries, such as theatres and orchestras, music, film, television and radio production, the printing and publishing trades, the multimedia sector, as well as design and advertising firms. In other contexts of analysis, the advertising industry might well be classified among producer services, just as the printing industry can be included among the traditional manufacturing sectors. Even universities, which are important providers of new knowledge and educational services, could be included as a distinct subsector of the culture industries, particularly when the ongoing commercialization of the university as an institution is taken into account. Commercialization has led some prominent universities to become major export-oriented culture industry establishments that attract foreign students and receive high education fees. The following analysis, however, focuses on the culture industry's core of commercial private enterprise and does not refer to universities (these were discussed in Chapter 3 as public research establishments that employ scientifically creative workers).

The "image production" activities of the cultural industries should not be conceived solely as the work of creating product images. The entertainment and media industries also play a key role in the propagation of lifestyle images. There is therefore considerable overlap between the culture and media industries. Most forms of cultural production are directly or indirectly organized as specific value chains within the media industry. In the framework of an increasing "mediatization" of social communication, consumption, and entertainment, the culture and media industries have a direct impact on large parts of the economy as well as a considerable influence on consumer patterns and lifestyles. The culture and media industries are a focus of the economic restructuring and commercialization of cultural production and are at the heart of the "culturalization of the economy," whose market success is increasingly founded on the construction of images and extensive marketing activities (see Featherstone 1994; Lash and Urry 1994; Scott 2008). According to Featherstone (1994: 399), "the awareness that culture industries ... can play a growing role in national and local economies has grown alongside the general expansion in the production and consumption of symbolic goods in contemporary Western societies."

The relation between culture and cities is to a large extent shaped by the "commodification of culture," that is, the subsumption of cultural activities in the capitalist economy. It also includes phenomena such as the formation of urban "entertainment districts" that enhance the attractiveness and economic development potential of urban areas. Such aspects have long been the subject of urban research (see Crane 1992; Kirchberg 1992; Wynne 1992; Kearns and Philo 1993; Zukin 1995; Hannigan 1998; Kirchberg and Göschel 1998; Biswas 2000; Roost 2000; Bittner 2001; Clark 2003; Benneworth and Hospers 2009). Cities are, of course, also places where cultural goods and services are produced for local, national, and international markets.

With regard to the culture and media industries, which today are frequently labeled as the "creative industries," our focus here is on those branches (and products) of social activity that are determined to a large extent by artistically creative work and the production and communication of symbolic meanings and images (see Throsby 2001; Amin and Thrift 2003). I use the term "culture industry" (or, likewise, the cultural economy sector) to refer to these activities. Today, cultural production includes a vast area of social activities which emerge from diverse realms of cultural practice, such as music, theatre, dance, writing, painting, and so on. Other areas of cultural production are strongly connected to the rise of modern technologies, such as film and music production, journalism and diverse new media sectors. Some of these activities are relatively "pure" forms of artistry (e.g., painting), while others have a more limited artistic component (e.g., journalism). Cultural products that inform, educate, or entertain (metaphorically, "food for the mind"), account for a high and growing share of economic activity in present-day society. Cultural production in this area is also increasingly subject to industrial production methods and market segmentation. Products are designed to target specific groups of cultural "consumers" and exhibit varying degrees of quality and sophistication. In the widest sense, "food for the mind" also encompasses the afternoon soap opera, which could be seen as the culture and media sector's "fast food" market segment. It would be inappropriate to confine an analysis of the cultural economy to "elite" segments of the market as opposed to "popular" culture, especially since most cultural products are distributed through mass media (print media, TV and radio, Internet). The culture industry's commercial imperatives are to some extent in structural conflict with value-based notions of art's social function, as expressed by the so-called "Himalaya option" – that is, as media content becomes more demanding and sophisticated, the pool of potential consumers shrinks. For this reason, "food for the mind" is served up by culture and media companies predominantly as one-size-fits-all commodities for mass-market segments. However, I do not intend to express a privileging of "high" culture, but rather to encourage more critical reflection on the capitalist dynamics that shape differential valuations of cultural products.

To help us grasp these dynamics, Throsby (2001) helpfully highlights the distinction between the economic and cultural value of commodities distributed by the cultural economy, and notes that their valuation depends on larger cultural factors. When "high" or "elitist" cultural norms are prevalent, cultural goods are valued in certain ways. Atonal classical music, for example, would represent a product with high cultural but low economic value, and a TV soap opera would represent a product with high economic but low cultural value. In marked contrast to this attempt to offer a critical assessment of the value of the products of the cultural economy, the mainstream debate on creative industries is characterized by a highly simplistic view of creativity: the positive (cultural) valuation of the culture industry's "creative" products is accepted as a self-evident truth and rarely questioned. Indeed, the view it encourages is that the culture industry's creativity is superior to other forms of creativity (such as the creativity required for technological research and development). It behoves us to ask if the invention of a new television show format such as *Big Brother* truly involves more knowledge and creativity than that required by scientists and engineers to develop new technologies.

The Institutional Order of the Cultural Economy: Creativity in a Capitalist Context

While Florida's "creative class" theory is based on the notion that certain urban environments are a stimulant to creativity, it offers no insight into the ways in which industries that thrive on the creativity of their workforce actually function. In addition, most scholarship in the debate on "creative industries" is quite uncritical of the specific economic and organizational frameworks within which creative work takes place. In this section, the culture industry's internal mechanisms for organizing creative performance are outlined in order to critically assess the contours of creative work in a capitalist context.

The term "culture industry" indicates a perspective that is directed toward the economic processes and institutional forms by which cultural goods are produced as commodities and distributed to consumers. However, the delimitation of specific industries is confronted with difficulties, definitional problems, and "fuzziness." These problems apply not only to the cultural economy, but also to traditional industrial branches, new industries, the financial sector, and the service economy. According to Scott (2000), the culture industry encompasses those branches of production whose products function as a carrier of symbolic meanings and images, as a means of entertainment, as tools for informing, convincing, and influencing people, or as means of image cultivation (social self-representation).

Throsby (2001) has schematized the culture industry as a system of concentric circles with the creative arts at the center. The inner circle is made up of traditional artistic activities. In the outer circles, cultural goods and services are created with a diminishing share of original and creative artistic output. The second circle in Throsby's concept includes film, television, and radio production, as well as journalism and the publishing industry. The third circle encompasses branches of activity which overlap with other industries, but are categorized under the culture industry insofar as their products and services are carriers of cultural meaning or involve "image-producing activities." This third, outer circle includes advertising and design agencies as well as architectural firms. While Throsby's concept is useful in certain respects, the contemporary entertainment and media industries represent a complex of activities that extends through all the above-mentioned circles of cultural production to flexibly combine and recombine various products and services.

The contemporary culture industry is heavily shaped by a capitalist mode of production, as cultural products are "to ever greater degree supplied through profit-making institutions" (Scott 2000: 2), even though there remains an array of cultural producers outside the realm of private entrepreneurial business (see Markusen 2008). The term "culture industry," however, should not be understood as an analogy to the institutional practices of Fordism, but rather as a term that emphasizes capitalist forms of cultural production. The organizational forms of the culture industry have adopted a Fordist model only in particular branches of activity (e.g., printing) and in particular historical periods (e.g., Hollywood film production in the 1920s). In the current era, the cultural economy sector is to an increasing extent a model for a flexibilized and networked form of social production, which has spread in design-intensive and innovation-driven subsectors of the economy in tandem with changing organizational forms of production in knowledge-intensive manufacturing branches. In this sense, the cultural industry represents an extremely "modern" industry. The culture industry is also an important driving force in the development of spatial forms of industrial organization which are of strategic importance for a knowledge-intensive and innovation-based model of economic development.

The following sections will explore the institutional order of cultural production as a "creative" industry. This entails a focus on institutional forms and the specific characteristics of the industry's economic and spatial organization. The industry's products and market segments, value chains and actors, as well as the "logic of action" and rules under which its actors operate are elucidated. The discussion emphasizes the institutional forms and practices by which cultural products are produced and circulated as commercial products, including the characteristic division of labor and organization of work in the cultural production sector. Attali's (1984) survey of the music industry marked the first analysis of the cultural economy from an institutional perspective, and Ryan (1992) was the first to employ this perspective in an examination of the entire culture industry (see also Caves 2002). Ryan (1992: 13) identifies the organization of production according to capitalist principles, in a manner that *combines* capitalist and artistic structures of creative production, as a particular feature of the contemporary culture industry (see also Throsby 2001). While this perspective for the most part neglects the public non-profit sector of the cultural economy (e.g., public theatres), with regard to the development of artistic innovation and creativity the non-profit sector is of particular significance (see Throsby 2001: 116f.). Concerning the private sector, two particularly relevant aspects of the culture industry's institutional order have to be considered (see Ryan 1992). On the one hand, the production process within the cultural economy's firms is divided into a "creative phase" and a "reproduction and distribution phase," whereby the creative phase clearly differs from the standard industrial practices used in the reproduction phase. On the other hand, the "truncated" product life cycle of commercial cultural products confronts firms with a particular set of marketing and sales problems.

Ryan (1992) begins his institutional analysis of the culture industry by highlighting a particular characteristic of *creative artistic* production: works of art are valued culturally according to the uniqueness and originality ascribed to them. To satisfy public demand for original creative works, the culture industry employs a unique division of labor; separate groups of workers are involved in the "creative" and "reproductive" phases of cultural production. The workers in the creative phase are considered by the culture industry's managers as the artistic workforce. In Western societies, artistic production is always considered as an individual performance, as the product of the creative personality. Artistic production thus can be regarded as a counterpole to the "abstract" – i.e., depersonalized – work that governs assembly line production methods of a Fordist industrial organization. The term "creative" industries implicitly tries to distinguish the culture industries from Fordist industrial structures, ignoring the fact that in many manufacturing sectors these forms of industrial organization have been substituted by "post-Fordist" structures of flexible specialization and work organization (see Leborgne and Lipietz 1991). Nevertheless, creative cultural producers cannot be put to work as abstract, anonymous factors of production like the employees of an assembly line. Likewise, artistic production that is valued for its originality cannot be divorced from the creative talent of the individual. This remains true despite the formation of various modes of "collective" cultural production (such as project teams) in the creative stage of product development. As a consequence, the creative workforce has retained a relatively high degree of individual autonomy in the workplace, even in large capitalist firms. Artistic insight and inspiration cannot be standardized; the *Eingebung* (inspiration) of the artist(s) in terms of a creative idea, on the basis of which a cultural product innovation is generated, cannot be rationally planned in advance. Creative work is thus unsuited to Fordist production methods, which rely on planned inputs and standardized work processes to achieve greater productive output. In order to resolve the contradiction between artistically creative production and capitalist industrial production, the culture industry pursues various rationalization strategies (discussed below).

Another major contradiction concerns the specific characteristics of cultural products that are marketed as commodities. Because cultural products are valued above all for their originality, their commercialization and mass distribution leads to an erosion of the qualities which distinguish them as products of artistic creativity. Capitalist growth imperatives are thus at odds with the creative endeavor: the mass reproduction of the creative work undermines its original attraction. As a consequence, cultural products have "truncated" product life cycles (Ryan 1992: 55). In contrast to the product life cycles of industrial consumer goods, newly released cultural products (such as books or music CDs) generally achieve – presupposing their success – initially high but rapidly diminishing sales figures. In some cases, the market success of cultural products can be revived at a later date through their re-release. As a result of these market conditions, cultural firms are forced to continuously invest in the development of new products. This ensures a continuous flow of original output, of "fresh" material for mass distribution. The cultural economy demands constant innovation in terms of new stories and designs in order to satisfy unpredictable consumer tastes (see Caves 2002). This means that firms in the cultural sector must maintain a high level of "risk investment" (Banks *et al.* 2000).

The cultural economy can be broadly subdivided according to various marketing conditions and "distribution systems" for cultural products. There are diverse interrelationships between the various cultural producers and suppliers of distribution services for cultural goods (e.g., between film producers, TV stations, and the advertising industry). A particular role in the cultural economy's institutional order is fulfilled by advertising and media firms. The marketing component of cultural production has expanded tremendously in recent decades, such that the "mediatized" elements (marketing, advertising, design) of the production process are now often more costly than the product's actual fabrication. Product differentiation, market segmentation, and product branding are among the most important marketing activities (see Klein 2001). The growing significance of advertising and media firms in the capitalist economy is intimately connected to the changing nature of consumption in a highly commercialized society: industrial firms no longer merely sell material products, but also the feelings and emotions attached to them. Marlboro, for example, does not simply sell cigarettes, but "rugged independence"; automobile manufacturers do not simply sell cars, but "chromed chariots." Brands deliver alluring lifestyle-related "ways of seeing." To an increasing extent, commodity fetishism now takes the form of brand fetishism.

The growing significance of marketing activities has been accompanied by the development of an ever-greater variety of advertising media (posters, brochures, promotional films, Internet advertising, etc.). Commercial advertisements function as "publicity products" (Ryan 1992) that imbue commodities with a specific image and make them recognizable, distinguishable, and desirable. For this reason, the advertising sector (including design agencies) can be categorized amongst the cultural economy sector. Media firms also play a significant role in the marketing and advertising business: public and private TV and radio programming is a semi-public good in that no single advertisement is sold to consumers. Media firms sell their capacity to reach large audiences to the highest bidder. Advertising revenue represents the key economic basis of private-sector media firms and provides an indication of the distributive efficiency of a given form of media or media supplier. Large advertising firms also develop close ties with the entertainment industry in order to become *integrated* communication service firms. The "publicity capital" (Ryan 1992: 74) thus created is playing an increasingly important role in product distribution.

In order to subdivide the cultural economy according to the conditions by which cultural products are marketed, it is useful to draw on the classical differentiation made between private and public goods (Musgrave 1969). Ryan (1992) distinguishes between three categories of products in the cultural economy. Firstly, there are *private goods* such as books, CDs, home videos, and paintings, which are distributed to individual consumers for their exclusive use. Private cultural commodities are predominantly produced by private sector firms, and, as a result of the need to market cultural products, producing firms also maintain marketing departments or work with advertising agencies. Secondly, there are the *quasi-private* goods of the cultural economy, such as theatre productions, music concerts, festivals etc. These goods are characterized by collective consumption that is spatially delimited by the viewer's gaze. In the performing arts, public performances represent the way in which the "original" product – that is, the "premiere" or first showing – is reproduced. These quasi-private products of the culture industry also require marketing; to this end, celebrity performers, or "stars," are created. Today, many cultural products are marketed with a combination of different distributional techniques: film and television enterprises, for example, which originally stood in direct competition to one another, now work together to market cultural products. Television rights for cinema films are sold; film studios help to produce TV series; the film distribution system (i.e., cinema chains) is used as an advertising medium; and film productions are reproduced as DVDs for home viewing, thereby transforming them into private cultural products. The trend toward cross-sectoral marketing is undermining traditional sectoral divisions in the culture industry.

Thirdly, there are the *quasi-public* goods of the cultural economy, such as radio and television programs, as well as Internet portals. These goods are presented to a wide public audience. In principle, everybody can receive these cultural products, and no consumers are excluded through pricing. Public-service television fees are not to be understood as a market price for television programs. Private television stations cannot directly finance their programming by sales to the audience; they rely instead on their access to consumers in order to collect advertising revenues. Indeed, there are no technical imperatives that insist that television programming must be a quasi-public good; TV programming has also been distributed as a private good (e.g., HBO) for a long time. Radio and television programs create a publicity effect for other categories of products and services; together with newspapers and the Internet, they represent the "publicity sector" of the cultural economy (see Ryan 1992). Private sector firms (including the producers of private cultural goods) "rent" the distributive capacity of the mass media for advertising purposes, and advertising has become the most important source of income for large media firms. The publicity sector of the cultural economy has risen to become a central connecting node of the diverse branches of the culture industry.

As the publicity sector occupies a central position in the cultural economy and the production of its quasi-public cultural products involves the "assembly" of pre-produced elements (e.g., films, TV shows etc.) and intermediate products (e.g., advertisements) into a continuous program flow, the expansion of this media sector creates various market opportunities for other producers in the culture industry and thus contributes to the accelerated expansion of the entire cultural economy sector. The related differentiation, increasing specialization, and inter-firm division of labor in the cultural industry is also a driving force of this economic sector's specific spatial forms of organization. Additionally, the institutional order of the cultural economy continuously generates new business opportunities and "impulses" for the expansion of the number of firms in this sector (particularly small and specialized producers and service firms).

Internal and external division of labor in the culture industry

The private enterprise form of cultural production must handle the specific challenge that the creativity and originality of artistic work can only be achieved when cultural producers' work arrangements offer a relatively high degree of individual (creative) autonomy. The counterpole to this constellation is Fordist industrial methods, which submit individual producers to an extreme division of tasks and rigid machine-based production flow. Today, in a manner similar to the cultural economy sector, corporations in research-intensive manufacturing sectors are forced to provide their R&D employees with work arrangements that allow for creativity and the development of innovative capabilities. The large cultural industry firms must organize the process of production in a way that enables employees to generate "original" artistic work which is capable of market success. Hence they must offer their creative workers a level of freedom in which experimental activity for developing novel "compositions" can unfold; this entails a certain degree of tolerance toward failure that occurs in experimental work. At the same time, the firm must bring this creative process under the firm's control, so that management can set guidelines for content creation. Against this backdrop, a subdivision of the production process into "creative" and "reproductive" phases has emerged in the culture economy (Ryan 1992). In the film industry, the creative phase encompasses story and screenplay development up to shooting and post-production (editing, effects, etc.). The reproductive phase, by contrast, encloses the re-production of the film reel itself and its conversion into home consumer formats (DVD, Blue-ray). In the music industry, the creative phase includes the composition and arrangement of the musical score, as well as its rehearsal, performance, and mastering in the studio. The reproductive phase encompasses the duplication and mass production of audio CDs. In the book publishing industry, the creative phase includes literary production and editing, while the reproductive phase involves mass printing. In cultural production, just as in the production of informational goods, the creative phase accounts for a higher share of production costs (per unit) than reproduction and distribution.

In the creative phase, a "craft-based" form of labor is dominant; the individual artistic skill and talent of the employee is most important. However, there are also various forms of specialization according to subsector (dancers, musicians, writers), production phase (writing, directing, editing),

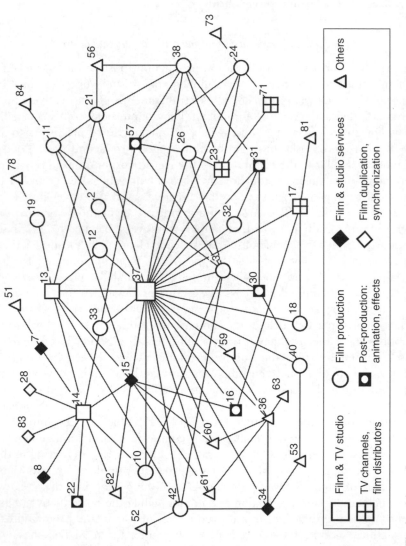

Figure 4.1 The local inter-firm network of business relations in the film industry cluster of Potsdam/Babelsberg.

and cultural form (orchestra, rock music). However, this type of artistic specialization is still vastly different from the specialization that takes place under the Fordist model of industrial organization. In the cultural economy's reproduction phase, the division of labor and forms of specialization are similar to those in other industries. Examples of the reproduction phase include book printing, DVD and audio CD production, etc. In these areas of activity, technological innovations and processes of intra-firm rationalization have replaced human labor and led to a partial dequalification of work. In many segments of the culture industry concerned with technical reproduction, the "machine system," "traditional" manufacturing occupations, and hierarchical management are predominant.

The cultural economy sector is also subject to a highly developed inter-firm division of labor. A large portion of creative experimental activities are carried out in the extensive "periphery" of the established corporate cultural economy sector, as many of the small peripheral firms and self-employed specialists are engaged in the production of particularly creative works. Furthermore, a growing share of the production processes is undertaken by small, independent subcontractors that carry out specific functions (e.g., digital effects in the film industry). There are always new opportunities to set up small firms which operate as subcontractors (i.e., specialized supplier firms) to larger corporations in the cultural economy sector, not only for specific services (e.g., casting agencies in the film industry), but also in the area of creative content production. On the regional and local level, the increasing inter-firm division of labor is articulated in the emergence of densely networked production clusters in the culture and media industries. The local production cluster of the film industry in Potsdam/Babelsberg, on the outskirts of Berlin, is representative of how local firms set up a dense network of business relations within a specialized local cultural economy district (see Figure 4.1). This local inter-firm transaction and communication network, which was investigated in 2000 (see Krätke 2002b), includes a variety of actors with different functions in the film industry, and reveals a high density of network relations as well as a strongly cohesive overall network structure. Beyond local inter-firm relations, the companies located in Potsdam/Babelsberg also have many cooperative partners in the city of Berlin and in other national and international centers of the film industry and cultural economy.

The inter-firm division of labor in the cultural economy leads to the emergence of a complex and highly differentiated "value-added network" of cultural production. Figure 4.2 maps this network for the film industry. The value-added network is based on the interlinkage of specific functions within a given area of cultural production (see Leyshon, Matless, and Revill 1998; Leyshon 2001). However, it can also be designated as a "value chain" with a view to the integration of successive inputs for product development, production, and final distribution.

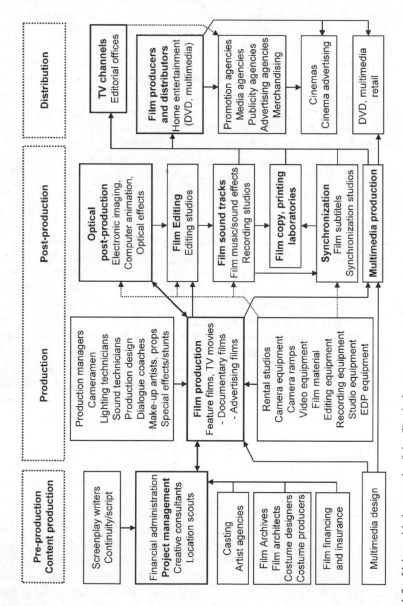

Figure 4.2 Value-added network of the film industry.

Two important aspects of work organization in the creative phase of cultural production are the project team and the *project-related organization* of the production process. A distinction should be drawn between project teams that are set up internally within the organizational boundary of a particular firm, and project teams that arise from inter-firm collaboration in a flexible project-related network (consisting of freelancers and employees from different firms). In the case of project teams that cross over firm boundaries, "the creative product is often a collective good, produced within a collective firm, where many entrepreneurial agents co-operate, and this is explained by the necessity to organize a complex work, where many dissimilar strategic capabilities need to be harmonized" (Belussi and Sedita 2008: 239). In integrating various artistic employees, the project team develops its own internal structure. The "creative management" of a project team depends on the consensus of the team members. This consensus is often established by means of artistic authority (e.g., of the film director or choreographer), as opposed to the administrative forms of authority that prevail in other phases of production and in other economic sectors. According to Ryan (1992: 134), the employees can be subdivided into "professional creatives" and "independent creatives." The latter receive a (mostly project-related) contract and thus act as individual subcontractors for a particular project. The group of independent creatives consists of a growing number of freelancers (who might be continuously re-contracted on a single-project basis). High-profile creative workers, or "stars," also make up this group. While the "stars" are also generally freelance employees, they are distinguished by their high "artistic reputation" or notoriety, and the fees they command. Other professional creatives, particularly those with standard full-time positions (e.g., studio musicians, orchestra members, dance or theatre ensemble members), have a far less personalized role. Their artistic skills are esteemed, and they often hold long-term positions. Some may succeed in climbing up from a subordinate position to become independent creatives or prominent "stars," provided they attain the necessary reputation. The independent creatives (individually subcontracted artists) are engaged in cultural production as suppliers of intermediate products to an artistic project (in most cases within the framework of a project team). They are dependent subcontractors in the sense that their performance is purchased and marketed by the hiring cultural firm.

In the case of project-related networks that cross firm boundaries, project teams are composed of various formally independent companies (including freelancers). The broad project-based organization of cultural production increases the market opportunities for small, independent firms and freelancers. Grabher (2001) regards such project-based networks of creativity as "project ecologies" which are characterized by collaboration, flexible network participation, and informal work relations. However, it remains unclear to what extent the branding of temporary project networks as "ecologies" advances a deeper understanding of network relations in the culture industries. Project-related networking can also be found in traditional manufacturing industries in the guise of flexible inter-firm networks of small and medium-size enterprises, and temporary project networks represent a quite ordinary feature of the construction industry. Nonetheless, the sphere of independent cultural producers and "free" self-employed actors is of major importance for the functioning of the culture industry: within the project-based organization of cultural production, these actors represent a flexible reservoir of skilled workers.

The industry's project-based organization implies the existence of *temporal* organizational structures (with a changing mixture of participants in every new project), and, as a consequence, the increased flexibilization of work relations. The widespread and extensive use of temporary contracts in the culture industry forms the basis of a freelance economy that conforms with neoliberal policy prescriptions for the flexibilization of work relations and reduction of fixed labor costs. From the individual freelancer's point of view, temporary contracts and relations with a variety of firms and organizations is often viewed as an opportunity to accumulate work experience in diverse jobs and projects, which in turn enhances a person's market value. In a more generalizing way, Scott (2000: 12) states that the employment relation in the culture industry "is typically intermittent, leading to frequently recurrent job search and recruitment activities." Hence local agglomerations of the culture industry can reduce risks of recruitment for both workers and employers.

Independent creative workers (musicians, authors, film and theatre actors, etc.) and small independent firms are the major source of artistic innovation in the culture industry, as they are not as strongly bound as the industry's large enterprises are to the compulsions of marketability and pressures to produce cultural products that mimic previously successful formats. On the other hand, the culture industry's large enterprises are able to make use of independent cultural producers with a great deal of flexibility and little risk. Furthermore, the large firms at the center of the culture industry (TV stations, film companies) generate an extensive demand for "intermediate products" and services, which in turn creates the basis for the continuous emergence of new freelance workers and independent specialist firms. A tremendous number of independent companies that provide a diverse range of specialized services are spread across the culture industry, including talent management agencies, design firms, marketing agencies, PR consultants, film editors, and so on. These firms are an articulation of the increasing inter-firm division of labor and specialization within the culture industry.

The "formatting" of artistically creative work in the culture industry

Cultural critics like Adorno (1991) have denounced tendencies within the culture industry toward standardized production that limits creativity in favor of the marketability of cultural products. The formatting of cultural products is a key strategy for rationalizing the creative phase of the production process. A classical example is the "novel factory," where professional writers create detective stories and "soap novels" according to given templates and content samples; today the scripts of certain TV series are produced in similar ways. Likewise, in the "film factories" of Mumbai ("Bollywood"), template-based film scenes are shot in an assembly line production system and sequentially put together as a new film for the mass market (as was done in Hollywood in its early days). "Bollywood" can be cited as an example of the rationalization of film production based on Taylorist principles. According to Ryan (1992: 154), the aspiration of firms in the culture industry to produce commodities for an unpredictable market is the imperative that drives the clichéd formatting of cultural productions. Indeed, while the general tastes of consumers might be relatively stable (concerning, for example, a preference for jazz or classical music), their acceptance of novel and perhaps eccentric cultural products is not predictable. Under these conditions, the culture industry adapts its production to the logic of repetition: the market success of past products dictates the direction and artistic contours of future productions. The commercial imperative enjoins the firm "to produce more of the same." The strategy of repetition can be divided into (1) a name-based approach, which concentrates on the recycling of specific celebrities, and (2) a type-based approach, for which the serial production of films or books of the same kind is essential. This concept culminates in the strategic product planning of the culture industry, which also makes use of professional market research techniques.

Formatting – the creation of an original according to given rules and templates – is a production concept in which capitalist imperatives shape the creative process in the hope of guaranteeing market success. The repetition of previously successful products manifests itself in the marginal variation of well-known types. The recurring sequels of a movie franchise (e.g., *Ice Age 1* to *Ice Age 3*) are an example of this repetition, as is the production of feature films according to rigid thematic templates, whether in Hollywood, Mumbai, or Hong Kong. In today's television shows, the principle of serial repetition is taken to the extreme, such that single episodes are barely distinguishable from one another. Success is achieved when a show's repetitive format is accepted by the audience.

The formatting of "creative" cultural production also signifies a trend by which cultural products are made increasingly redundant. Adorno's critique of the culture industry (1991) is thus also applicable to the contemporary media industry. According to Lutz Hachmeister, manager of the Cologne television and film festival:

> Redundancy, cannibalization, the overstretching of journalistic brands: these are phenomena which justify growing discontent with the contemporary

media industry. The core of journalism was characterized for a long time by an intention to generate political or cultural impacts. Pure money making motives and bare popular entertainment in journalism have always existed, but, nevertheless, generally one knew for or against which ideas, actions or developments something had been written, transmitted or broadcasted. Today, the accumulation of capital dominates as a leading philosophy in the journalistic sector as well, and the constantly rattling media-machines combine with the daily terror of the content economy.... The media industry has passed over from the production of politically, intellectually or aesthetically motivated statements to the mere occupation of places in markets, to the building of chains of capital valuation ... The media industry must newly determine the relation between projects which are motivated by content and those which only serve business imperatives. Otherwise, it will sink into the morass of the rotted content which it produces itself. (*Tagesspiegel*, March 16, 2001, author's translation)

Formatting has the function of rationalizing the "free play" of creative forces in cultural production in order to align them with products that have enjoyed market success. The cultural products that are produced according to given templates reinforce the commercial degradation of artistic creativity. Past a certain point, the nearly uniform shape of pre-formatted cultural products ultimately undermines their market success, as audiences become oversaturated with a given product series. For this reason, the culture industry's firms are forced to expend great sums on the marketing of their products in order to make them distinguishable and attractive in the market. Marketing activities now typically account for more than 50% of the budgets of today's Hollywood films, a fact that underscores the expanding significance of marketing in the circulation of cultural products. Marketing strategies are particularly focused on the creation of celebrities and styles that function in much the same way as "brands" in other industries. The positioning of a product on the cultural market incorporates two phases: (1) the "packaging" of the product, and (2) the subsequent advertising campaign. "Packaging" refers above all to the product design, which involves a large number of specialists (designers, advertising agencies, stylists). The purpose of advertising is to increase a product's visibility and reach customers in a highly competitive market. With regard to the creation of celebrities, packaging and product design take the form of image construction. This can include a complete marketing of the persona to achieve a specific product-driven image.

With regard to the marketing strategies of the culture industry's firms, the publicity sector (see above) also plays an important role. Cultural products like books, feature films, and music CDs require rapid and widespread publicity at the time of market entry. Aside from "paid publicity," which brings substantial income flows to the advertising industry and media companies, "free advertising" also exists, by which cultural products are inserted in various ways into the programs of the publicity sector. Today, the marketing of cultural products has achieved a new dimension by means of "reciprocal" advertising and product coupling. One example of reciprocal advertising is a celebrity appearance on a TV talk show: the celebrity obtains an opportunity to market his or her latest film, while the TV show benefits from increased viewership. Product coupling means that one cultural product is "derived" from another: the music soundtrack of a film, for example, might be marketed in tandem with the film's release, or a book based on a film might be written to capitalize on that film's success. The effect is that one cultural product takes the role of an advertising medium for another. Symbiotic advertising relations have evolved in the cultural economy between the producers of private and quasi-private cultural products and the producers of quasi-public products. The publicity sector is a producer of cultural products and, at the same time, functions as an advertising machine for all products of the culture industry. Celebrities and styles are "positioned" on the market in order to generate revenues and capture market share, yet, in the long term, market imperatives require their replacement. This process of placement and replacement is at the heart of the creation of fashion cycles of cultural production.

In this way, the cultural economy is a "trend machine." The culture industry also sends out trend scouts to cities like New York, Los Angeles, London, Paris, and Berlin – that is, cities which are perceived as "cutting edge" on the cultural front – in order to discover new cultural trends for the purpose of repackaging lifestyle elements and creating commercially exploitable new fashion styles. Today, the designers of large fashion retailers like Zara and Mango need only four weeks to create and introduce a new collection based on the ideas of their trend scouts. In this way, the design-intensive branches of the culture industry are continuously generating new trends which encourage the accelerated circulation of capital.

When celebrities and styles are positioned in product markets, they are quickly imitated by the public and by other cultural products (the spread of the Beatles' haircut in pop music is a good example of this). A new fashion cycle originates from this process of imitation. However, after a certain period of time the market becomes saturated by a specific fashion and consumers crave change. In this process, the "truncated" product life cycle of cultural products (see above) is replaced by a truncated life cycle of celebrities and styles, a dynamic that maintains the systemic instability of the cultural market. The rationalization and marketing strategies of the culture industry can only temporarily overcome the fleeting market success of particular cultural products. While fashion cycles compel the culture industry to con-stantly develop new product innovations, celebrities, and styles, this market pressure does create economic opportunities for small and independent cultural producers. The notion of fashion cycles indicates a revolving sequence of innovations in the cultural economy that depends on the competitive interplay between established large firms and small firms engaged in experimental product innovation (Scott 2000: 37). Market control of formatted mainstream products by large firms opens up market niches for innovative products that are explored by more risk-taking "experimental firms" (such as the independent labels in the music industry). As some of these innovative products achieve market success, the established large firms will start to "imitate" or take over the innovation, and in this way create a new mainstream, which in turn leads to the emergence of new possibilities for experimentation by small firms in the culture industry's creative "periphery."

In light of increasing product specialization and market segmentation, cultural productions of a relatively small scale can easily achieve market access. And as small, specialized producers are in a position to serve the market (e.g., in publishing, radio, or the performing arts), this leads to greater competition in cultural markets. The sequential character of fashion cycles and marketing imperatives have a significant impact on the creative phase of cultural production, as they generate a steady demand for commercially viable "new" content and original products. This demand is boosted by the symbiotic relationship between the cultural economy's publicity sector and the culture industry producers. New market opportunities and start-up chances for small independent cultural producers and freelancers thus emerge, particularly with regard to artistically creative work in the culture industry, and fuel the specific dynamics of urban cultural production clusters.

Global Centers of the Culture Industry and the Production of Lifestyle Images

The urban centers of the culture and media industries are characterized by interorganizational networks at both the local and global level. According to Held *et al.* (1999: 16), "globalization" can be defined as a process or a bundle of processes that involve the transformation of the organization of social relations in terms of their geographic extension, intensity, speed, and impact. These processes also generate transcontinental flows and networks of activities. "Flows" refer to the movements in time and space of physical goods, persons, symbols, and information, whereas "networks" describe the structured interactions between social, political, and economic actors and activity centers. Cities might be regarded as *a process of networking* that is unfolding on different but intertwined spatial scales, resulting in the interplay of local, regional, and global networks that are constitutive forces in the production of urban space. The connection between globalization and urban development has become a central theme in urban research (see Chapter 1). Many urban researchers emphasize that globalization primarily proceeds outward from specific urban centers, which gradually integrate other urban areas into globalization processes (so-called "globalizing cities"). The cultural economy is of key importance in this process.

With his analysis of leading global cities that act as command and control centers in a "new international division of labour," Friedmann (Friedmann and Wolff 1982; Friedmann 1986, 1995) made an influential contribution to the analysis of the global urban system in contemporary capitalism. Building on Friedman's conceptualization, Knox (2002) emphasized that global cities are also home to the world's most influential media corporations. Sassen's global city concept (1991, 2000) focused on the function of cities as providers of global financial and corporate services. Initially, her analysis concentrated on London, New York, and Tokyo – three global cities which invariably score at the top of all functional rankings of the global city system (Short *et al.* 1996). However, the processes of globalization are essentially affecting all cities (Marcuse and van Kempen 2000; Scott 2001) and lead to the active or passive integration of a multitude of other cities into the global economic system.

Most analyses of global cities reveal a tendency to reduce the high-ranking cities to their function as centers for the provision of specialized corporate services. In other words, they neglect the role these cities play as locations for industrial manufacturing. The industrial sphere is only mentioned tangentially in reference to the role played by global cities as centers for the generation of knowledge and economic innovation (see Sassen 1991). Research on the specific function of global cities and "globalizing cities" in the industrial development process has been carried out predominantly in the field of regional studies. Existing scholarship on new industrial spaces and technology districts contains many references to the key role that global cities and metropolitan regions continue to play in industrial development (Scott 1988a, 1997; Storper 1997; Rehfeld 1999; Krätke and Borst 2000; Schamp 2000; Krätke 2007; Wall and van der Knaap 2009). Most global cities provide central locations for new knowledge-based production chains and for highly innovative production clusters in the fields of information and communications technology, medical engineering, biotechnology, the media, etc. These urban innovation centers for "new" and "old" industries are often characterized by extensive networking within the metropolitan region and by strong supra-regional ties with the centers of innovation in other metropolitan regions at the national, international, and global scale (see Chapter 3). Transnational links between urban production and innovation centers might be considered a major element at the heart of the phenomenon of "globalizing cities" (i.e., integrating new cities into the globalization dynamic). The development of the global urban system is determined by a selective geographic concentration of global service capacities as well as "innovative" production clusters and industrial innovation capacities. In global city regions, both of these elements regularly overlap, which means that the economic prosperity of such cities can be based both on capacities in the field of specialized corporate services and on highly innovative regional industries. Scott (2001) has emphasized the diversity of economic sectors that tend to form clusters in global city regions; for Scott, it is the clustering of multiple economic sectors that transforms these geographic production centers into "regional motors of the world economy."

The formation of a "world city network" that comprises both the established prominent global business centers and the large number of "globalizing cities" is the subject of research carried out by the Globalization and World Cities Study Group and Network (GaWC). GaWC researchers have classified a large number of cities by evaluating the global competence of their service providers in terms of the local presence of globally operating service firms with a transnational network of branch offices (Beaverstock, Smith, and Taylor 1999; Taylor 2004). The GaWC approach conceptualizes the world city network as an "interlocking network" that allows relations between cities to be measured through data collected on firms (Taylor 2004). An interlocking network denotes a specific type of network (see Knoke and Kuklinski 1982) that consists of a nodal level (the cities), the overall network level (all nodes and links, cities connected) and the sub-nodal level of firms (corporate service firms, media firms, etc.). The locational strategies pursued by multinational firms interconnect the cities to create a global urban network. Intra-firm flows of information and knowledge between branch offices or enterprise units are the constituent components of the world city network. The first GaWC analysis used 100 office networks of global service firms across 315 cities worldwide (Taylor and Hoyler 2000; Taylor and Walker 2001; Taylor, Catalano, and Walker 2002). This analysis was repeated in 2004 in order to appraise the connectivity changes in the world city network between 2000 and 2004 (Taylor and Aranya 2008). In 2008, the data collection was revised and improved, leading to a renewed analysis that covers the office networks of 175 global service firms across 526 cities worldwide (Taylor *et al.* 2009). The results of this new analysis indicate that the globalization process of advanced producer services has further continued, with the expansion of offices in many cities and the extension of office networks into new ones. According to Taylor et al. (2009), this indicates the expansion and increasing integration of the world city network. More specifically, the analysis confirms the premier position of London and New York at the top level of global service centers, the rapid advance of Shanghai, Beijing, and Sydney, and the rise of cities in emerging markets such as Mumbai and Kuala Lumpur. The rise of emerging markets' cities has largely taken place at the expense of leading West European cities such as Amsterdam, Frankfurt-Main, and Zurich (Taylor *et al.* 2009). However, the analysis also reveals many cities with a relatively stable position in the world city network (such as Paris, Singapore, and Toronto).

The GaWC approach to the analysis of the world city network yields empirically based assessments of cities in globalization. Yet the global service providers' organizational networks reveal considerable variation in the corporate geographies of globalization. For this reason, information concerning international financial centers, for instance, does not permit forecasts about the locational centers of global firms in the advertising industry, pharmaceutical industry, or cultural economy, etc. All cities included in the world city network will be characterized by specific profiles of globally connected economic functions. Thus the world city network includes global cities focusing on advanced producer services as well as many other cities with differing profiles of their globally connected activities.

The globalization of the culture and media industries

The current phase of globalization entails a global circulation of symbols and images that is based on the worldwide distribution of cultural commodities and media formats. New communication technologies and the emergence of large multinational groups within the culture and media industries contribute to a global flow of cultural forms and products whose reach, intensity, speed, and diversity far exceed the cultural globalization processes of previous eras (see Held et al. 1999). Since the 1970s, the progressive deregulation of the media industries has fostered a shift in market share from the public to the private media sector and the increasing globalization of the corporate culture and media sector (Robins 1995; Pratt 2000). The global enterprises of the cultural economy are well aware of the cultural diversity and differentiation of their global audiences, customers, and consumers, and have long adapted their products and programs to specific regional or national tastes and cultural preferences. The trend toward cultural market differentiation is at the same time a driving force for the organization of global production networks in the culture and media industries, with "local" anchoring points in different countries and regions. The increasing concentration of capital has led to the formation of huge media conglomerates that have created a global network of branch offices and subsidiaries. These global media groups have set up local anchoring points particularly in those centers of the worldwide urban system that are recognized as "cultural metropolises" and function as centers of cultural production activities. These cities, however, are not always global centers of the corporate service sector, and may have sectoral profiles which differ from the economic structure of most prominent global cities (see Krätke and

Taylor 2004). Nevertheless, the culture and media industries are prime movers of globalization processes in the urban system, in which urban cultural production clusters act as local nodes in the global networks of large media groups.

The large media groups are pursuing a policy that involves the integration and recombination of value chains in the cultural economy at both the national and global level. As a result, global production networks have developed that incorporate TV and film production firms, film laboratories, special digital effects firms, film distribution agencies, TV stations and cinema chains, distribution firms and firms dealing in cinema and television licenses, etc. A media conglomerate's reach can also extend to other sectors of the culture industry, such as the music industry, print media, advertising industry, and Internet. New information and communication technologies and new high-performance network infrastructures provide the media industry with considerable opportunities to develop innovations, including new media formats, new digital production technologies, and new forms of marketing, such as online information services, web TV, interactive cable TV, etc. (Baldwin, McVoy, and Steinfield 1996). The globalization strategy pursued by large media groups is geared in the first instance toward market extension through the establishment of branch offices and subsidiaries in the major international centers of the culture and media industry. Secondly, the globalization strategy of media firms reveals a strong orientation toward accessing specific creativity resources: a presence in the leading centers of cultural production and integration in local clusters offers global media conglomerates the best chance of incorporating the latest trends in the culture industry as quickly as possible. The "global players" of the culture industry are networking at the local level with small specialized producers and service providers. In this way, they are actively establishing global ties amongst various international urban centers of cultural production. The establishment of a global locational network of business units which are at the same time integrated into local clusters of the culture industry enables media conglomerates to tap the globally distributed creative potential that resides in cultural production clusters.

The production cluster of the film industry in Potsdam/Babelsberg on the outskirts of Berlin can be taken as an example of how firms not only set up dense cooperative network relations within a local culture industry district, but are also integrated into the supra-regional networks of global media firms. In the case of Potsdam/Babelsberg, the local cluster firms are directly linked with the resident business units of global media firms from Paris, London, and New York, and indirectly connected to other global players in the film and TV industry through their business relations with media firms that are based in Berlin (Krätke 2002b). In other words, the global firms of the culture and media industries are locally interacting with the small

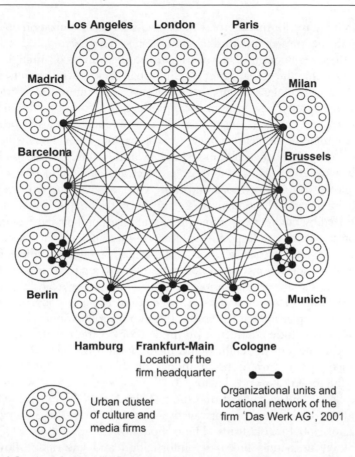

Los Angeles   London   Paris

Madrid

Barcelona

Berlin

Hamburg   Frankfurt-Main   Cologne

Milan

Brussels

Munich

Location of the
firm headquarter

Urban cluster
of culture and
media firms

Organizational units and
locational network of the
firm 'Das Werk AG', 2001

Figure 4.3   A global media firm's network of branch offices and subsidiaries in the national and international urban system.

specialist producers and service providers. At the same time, they are running a global production network with widely dispersed branch offices and subsidiaries that permits networking with urban centers of cultural production on a global scale. This interrelation between global intra-firm networks and local inter-firm networking has been visualized in Figure 4.3, which displays the network of business establishments maintained by the firm Das Werk AG (a film company specializing in post-production and digital effects).

The premier role of a few global cities like London, New York, Paris, etc. in generating "radical cultural product innovation" has been emphasized by Lorenzen and Frederiksen (2008), who argue that radical product innovation entails the creation of new knowledge as well as the combination of previously unrelated knowledge bases. The depth of specialization and high diversity which are required for this interplay of localization and urbanization economies might only be present in leading global cities. Lorenzen and Frederiksen develop their argument further with regard to the impact of multiple cluster formations within the global city region: in urban regions with clusters that are outstanding technological centers of excellence, the cultural industries may cooperate to develop new technological products in terms of a "fusion of new technologies and culture" – in this regard, the multimedia industry provides a striking example of the generation of radical product innovations which stem from the interaction between high technology and cultural production clusters (see also Scott 2000). However, there is no clear delimitation of a group of "truly" global cities, since more and more cities all over the world are now involved in the globalization process, and even the major global cities are characterized by different economic profiles in terms of their particular mix of subsectors and clusters. The positive interaction effects of localization economies (specialization and excellence) and urbanization economies (diversity and multiple cluster formations) might not be restricted to a narrow group of global cities, notwithstanding the plausible argument that those major global cities which function as leading centers of the cultural economy offer a favorable socioeconomic environment for "radical" cultural product innovations.

An empirical study conducted by the author on the network of globally interlinked centers of the culture and media industries assessed the relative importance of the various urban nodes of the global cultural economy (Krätke 2003; Krätke and Taylor 2004). The network of "world media cities" is based on the concept that the premier global centers of the culture and media industries can be portrayed as nodal points in the organizational networks of global media firms. These should be interpreted as a locational fabric of business units linked by information and knowledge flows that enable the firm to absorb and react to specific regional or local "impulses" and customer demands on a worldwide scale. Thus, a "global" media city is characterized by an overlap between the locational networks of various global media firms in the urban economic space. Local and global firms of the culture and media industries are linked in a functional context that fosters the formation of an urban cultural economy cluster, whose international business relations are primarily handled via the global media firms that are present in the city. The aforementioned analysis revealed that the branch offices and subsidiaries of global media firms are selectively concentrated in just a handful of global cities (see Krätke 2003). The seven cities of the "alpha" group of the 284 cities surveyed accounted for as much as 30% of the 2766 registered office locations, while the 15 cities in the "beta" group accounted for 23% of registered office locations. In this way, over 50% of the branch and subsidiary offices of global media groups are concentrated in just 22 global cities. The group of "alpha" media cities included New York, London, Paris, and Los Angeles, which are ranked as premier global cities in virtually every analysis of the global urban system. However, among the other cities that qualified as premier global media cities, there were interesting deviations from standard conceptions of the global city system. The "alpha" group of global media cities also included Berlin, Munich, and Amsterdam, that is, three cities that have been ranked as (third-rate) "gamma" world cities in global city research that focuses on corporate services (Beaverstock, Smith, and Taylor 1999). In this way, Berlin, Munich, and Amsterdam had achieved a degree of integration in the location networks of global culture and media firms to qualify them as premier international centers of the cultural economy.

In recent times, Watson (2009) has presented an analysis of the global urban networks of digital music production in order to illustrate the transnational dimension of relational spaces of creativity. This research employs social network analysis methods and assesses the connectivity of cities in global networks of music production. Each recorded music album might be regarded as a discrete "product innovation" with new content that is created in a temporary project network combining skilled creative workers (such as musicians, sound engineers, etc.) in recording studios. Today, such musical recordings can be coordinated on a global scale by networking studios in geographically distant locations (Watson 2009; Watson, Hoyler, and Mager 2009; Leyshon 2009). Based on albums appearing in the top 10 iTunes download charts, Watson's study reveals the dominance of London, New York, and Los Angeles as central nodes of global networks of musical recording. This valuable research measures the significance of *production locations* as nodes of transnationally networked music production. However, it concentrates on recording activities as a partial process within the music industry's value chain and doesn't measure the musical *creativity* unfolding in these urban locations, which resides in the local creative milieu of the respective cities' music industry (see also Chapter 5).

Urban centers of the culture industry and the production of lifestyle images

With regard to the point of departure of this chapter – the comprehensive merging of culture and markets – it is useful to outline the broader societal impact of urban centers of the culture industry by focusing on the point that cultural economy firms operate as "lifestyle producers" in the global urban network (Krätke 2002c). In their role as "lifestyle producers," these firms generate the imagery on which many lifestyle groups are based. The contemporary "lifestyle producers" are primarily active in the cultural economy sector and geographically concentrated in specific cities and regions within the global urban system. In the cultural globalization process, these cities and regions operate as key locations for the generation and distribution of lifestyle images.

In the globalizing cities of today, individual patterns of living and lifestyles are less and less an expression of spatially delimited "local" cultures. The correspondence between culture and geographic territory is evaporating. The forces of globalization are leading to an interpenetration of social worlds across local, regional, and national boundaries (see Noller, Prigge, and Ronneberger 1994; Noller 1999), and cultural differences manifest themselves in terms of varying patterns of living and lifestyles without any clear-cut territorial anchoring. Cities are becoming transcultural locations by hosting a mixture of cultures and by providing for the coexistence and interplay of different cultures and lifestyles in one and the same place (Zukin 1995). One contributing factor in this respect is the globalization of the culture and media industries. Major centers of the urban system are the production locations of material and symbolic cultural commodities for a global market. Moreover, in world cities, particularly in the group of global media cities, lifestyle images are "filtered out" from the local worlds of life and work, and are spread or distributed globally via the culture and media industries. While this doesn't represent a trend toward the homogenization of cultures, this process certainly exerts an influence on the lifestyles of the global economic elite and other social strata, and also leaves its stamp on market-relevant elements of youth cultures. Contemporary youth cultures exhibit particularly "fluid" cultural forms. Communicated via the media, youth cultures are subject to global proliferation and intermixture. The images spread by MTV are a relevant example here. Cultural images disseminated globally by the media have a far greater influence on cultural identification and self-expression in the age group of 13- to 20-year-olds than among those over 40. Youth cultures are heterogeneous, greatly dependent on media communication, and globalized with regard to many elements of style and self-expression.

As consumption habits are shaped to a large extent by lifestyle images in this era of globalized media, the production locations of lifestyle images are to be found primarily in the prominent urban centers of the culture and media industries. If the specific societal impact of a cultural economy is taken into account, this field of production does not constitute just one economic sector among others, but a specific sector of activity that has a direct influence on large sections of the economy and a considerable impact on social communication as well as consumption patterns and lifestyles. In virtually all branches of the economy, market success is based largely on the construction of images and their communication via the media. In this respect, the culture and media industries have long functioned as "key industries" (Lash and Urry 1994). The image production activities of the cultural economy (see Scott 2000) do not just include the product images created by advertising and design agencies, but extend to the lifestyle images that are disseminated by the entertainment and media industry. In conjunction with the increasing mediatization of social communication and the consumption sphere, the cultural economy functions as a "trend machine," absorbing the trends that develop primarily in leading cultural metropoles and global media cities. The culture and media industries exploit these trends commercially by packaging and repackaging "lifestyle" elements – for example, the new forms of hip-hop and rap music generated by urban subcultures. "Thus is the creativity embedded in the web of life appropriated by capital and circulated back to us in commodity form so as to allow the extraction of surplus value" (Harvey 2006: 92). The commodified elements of particular subcultures are subsequently transmitted worldwide, thereby reinforcing the processes of cultural globalization. The global export activities of the culture and media industries are of significance at the "receiving end" because of their impact on everyday cultures, value systems, practices, and ways of life. Imported cultural commodities incorporate symbolic messages and penetrate cultural development processes in "reception locations." These reception locations are situated at a greater or lesser "cultural distance" from the export centers and, therefore, process, mix, and recombine the exported messages or images in different ways.

Conclusion

This chapter began with the observation that much of the scholarship on "creative industries" and the cultural economy is highly affirmative of the neoliberal economic trends dominating creative work in the culture and media industries. This observation underlines the need for a deeper analysis of the functioning of industries which thrive on the creativity of their workforces. In order to arrive at a critical assessment of the role of creativity in a capitalist context, the chapter discussed the specific economic and organizational framework of the culture and media industries and outlined the internal mechanisms by which creative activities are organized at the firm level and within inter-firm networks.

As a result of specific market conditions in the cultural economy – that is, the unpredictable market success and "truncated" product life cycle of cultural products – culture industry firms are forced to continuously invest in the development of new products. The cultural economy demands constant innovation in terms of new stories and designs in order to satisfy unpredictable consumer tastes. Corresponding to these conditions, the cultural economy is also characterized by highly developed inter-firm division of labor. A large portion of creative experimental activities are carried out in the extensive "periphery" of the established corporate sector of the cultural economy, as many of the small peripheral firms and self-employed specialists are particularly engaged in the creation of innovative products or styles. Furthermore, a growing share of the production processes is undertaken by small, independent subcontractors that carry out specific functions. Due to the necessity to organize a complex work, where many dissimilar capabilities need to be harmonized, the creative product is often a "collective" achievement, produced within a "collective firm," where many entrepreneurial agents cooperate. Hence the organizational form of temporary project teams and the project-based organization of the creative process is particularly widespread in the culture industry. On the regional and local level, the increasing inter-firm division of labor is articulated in the emergence of densely networked production clusters in the culture and media industries.

Creative workers in the culture industry cannot be put to work as abstract, anonymous factors of production like the employees of an assembly line. Creative work is thus unsuited to Fordist production methods, which rely on planned inputs and standardized work processes. Artistic production that is valued for its originality cannot be divorced from the creative talent of individual workers. This remains true despite the formation of various modes of "collective" cultural production in the creative stage of product development. As a consequence, the creative workforce has retained a relatively high degree of individual autonomy in the work process in terms of the opportunity for experimental activity in developing novel forms. At the same time, the firm must bring this creative process under the firm's control, so that management can set guidelines for content creation.

In this context, two particularly relevant aspects of the institutional environment were considered: the division of the production process into a "creative phase" and a "reproduction and distribution phase," and the strategy of "formatting" creative work. Formatting – that is, the creation of an original according to given templates – is a production concept in which capitalist imperatives shape the creative process in the hope of guaranteeing market success. This represents the central approach for rationalizing the creative phase of cultural production. The repetition of previously successful products is manifested in the marginal variation of well-known types. In this way, the "free play" of creative forces in cultural production is rationalized in order to align them with products that have enjoyed market success. Accordingly, celebrities and product styles are consciously created and "positioned" on the market in order to generate revenues and capture market share, and thus the cultural economy also functions as a "trend machine." When celebrities and styles are positioned in product markets, they are quickly imitated, and from this process of imitation a new "fashion cycle" of cultural production originates. In this process, the "truncated" product life cycle of cultural products is replaced by a truncated life cycle of celebrities and styles. The notion of fashion cycles indicates a revolving sequence of innovations in the cultural economy that depends on the competitive interplay between established large firms and small firms engaged in experimental product innovation.

The analysis of the functioning of "creativity under the command of capital" leads to the conclusion that there is little justification for limiting the idea of "creative industries" to the cultural economy, excluding innovative activities in other industrial sectors. Furthermore, the widespread uncritical use of the terms "creativity" and "creative industries" encourages the self-idealization of cultural economy actors comparable to the hype that surrounded the so-called New Economy. The analysis of the subsumption of the culture industries' creative work under the imperatives of capitalist production calls into question the prevailing superficial view that the culture industry's creativity is "superior" to other forms of creativity. The cultural economy for the most part represents a capitalist entertainment industry whose organization and outputs are geared toward the imperatives of market success and capital accumulation. The need to adjust the particular features of artistically creative work and cultural products in line with these imperatives does not change the industry's essential character, that is, organizing cultural production as a distinct sector of capital accumulation. The culture industry can be regarded as a prototype of the flexible organization of industry due to its reliance on inter-firm networking, flexible work relations, and the cross-marketing of new products in ever shorter cycles. The cultural industry's subsumption in the dynamics of capitalist production has been further intensified by its inclusion in the process of economic globalization.

The globalization of large media conglomerates represents a significant trend in the present-day culture and media industries. These "global players" network locally with specialized producers and service providers in urban cultural-economy clusters, while at the same time establishing a global network of branch offices and subsidiary firms, effectively linking urban centers of cultural production worldwide. The leading urban centers of the global economy are in many cases functioning as epicenters of globalization in the cultural sphere. The content and designs produced in these locations exert a direct impact on consumption patterns and lifestyles worldwide. For the process of globalization, therefore, global culture and media firms are at least as influential as the global providers of corporate services, because they create a cultural market space of global dimensions.

In conclusion, the cultural economy represents a model for a flexibilized and networked form of social production which has spread in design-intensive and innovation-driven subsectors of the economy. With regard to its prominent role in the formation of new "city industries," the culture industry is also an important driving force in the development of spatial forms of industrial organization which are of strategic importance for a knowledge-intensive and innovation-based model of economic development. The next chapter will deal with the development of the cultural economy in the metropolis of Berlin in order to investigate the organization of cultural production at the local level, and to assess its impact on urban labor markets and sociospatial polarization.

5

Local Clustering of the Cultural Economy in the Metropolis of Berlin

The Urbanization Economies of Artistically Creative Occupations

Introduction

A most important characteristic of present-day cultural production is the formation of local clusters within large cities or metropolitan areas – that is, the local concentration of culture and media industries in specific inner-city districts (Scott 2000; Krätke 2000, 2002a). A distinction must be drawn between the notion of "cultural entertainment quarters," which denotes a well-established and publicly visible urban area with a high concentration of cultural establishments and strong visitation by cultural consumers and tourists, and the notion of "cultural economy districts," which designates the Marshallian industrial districts organization of cultural production in large cities with a clearly recognizable local clustering of cultural industries (Cinti 2008). However, there are cities (such as Paris and Berlin) where, in specific urban areas, the functions of cultural entertainment quarters and cultural economy districts overlap. From the perspective of economic geography, the cultural economy district approach offers deeper insights into the sociospatial organization of cultural industries.

Analyses of the urbanization economies of cultural production emphasize that artistic creativity is positively stimulated by specific sociospatial environments. The cultural economy's creative actors are embedded in locally concentrated communities, which additionally benefit from an interaction with a diversity of milieus and actors who are present in the same urban area. Cultural economy districts create a favorable environment for artistically creative work, as they encourage an exchange of knowledge and offer opportunities for interpersonal and interorganizational cooperation in the production of cultural goods and services.

The Creative Capital of Cities: Interactive Knowledge Creation and the Urbanization Economies of Innovation, First Edition. Stefan Krätke.
© 2011 Stefan Krätke. Published 2011 by Blackwell Publishing Ltd.

A characteristic feature of present-day cultural industries' institutional order is the pronounced inter-firm division of labor and selective clustering of cultural producers within the urban system. While most accounts have highlighted the prominent role of large cities and metropolises as locational centers of the cultural economy, the rise of "creative" small cities has only recently received attention (Waitt and Gibson 2009). The locational patterns of different branches of the culture and media industries – which have been mapped by economic geographers in selected "global cities" such as Los Angeles, London, and Paris – support the theory that the cultural economy sector tends to produce local agglomerations of specialized firms (Scott 1997). Among the examples which substantiate this proposition are the metropolitan regions of London, Paris, New York, and Los Angeles (Braczyk, Fuchs, and Wolf 1999; Scott 2000; Coe 2000, 2001; Oakey, Kipling, and Wildgust 2001; Simmie 2003). Such agglomerations of specialized firms have also been referred to as regional "production clusters" (see Porter 1993, 1998, 2001).

The basic forces behind the selective geographic clustering of cultural industries in large cities and metropolitan regions are economic externalities, which can be differentiated into externalities derived from specialization ("localization economies") and those derived from diversity ("urbanization economies"). In Chapter 3, it was argued that the scientific and technological creativity and innovative capacity of research-intensive manufacturing sectors are strongly based on knowledge networking and spillovers between the related knowledge bases of specific sectors' cluster firms. However, in metropolitan regions these cluster firms also make use of a diversified economic structure which enables them to draw on and combine knowledge resources from other industries (Simmie 2003). In a similar way, the culture industry clusters in metropolitan regions that particularly rely on artistic creativity make use of externalities that stem from both specialization and diversity. The specific properties of artistically creative work seem to privilege the benefits derived from urbanization economies (e.g., a variety of cultural economy actors and the stimulating effects of urban sociocultural diversity). "Contrary to localization economies, where co-location, rather than a particular place, is key, urbanization economies hinge upon a range of place-specific and ideographic factors that are invariably urban" (Lorenzen and Frederiksen 2008: 159). Particularly in the culture industries, where production is frequently carried out by project teams and relies on a highly flexibilized, freelance workforce (see Chapter 4), knowledge and innovative ideas are not only exchanged between firms, but also to a large extent outside the sphere of inter-firm interaction, that is, in the sphere of urban social life (see Storper and Venables 2004; Meusburger 2009). In exploring artistic creativity and the local clustering of culture and media industries, this chapter thus focuses on a type of clustering that is primarily informed by the notion of urbanization economies. "Whereas non-urban clusters mainly enjoy localization economies in the guise of the positive externalities arising from co-location of a particular group of firms, an urban cluster may enjoy such localization economies in combination with economies arising from co-location with other clusters – plus a broad array of other positive externalities related to urban location" (Lorenzen and Frederiksen 2008: 156). With reference to Lorenzen and Frederiksen (2008: 161) we might say that the creative capital of major cities and metropolitan regions in the urban system is in particular based on the "interaction effects" of urbanization and localization economies.

In this chapter, the cultural economy of the Berlin metropolis will be taken as a case study area for investigating the clustering of artistically creative workers at the local level and the related emergence of a locally bound creative milieu of cultural producers. The Berlin metropolis represents a city that thrives on the "urbanization economies" of artistic innovation. It is a good example of the local clustering and rise of new "city industries" that prefer to concentrate in the densely built inner-city area. At the same time, there is broad international interest in the recent development of this city, which had been an outstanding economic metropolis and innovation center before becoming a divided city (with the territorially isolated West Berlin economy drawing on subsidized industrial branch plants) after World War II. In the context of our investigation, the most important specific feature of Berlin is the mismatch between flourishing creative industries and regional economic growth. The Berlin economy is comparatively weak even while the creative industries are expanding – in the words of the city's mayor, Berlin is "poor but sexy." The Berlin case may (along with Montreal and perhaps some other cities) provide a counter-argument to Florida's causal claims regarding the relationship between creative industries and growth.

Berlin's economic development path since 1990

Berlin's reinstatement as the capital of Germany has raised great expectations of its transformation into a major economic metropolis of Europe. Yet the city has not been able to fulfill these expectations. Berlin's socioeconomic restructuring in the 1990s led to a tremendous loss of manufacturing jobs in traditional industries, a rise in unemployment, and the spread of urban poverty. At the same time, the city has been a prime playground for speculative real estate investment, which left behind a huge pile of unoccupied office space. On the other hand, new islands of economic growth have developed, particularly in knowledge-intensive economic activities. From 1991 to 2007, employment in Berlin's manufacturing sector decreased by 178 000 jobs (leaving no more than 86 000 workplaces); the parallel increase in service sector jobs could by no means compensate for this loss of manufacturing jobs. The decline of Berlin's manufacturing industries has partially been triggered by the closure of production sites in the eastern part of the city (former GDR plants; in addition, the decline resulted to a large extent from the structural weaknesses of the manufacturing industries in the western part of the city, which for decades used the special Berlin subsidies to expand the assembly line production of simple mass products (Krätke and Borst 2000). The termination of these special Berlin subsidies after 1990 led to factory closures and relocations. Today, the traditional manufacturing industries are much less represented in Berlin than in the other urban economic centers of Germany.

A historically specific property of Berlin's economy is the comparatively weak representation of corporate headquarters. As a consequence of the division of Germany after World War II, and West Berlin being an island within the territory of the GDR, Berlin suffered an exodus of corporate headquarters. Since 1990, the city's new role in the German and European urban framework spawned hopes that it would be able to re-establish its position as an economic center with a high level of economic centrality in terms of corporate command and control capacities. The newly acquired role of capital city encouraged some prominent national and international companies to set up selected divisions and directional centers in Berlin. In this way, a number of new corporate headquarters have been located in Berlin since 1990 – however, in comparison to the other large urban economic centers of Germany, Berlin still has quite a weak position in terms of entrepreneurial control capacity (Krätke and Borst 2000). Berlin's newly acquired political centrality in terms of capital city functions has triggered growth in the city's service economy. Yet despite the registered growth of producer services in Berlin since 1990, the relative concentration of so-called "advanced producer services" is still much lower than in the other centers of the German urban system. Compared to other economic metropolises, the erosion of Berlin's manufacturing industries has undermined the city's long-term growth potential in the subsector of advanced producer services.

In the 1990s, Berlin was also a prime playground for the activities of professional subsidy hunters in the real estate business. In the course of German reunification, national and international real estate firms expected a continuous growth of demand for new office and commercial space in the metropolitan centers of the urban system. A wave of real estate acquisition, conversion, and large-scale building projects particularly affected East German cities (Krätke 2004b). This, combined with the former Berlin government's belief that office building sites were a sign of economic progress and offered a promising future for the respective city, led to the government agreeing to new office projects of any size and number; the city's own financial corporation actively took part in large-scale speculative real estate investments in East Germany. Within a couple of years, the speculative real estate boom in East German cities turned into a real estate market crisis, leaving the city of Berlin with an unexpected financial burden of roughly €60 billion. In a broader view, the speculative activities and related real estate policies resulted from the ideological concept of a metropolitan urban economy that bets on financial investments (including real estate business). Such a metropolitan economy had received the strongest support from Berlin's political class, which confused regional economic development with finance and real estate business and had actively taken part in these activities. Since the mid-1990s, Berlin has suffered from a "home-made" financial crisis. A new urban government is striving to consolidate the city's financial situation by measures which include cuts in social expenditure and public services.

The problematic trends mentioned above do not, however, represent the whole story of Berlin's economic restructuring process. New islands of economic growth have developed in Berlin, particularly in selected "knowledge-intensive" activities such as the software industry, biotechnology, medical engineering, and the culture industries. The most important growth sector of Berlin today is the cultural economy (including the media industries), in which the city has reached the position of a first-rank center of the German and European urban system. As a vibrant "cultural metropolis," Berlin also reveals a positive record in the realm of urban cultural tourism and related service industries. Berlin also shows a high rate of growth in the software industry and is home to more than 1700 specialized firms. In addition, Berlin has become (besides Munich) a leading center of the European "life sciences" sector which comprises biotechnology, medical engineering firms, the pharmaceutical industry, and medical research. On this basis, the Berlin metropolis has achieved a strong position among the regional centers of knowledge-intensive economic activities in Germany.

Despite the economic growth in these subsectors of Berlin's economy, the overall process of economic restructuring in Berlin has led to a considerable rise in unemployment and the number of people dependent on public social assistance. Growth in a few selected subsectors of a large metropolis with roughly 3 million inhabitants could not compensate for the aggregated loss of jobs in the city's traditional employment sectors. The losers are predominantly concentrated in the inner urban districts of West Berlin, namely the traditional industrial workers' districts like Wedding, Tiergarten, and Kreuzberg. At the same time, other inner urban districts are becoming more and more attractive to "new urban scenes" and subject to gentrification processes. The most obvious case is the district of Prenzlauer Berg adjacent to the eastern city center. A further candidate is the adjacent inner urban district of Friedrichshain, which has moved into the "pioneering phase" of a future gentrification. In sum, the Berlin metropolis is on the path toward developing a more pronounced polarization of its sociospatial fabric.

Today, Berlin still exhibits the general characteristic of a comparatively "weak" metropolitan economy, with an aggregated growth rate scoring continuously below the German average and the performance of metropolitan regions such as Frankfurt-Main, Munich, and Stuttgart. Growth in the above-mentioned knowledge-intensive subsectors has not outweighed the economic decline and weak development in other sectors such as traditional manufacturing industries and less skilled services. However, in the world economic crisis of 2008 onward, Berlin's economy experienced a comparatively small decrease of its growth rate due to the weak presence of manufacturing industries. The economic downturn of 2009 (following the outbreak of the financial crisis in 2008) has hit metropolitan regions with a strong base of export-oriented manufacturing industries much more strongly.

The next section concentrates on Berlin's cultural economy.

The Rise of the Cultural Economy in Berlin's Inner-City Area

The German regional system contains a number of competing urban centers in the cultural economy. The culture and media industry firms and workers are selectively concentrated in large metropolitan regions (Krätke 2002a). Major centers of the cultural economy are the metropolitan regions of Berlin, Munich, Hamburg, Cologne, and Frankfurt am Main. A high *relative concentration* of artistically creative occupations can be taken as an empirical indicator of cultural economy clusters in Germany's urban and regional system. In 2005, the location quotient for artistically creative workers was particularly high in Berlin, Munich, Hamburg, Cologne, and Leipzig (between 2.0 and 10.00; see Figure 5.1). And while the metropolitan region of Frankfurt am Main, which includes the subcenters of Mainz and Wiesbaden, had a second-tier concentration of artistically creative workers (1.25–2.00), in terms of absolute numbers it is a prime location for artistically creative workers in Germany's culture and media industries (see Figure 2.10).

The urban centers of the cultural economy are characterized by divergent sectoral profiles – that is, particular subsectors of the cultural economy are concentrated in specific cities. Nevertheless, in the leading urban centers of the culture and media industries, the absolute employment figures are highest across *all* subsectors (see Figure 5.2). This highly selective geographic concentration facilitates the optimal use of cross-sectoral "impulses" and network relations within a given urban area. The most important centers of the cultural economy in Germany can be identified by locating the prime urban centers in *different* subsectors in terms of absolute employment numbers (see Figure 5.2).

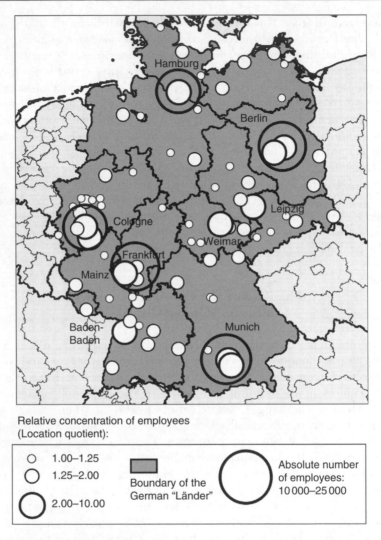

Figure 5.1   The relative concentration of employees in artistically creative occupations in Germany's urban and regional system, 2005.

As shown in Figure 5.2, the German regional system has five "prime" centers of the culture and media industries: Berlin, Munich, Hamburg, Cologne, and Frankfurt am Main. Two additional media cities – Düsseldorf and Stuttgart – have a comparably high concentration of employees in just two subsectors: advertising and publishing. The fact that Germany's urban and regional system contains several prominent cultural economy centers is partly due to the fact that large culture and media firms frequently establish

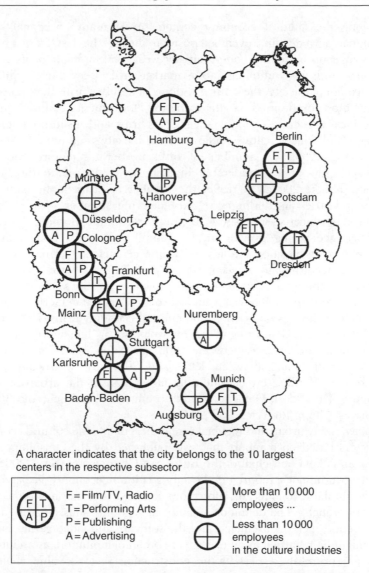

A character indicates that the city belongs to the 10 largest centers in the respective subsector

F = Film/TV, Radio
T = Performing Arts
P = Publishing
A = Advertising

More than 10 000 employees ...

Less than 10 000 employees in the culture industries

Figure 5.2 Regional centers of the culture and media industries in Germany according to sectoral profile, 2000.

branch offices in various important centers of the urban system in order to take advantage of local production capacities and creative resources. Thus, the various regional clusters of the culture and media industries in Germany are interlinked by the organizational networks of large media firms who strive to be present in all prominent centers and make use of local inter-firm cooperation and communication networks.

Among the cultural economy centers of Germany's regional system, Berlin has strongly improved its position during the last 20 years. This stands in contrast to the comparatively weak development of its regional economy and its continuing labor market crisis (see above). Since the reunification of the city, the culture and media industry firms have considered Berlin's most important strengths to be the "local media culture," in terms of the local clustering of many specialized firms and institutions, the high availability of skilled creative employees, and the city's cultural attractiveness. During the 1990s, the number of firms in Berlin's culture and media industries grew at a considerably higher rate compared to the German average (Krätke 2002a). In 1998, the number of firms in the culture and media industries in Berlin even exceeded the number of firms in the advanced producer-services subsector. In the meantime, Berlin has continued to experience strong growth in its culture and media sector, and has strengthened its position among the prime centers of Germany's cultural economy. According to a recent report published by Berlin's government (Senatsverwaltung für Wirtschaft 2008), growth in the city's cultural economy between 2000 and 2006 was much stronger than the German average. In 2006, the city was home to 22 900 cultural economy firms (75% of which were "micro-firms" consisting of one or two persons). The figure corresponds to a growth rate of 33% between 2000 and 2006 (see Senatsverwaltung für Wirtschaft 2008). Between 1998 and 2006, the artistically creative workforce in Berlin grew considerably faster than in the urban regions of Hamburg, Düsseldorf, Cologne, Frankfurt am Main, Munich, and Stuttgart (Senatsverwaltung für Wirtschaft 2008).

Today, many urban and regional researchers define the cultural economy's subsectors based on a report that was published by the consultancy Kern European Affairs on behalf of the European Commission (KEA 2006). The Berlin government's report on the city's cultural economy is based on a largely similar grouping of subsectors (apart from the inclusion of the software branch). The definition of cultural economy subsectors used in the Berlin report includes architects and the software and video games industry. This might be regarded as an excessively broad delimitation, as architectural firms are primarily a part of the construction sector's value chain, and software firms mostly act as specific technology-related service suppliers in the value chains of other industries (see Howkins 2001). In any event, the high number of firms and employees located in Berlin clearly confirms its position as a prime center of Germany's cultural economy. Regrettably, the city's cultural economy report is characterized by a broad ignorance of existing research on the culture and media industries in Berlin and at an international level (see literature cited in Chapter 2). Nevertheless, the report presents relevant empirical data on recent developments in the various subsectors of Berlin's cultural economy.

The rise of new "city industries" and the cultural economy's spatial organization

With regard to the spatial organization of an urban region's economy, for a long time the city was characterized by an urban center composed of an agglomeration of business-service firms and corporate headquarters. Manufacturing industries, on the other hand, were either concentrated on the urban core's periphery or undergoing a process of relocation to the outer fringes of the metropolitan region. This rough picture of the metropolitan economy's spatial organization has been challenged by a new trend: key metropolitan subsectors of productive activity have been regrouping to form new local clusters within the metropolis itself (Scott 1988b; Krätke 2000). A number of traditional local areas of production activity in the inner-city area of the metropolis are subject to a process of restructuring and "upgrading" by a new mix of production activities, which predominantly include knowledge-intensive high-technology subsectors such as the software industry, the pharmaceutical industry and biotechnology, medical engineering, and the diverse cultural products industries. These subsectors are forming new "city industries," which lead to a revitalization of productive activities in the inner-city area (Krätke 2000; Indergaard 2004; Hutton 2006, 2008). As a consequence, however, there are an increasing number of competing and conflicting claims for the use of inner-city space.

Hutton (2008: 18) emphasizes that new city industries are constantly threatened by expanding spatial demands of the commercial/financial sector. "The role of the latter in driving inflationary pressures within the ... property market suggests a profile of 'precarious reindustrialization' in the metropolitan core." Particularly in the framework of inner-city "redevelopment" projects, the small experimental producers of the cultural economy are prime candidates for displacement. The inner-city areas of metropolitan regions represent a "contested" social space, not just with respect to residential gentrification processes, but also with regard to various production activities.

The formation of new intra-urban industrial districts of research-intensive industrial subsectors and the culture industries can be regarded as a spatial articulation of economic restructuring processes in favor of an increasingly knowledge-intensive urban economy. In his account of the "new economy of the inner city," which is based on detailed case studies (showing a marked variation in the particular reindustrialization processes and experiences of individual cities and inner-city districts), Hutton (2008: 248) underscores that "the last decade and a half or so has seen a significant reassertion of production within the inner city," which suggests a recovery of the inner city's role as incubator of experimentation and innovation. The rise of new "city industries" that prefer to locate and expand in the inner-city area lies at the heart of the resurgence of urban economies. New "city industries" are expected to take on the role of core growth sectors, which might compensate for the decline of Fordist industries.

The restructuring of the spatial organization of metropolitan economies corresponds with a trend toward reagglomeration witnessed in numerous industries (cf. Scott 1988a), particularly in R&D-intensive manufacturing sectors, design-intensive subsectors, and cultural-product industries (see Scott 2000). New or revitalized local agglomerations of such industries are located both in the inner-city areas of large cities, as well as in the outer zones and fringe areas of metropolitan areas. Here, the emerging local clusters of knowledge- and research-intensive manufacturing activities are frequently labeled as new urban "technology districts." A recent empirical analysis of industrial location at the intra-metropolitan level (Arauzo-Carod and Viladecans-Marsal 2009) confirmed that new manufacturing firms of high-technology industries in particular

> prefer to locate their establishments within, or as close as possible to, the central city itself. These results suggest that even though a suburbanization process exists and some firms may indeed move away from the center of the metropolitan area, they prefer to locate their activity close to the central city because it allows them to maintain fluid communications with the center and so benefit from the greater advantages of agglomeration. (Arauzo-Carod and Viladecans-Marsal 2009: 556)

The formation of new production spaces on the intra-metropolitan level is fostered by the continued "unbounding of the metropolis" in terms of the extraordinary expansion of its spatial scale (see Soja 2000) toward the formation of a metropolitan region which might include several secondary cities and urban subcenters besides the central city and its core area. Similarly, the debate on globalizing cities is increasingly related to the expanding spatial scale of a global city region that exceeds former administrative boundaries of the city.

The formation of intra-metropolitan "technopoles" – in terms of specialized districts with specific infrastructures and buildings for research-intensive new industries that are in most cases located outside the inner-city core area (such as the Berlin Adlershof technology district or the "cité scientifique" in the metropolitan region of Paris) – might be regarded as a particular type of restructuring of the urban regions' space economy. Furthermore, an increasing specialization of urban economic functions leads to an increasingly polycentric structure of the urban regions' space economy. Specific functions such as back offices, logistics, and large-scale entertainment and sports facilities are relocated within a metropolitan region to decentralized locations (Hall 2001). A most important development is the formation of "edge cities" (Garreau 1991), in terms of new subcenters and local economic growth poles that are often located on the fringe of the metropolitan area. The edge city has been defined as "a suburb in which business activities, employment centers, commercial and cultural facilities are brought together with the residential function. These suburbs are not primarily residential any more" (Marcuse and van Kempen 2000: 15). However, edge cities might also be defined in a broader sense as new intra-metropolitan subcenters that can take on a great variety of forms. Hall (2001) does not restrict the usage of the term "edge city" to particular "suburban" spatial environments. He distinguishes four types: (1) the "external edge city" that is often located on the axis of a major airport (for example, London Heathrow or Paris Charles de Gaulle); (2) the "outermost edge city complexes" for back offices or R&D functions that are typically located at major train stations at a comparatively large distance from the city center (such as Reading in the metropolitan region of London); (3) "internal edge cities" that result from pressure to expand the traditional urban business center or from speculative reconversion and development of old industrial sites or redundant harbor areas in proximity to the traditional city center (such as the London Docklands or Paris La Défense); (4) "specialized subcenters" such as new entertainment districts with exhibition and convention centers. Some of these are located on reconverted sites close to the traditional city center; others are developed in formerly separate towns that have become progressively embedded in the space economy of a wider metropolitan region. The development of edge cities is often included in the large cities' growth strategies in terms of a spatially focused expansion strategy. Further relevant trends in the reshaping of the urban regions' space economy comprise the formation of new spaces of consumption and spectacle (including the development of specifically attractive "shopping districts" and cultural quarters), which serve in inter-urban competition as major consumerist cultural assets. The cities' cultural industry districts, as well as specialized intra-metropolitan technology districts, might be regarded as representing specific variants of the formation of new "specialized subcenters" of the urban economy.

In Berlin, the culture and media industries are selectively concentrated in various subdistricts of the inner-city area and the two city centers (i.e., the city's traditional center in former East Berlin and the western city center of the formerly divided city). Many of Berlin's inner-city districts qualify as cultural production sites rather than as "service industry" locations. Moreover, there are specific local agglomerations of particular subsectors. Film production, for instance, is clustered in the western city center as well as in some of the trendy districts of the east. A large number of film and TV industry firms and related service companies are also located in the so-called "science and technology" district of Adlershof in Berlin's outer-urban zone. If Berlin's fringe area is included, the traditional film production site in Potsdam/Babelsberg (which was established by UFA and DEFA studios) – newly rechristened "Media City Babelsberg" – would have to be regarded as a local media industry cluster in the Berlin metropolitan region. Other branches of the cultural economy, such as the printing and publishing trades or the music industry, are locally clustered in different inner-city districts. The printing and publishing trade is an outstanding example of a classical "city industry." It has formed local clusters in the area between the two city centers as well as in the district of Kreuzberg. Altogether, the locational distribution of Berlin's cultural economy provides another example of the phenomenon of local cultural-economy clustering, which was initially illustrated with reference to Los Angeles, London, and Paris (see Scott 2000).

An analysis of the locational fabric of Berlin's cultural economy should not only refer to the locational patterns of various subsectors, but also address the question as to whether related subsectors in the cultural economy overlap in particular urban districts. Indeed, some of Berlin's prominent inner-city districts are characterized by a close propinquity of firms and actors who are active in different culture and media industry subsectors (see Krätke 2002a). Regional research has long established that local agglomerations of complementary production activities offer particular developmental advantages by enhancing the learning capabilities, and, in turn, innovation capacities, of co-located actors (see Storper 1995, 1997). This observation is closely related to the notion of urbanization economies (see above).

The author has identified numerous local industrial agglomerations in Berlin (Krätke 2000). These are distributed across all zones of the city's urban territory and can be subdivided into two groups based on their respective activity profiles. (a) The first group consists of several industrial agglomerations in Berlin's urban periphery (i.e., located outside of the commuter-train ring, or S-Bahn ring, that encircles the urban core of the city, but within the city's administrative boundaries). These agglomerations are characterized by a concentration of firms in the research-intensive high-tech and medium high-tech industries. Moreover, most of these agglomerations are situated on traditional industrial sites in Berlin's urban area. On the one hand, the location of these agglomerations is an expression of industrial restructuring and "upgrading" processes, which have resulted in an increased share of R&D-intensive industries occupying old industrial sites. On the other hand, in East Berlin these agglomerations are also a result of the privatization of former East German industrial complexes (so-called "combines"). The industrial sites formerly inhabited by East Germany's vertically integrated state combines are now home to a relatively large number of individual companies operating in close proximity to one another. The Adlershof "science and technology district" is a prominent local industrial agglomeration that is located on Berlin's urban periphery; while its sectoral profile is dominated by R&D-intensive high-tech industries, it is also home to a local cluster of mostly technology-related media firms. (b) The second group consists of a series of agglomerations located in the inner-city area, particularly in a ring of districts around the former city center of East Berlin (e.g., the districts of Prenzlauer Berg, Friedrichshain, and Kreuzberg). Culture and media industry firms dominate the sectoral profiles of these agglomerations. The analysis of Berlin's space economy emphasizes that the majority of empirically identifiable local industrial agglomerations are situated in the inner-city area of Berlin, and that these agglomerations represent local clusters of mixed activity in the culture and media industries (Krätke 2000). This finding has also been confirmed by the city government's new cultural economy report (Senatsverwaltung für Wirtschaft 2008).

The Mitte district in the eastern city center reveals the greatest density and variety of cultural economy firms, actors, and institutions. This local agglomeration of culture industries and artistically creative actors includes much more than just private sector firms in various cultural economy subsectors. It also encompasses a great variety of "informal" cultural institutions and "experimental" cultural producers in the non-profit sector. Due to the lack of profitability pressures, the non-profits can focus on artistic innovation and quality in ways that commercial firms cannot (Markusen 2006b). The cultural economy's "creative periphery" of non-profit artists' spaces functions as a most important generator of innovation impulses for the whole sector. Markusen (2006a) emphasizes that the spaces and organizations which form the infrastructure for artists to develop their creativity not only include artist-employing and -presenting commercial establishments, but also a multiplicity of other artist-centric spaces such as artists' clubhouses, artists' live/work and studio buildings, and small-scale performing arts venues, where artistic work is developed and exhibited. She argues that such spaces can make a substantial difference to the ability of a city to home-grow, attract, and retain artists.

In the Berlin Mitte district, the spatial density and variety of established and experimental cultural producers has led to the emergence of a particularly energetic creative milieu and "creative atmosphere," and strongly contributes to the vibrant cultural life and attractiveness of this "cultural producers district." The cultural economy of Berlin cannot be accurately described purely with reference to the venerable cultural institutions and commercial producers of the cultural economy. Berlin's cultural lifeblood is drawn from the presence of diverse and innovative small-scale cultural producers and their interaction with established cultural institutions and private sector firms. The city's "cultural producers districts" thrive on formal and informal interorganizational networking amongst the variety of actors and the resulting "creative atmosphere" within a local agglomeration of cultural producers.

Based on this general analysis of the spatial organization of Berlin's cultural economy, a more detailed account of local clustering of the

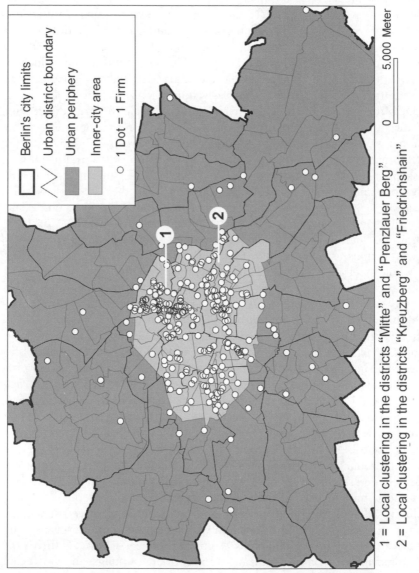

1 = Local clustering in the districts "Mitte" and "Prenzlauer Berg"
2 = Local clustering in the districts "Kreuzberg" and "Friedrichshain"

Figure 5.3 Locational distribution of the culture and media industries in Berlin: multimedia firms, 2008.

multimedia sector and the music industry follows here. Individual firms and their specific inner-city locations can be identified with reference to the 2009 edition of the German "Media Handbook" (Medienhandbuch 2009). The Berlin culture and media industries contain a cluster of multimedia firms of considerable size. Today, many well-known multimedia agencies are located in Berlin, and the start-up rate in the city has also been quite strong in recent years. As a result, Berlin is now a key location for Germany's multimedia industry. The multimedia subsector of the cultural economy creates knowledge-, design-, and technology-intensive products with a high component of IT know-how. The multimedia value chain represents a process that integrates production activities and the provision of specialized services. The value chain includes the provisioning of hardware and software as well as technological network infrastructure; the supply of content in the field of digital image, sound, and text production; the integration of diverse media and design of multimedia products; post-production activities in the field of digital processing; the technical reproduction of multimedia products; and the provision of online services. With regard to marketing activities in the offline and online spheres, multimedia producers are frequently interlinked with publishing firms and TV broadcasters.

Knowledge- and technology-intensive multimedia firms can be regarded as an important subsector of the so-called "creative industries." Within the urban spatial fabric of Berlin, multimedia firms are concentrated in a number of local agglomerations, most of which are located in the densely built and mixed-use inner-city area (see Figure 5.3), circumscribed by a commuter-train ring (the so-called "S-Bahn" circle).

The largest local agglomeration of multimedia firms can be found in the eastern city center in the Mitte district. This agglomeration extends to the central part of the adjacent inner-city district of Prenzlauer Berg. Note that the "official" names of Berlin's districts are now different due to an administrative reform that combined the former districts into larger administrative units. However, we refer here to the former district names, as they are well established, still commonly used, and allow for a more detailed representation of Berlin's spatial structures. Within the eastern city center (i.e., the district of Mitte), multimedia firms are strongly clustered on Chaussee Strasse (which has been labeled Berlin's "Silicon Alley"), among other locations. A second prominent agglomeration of multimedia firms is located in the trendy inner-city districts of Kreuzberg and Friedrichshain (see Figure 5.3). It is important to note that most local agglomerations of the multimedia sector in Berlin coincide with local concentrations of other culture and media industry subsectors (particularly the film industry). In particular fields of competence, the multimedia sector's activities complement or overlap with some technology-intensive activities in the film and television industries. In Germany, the metropolitan region of Berlin (including Potsdam/Babelsberg) has a leading position in film industry post-production activities. In 2000, 25% of the identified 211 specialist firms for digital image processing and computer animation in the German film industry were located in the Berlin metropolitan region. Munich and Hamburg each accounted for 13% of the remaining total; Frankfurt am Main, 9%; and Cologne, 7% (Krätke and Scheuplein 2001). The digital post-production and computer-animation subsectors represent a field of intersection between the media and information technology industries (including the software industry). These subsectors have positively contributed to the strong position and dynamism of Berlin's multimedia sector.

The concentration of the multimedia sector in the above-mentioned inner-city districts can be ascribed to several influencing factors. Firstly, actors in the multimedia sector prefer "mixed-use" inner-city districts that allow for the local integration of work and leisure time. This is essential for people who work long hours, and who require services such as restaurants and supermarkets in close proximity to the workplace. Furthermore, the employees of multimedia firms such as Jamba and doohoo prefer to live in the inner-city districts where they work. Most start-up firms in the sector recognize this fact and choose to locate their offices accordingly. Secondly, the architectural and urban-design features of the built environment in Berlin's "mixed-use" inner-city districts are highly attractive. This accords with Helbrecht's notion of place-specific "geographic capital" in terms of the "look and feel" factor of particular urban districts (see Helbrecht 2005). Thirdly, these districts are characterized by a dense local agglomeration of firms and actors in the same or complementary fields of activity. As soon as a certain degree of agglomeration is reached, a locational concentration of firms produces a self-reinforcing growth dynamic. In the case of firm relocations to Berlin or local start-ups, it is evident that firms seek out business locations in close proximity to other firms in the same or complementary fields of activity (i.e., firms which are competitors or suppliers in a different section of the same value chain). The various firms within a local cultural-economy agglomeration share the same concerns and are confronted with the same market structures, so that local clustering creates an economic environment that offers valuable opportunities for inter-firm communication, learning, and the spread of "impulses" for innovation. The local concentration of multimedia firms on Chaussee Strasse, for example, is an attraction factor for start-up firms. Start-up firms emphasize the advantages associated with establishing an office in close proximity to a variety of complementary media firms. By choosing a location on Chaussee Strasse they are likely to find, on the same floor or in the next-door building, a variety of firms that represent the whole value chain of the multimedia sector. During lunch breaks, local employees encounter one another at food stalls or in the supermarket queue, and in the evenings, they frequent the same pubs and cafés. The communal feeling among local firms is the street's most important point of attraction. In other words, this local agglomeration offers socially produced locational advantages.

The music industry is another example of a subsector that is selectively concentrated in Berlin's inner-city area. Friedrichshain and Kreuzberg are the key districts in which the music industry is located; a second significant agglomeration of music firms is situated in the districts of Prenzlauer Berg and Mitte (see Figure 5.4). Spatial overlap with the multimedia-firm agglomerations described above is also clearly visible.

An analysis of the spatial distribution of selected sectors of the cultural economy in Berlin (Krätke 2002a) reveals that there are three districts with an extremely high concentration of firms and micro firms: (1) the districts of Mitte and Prenzlauer Berg; (2) the districts of Kreuzberg and Friedrichshain; and (3) the central areas of the districts of Charlottenburg and Wilmersdorf. The cultural economy report released by the government of Berlin in 2008 also identified these local agglomcrations (Senatsverwaltung für Wirtschaft 2008; see also Mundelius 2006; Lange 2007; Ebert and Kunzmann 2007). A key feature of the built environment in these districts is a high concentration of refurbished turn-of-the-century *Gründerzeit* buildings – which are coveted for their high ceilings, ornamental façades, and stuccowork – in conjunction with the so-called "Berlin mix," which designates a particular intermingling of housing, small businesses, and productive activities in Berlin's dense inner-city areas. On the whole, an assessment of the locational distribution of Berlin's culture and media industries reveals a number of inner-city districts which function as cultural production spaces and which contain various overlapping local agglomerations of cultural economy firms and actors.

The finding that Berlin contains a number of spatially overlapping local agglomerations of firms and actors from different subsectors of the culture and media industry might indicate that the actors involved share common locational preferences, such as the high regard for a local environment that offers a "creativity-boosting atmosphere," regardless of the actual existence of formal inter-firm ties or cooperative relations. This point reminds us again of the significance of urbanization economies and offers a new perspective on the multidimensional function of urbanization economies within particular districts of the urban territory.

Urbanization economies and the local concentration of the creative economy in specific inner-city districts

This chapter began by highlighting the general finding that the largest and most diversified urban clusters of cultural production have taken root in large cities and metropoles. More specifically, in the metropoles of the European urban system, most artistically creative activities are locally concentrated in specific districts of an "inner-urban ring" which surrounds

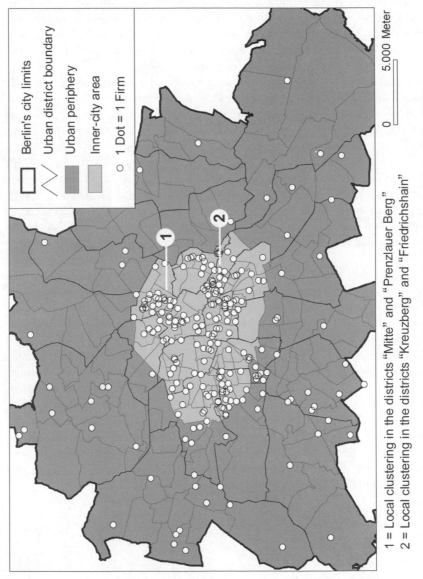

1 = Local clustering in the districts "Mitte" and "Prenzlauer Berg"
2 = Local clustering in the districts "Kreuzberg" and "Friedrichshain"

Figure 5.4 Locational distribution of the culture and media industries in Berlin: music industry firms, 2008.

an urban core "hub," the city's central business district. Knowledge-intensive creative activities – particularly in artistically creative industries – require urban settings that provide openness and diversity in terms of opportunities for social exchange and cross-fertilization between various actors and branches of activity (see Gertler 2003). According to Landry (2000: 35), the inner urban ring districts are usually

> the home of the less well-established creative and knowledge industries – such as design and Internet companies, young multimedia entrepreneurs or even artists – that provide the *buzzing atmosphere* on which cities thrive, experimenting with new products and services.... The buildings in inner urban rings are usually a mix of old warehousing, small industrial buildings and older housing with a large element of *mixed uses*. Lower prices enable younger, innovative people to develop projects in interesting spaces that in the center only companies with capital can afford. As these companies grow and become more profitable they move into the hub or gentrify their own areas. This inner ring provides a *vital experimentation and incubation zone*. As these inner areas themselves become gentrified the pioneers move out to low rent, run-down areas, and the cycle turns. (Author's emphasis added)

The "buzz" metaphor (see Storper and Venables 2004) effectively captures the essential property of urbanization economies, which is to facilitate creativity-boosting social exchange and cross-fertilization amongst different actors and branches of activity in a densely and diversely populated local area. Economic activities that depend on creativity require stimulating environments where face-to-face contact is convenient and efficient. Urbanization economies include the notion of proximity-based knowledge spillovers and the rapid spread of innovation "impulses" between different clusters (or subsectors) of the urban economy.

The performance of creative industries is also dependent on sociocultural aspects of urbanization economies (Gertler 2003) such as institutional and cultural diversity. As Thiel (2005: 159) has emphasized, "a diverse socio-cultural context helps to avoid the potential irreversibility of wrong choices in an uncertain labor market both by firms and by individuals, by constantly providing alternative options for action." Large cities and metropolitan regions are most likely to offer the sociocultural diversity which is essential for the functioning of urbanization economies beyond the opportunities for interorganizational knowledge networking that are related to the process of local cluster formation. Urbanization economies that are based on sociocultural diversity and cross-fertilization amongst different professional milieus in the urban social space might also be referred to as "Jane Jacob's externalities."

However, the concept of urbanization economies is applicable on the macro level of an entire city or urban region as well as on the micro level of particular inner-city districts. On the micro level, the functioning of urbanization economies is somewhat easier to grasp. The clustering of diverse cultural industries in a particular inner-city district fosters the spillover of new concepts and approaches from one subsector of cultural production to another. At the local level, this kind of cross-fertilization is reinforced by the mobility of artistically creative freelance workers who frequently offer their skilled work to various culture industry subsectors at the same time. Lorenzen and Frederiksen (2008: 171) emphasize the creative impact of inter-sectoral local labor mobility by noting that,

> even when firms from different cultural industries are non-related in terms of knowledge base and collaboration, chances are that they still benefit from being co-located, because of external economies arising from diversity on the labour market. In the cultural industries, most new product ideas are made by individuals, not firms, and when diverse cultural industries co-locate, such local labour flows among firms bring about not just talent, but also ideas – and a great potential for novelty.

On the urban macro level, the function of urbanization economies is also dependent on the accessibility of diverse areas within a city. If a large city or metropolitan region does not have a functioning local transport system (as for example in London, where the urban transport system has been extremely run down by privatization, lack of maintenance, and overpricing), the urban area in practical terms becomes a highly fragmented territory that offers urbanization economies only at the level of particular inner-city districts.

The local concentration of cultural economy branches in specific inner-city districts is not solely determined by the economic forces that drive the formation of local and regional production clusters in knowledge- and design-intensive sectors of activity. Local clustering also supports the functioning of a professional milieu in specific branches of the cultural economy "by providing random opportunities for social relations to be built ... as well as by fostering rivalry among the professionals themselves and by providing places at which the necessary sociability can be produced in everyday life" (Thiel 2005: 144). In local clusters, geographic proximity and the relational overlapping of interorganizational and social networks is a decisive supporting factor for artistic creativity (Belussi and Sedita 2008).

With regard to the case of Berlin, the local areas in which the aforementioned social and professional networks (consisting of loosely connected "weak" ties) are formed and sustained in everyday life can be identified through the locational distribution of artists according to their place of residence in Berlin. The analysis is based on data provided by the German Social Security Fund for Artists, comprising musicians, writers, performing and sculptural artists. This grouping predominantly consists of self-employed artists. In July 2007, a total sum of 27 324 artists were registered in Berlin, which amounts to a share of 17% of all artists in Germany. The major local concentrations of artists in Berlin are to be found in the inner urban districts of Mitte, Prenzlauer Berg, Friedrichshain, and Kreuzberg (see Figure 5.5). The local concentration of artists lies at the heart of these local areas' function as "trendy districts" in the Berlin context. Compared to the locational distribution of cultural economy firms in Berlin (see Figures 5.3 and 5.4), there is a clear overlap between the artists' major places of residence and the local clustering of cultural economy firms in the aforementioned districts. Hence in the cultural economy of Berlin, a pronounced spatial overlap between living and working environments of the artistically creative workforce forms the basis of the local interplay amongst professional, social, and interorganizational networks of the cultural economy actors. These conditions foster the emergence of a highly dynamic and particularly inspiring local "creative milieu."

Furthermore, the local clustering of creative industry professionals corresponds to specific urban lifestyles (Krätke 2002a). In Berlin (as in other urban centers of the cultural economy), artists and creative workers in the culture industries prefer inner-city locations in which living and working environments merge with leisure-time activities. The character of a district in terms of its "look and feel" (Helbrecht 2005; see also Pratt 2009), which is to a large extent determined by its residents, is thus a specific attraction factor. For employees and freelancers in the media and culture industries, a local connection between working, living, and leisure is an attraction factor that is in harmony with their lifestyles. However, due to the unbounding of work times of creative freelancers, these local work–life combinations in specific inner-city districts might not be interpreted as a matter of "free choice," but rather in terms of a need to rely on opportunities for coupling work relations, communication within the diverse community of creative workers, and everyday life. Such opportunities are developing particularly in mixed-use inner urban ring districts.

Moreover, culture industry workers frequently seek out locations in a "sub-cultural" urban district that they regard as a stimulating environment while at work or when pursuing leisure activities. The particular "urban atmosphere" and street life in mixed-use inner-city districts that are home to diverse cultural scenes is conducive to creative inspiration, particularly for the cultural economy's experimental producers and artistically creative workers. In this way, local media and culture industry clusters exhibit a direct link between distinct lifestyle forms and the organizational modes of cultural production, and thus a clear overlap between the geographies of production and consumption (Krätke 2002c). This point again highlights the interaction between professional milieus of creative workers and the urban space. Of relevance here is not only the dynamics of local clustering and the formation of interorganizational networks and labor pools of artistically creative workers, but also (as

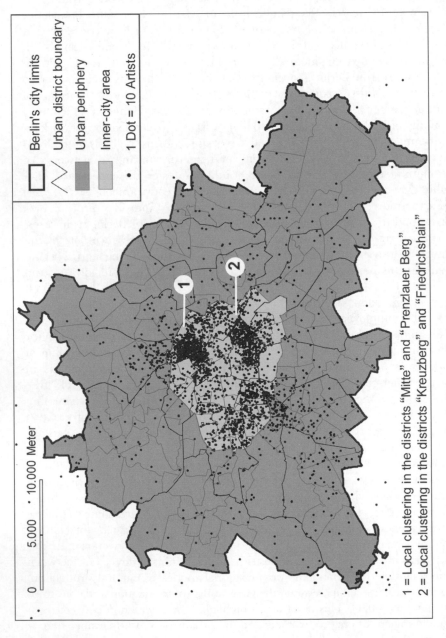

Figure 5.5 Locational distribution of artists in Berlin according to place of residence, 2007.

1 = Local clustering in the districts "Mitte" and "Prenzlauer Berg"
2 = Local clustering in the districts "Kreuzberg" and "Friedrichshain"

Legend:
- Berlin's city limits
- Urban district boundary
- Urban periphery
- Inner-city area
- 1 Dot = 10 Artists

0   5.000   10.000 Meter

mentioned above) the emergence of a locally bound "creative milieu" in terms of the "innovative milieu" approach (see Camagni 1991a, 1991b, 1999; see also Meusburger, Funke, and Wunder 2009). According to Thiel (2005: 144):

> the milieu in this sense offers the necessary cultural proximity between its members but also fosters the rivalry among them that drives its sustainable progress. Its functioning is yet underpinned by the urban context around it which both offers the members of the milieu [*sic*] to realize their lifestyles and guarantees the openness that provides the milieu with the necessary "external energy" it needs to maintain innovativeness over the long run.

Allen Scott's notion of the "creative field" as a dense network of social and economic interactions (Scott 2000, 2006) might be taken as an expression for the interplay of local agglomerations of specialized firms with urbanization economies in terms of the interacting professional and social milieus in particular cities and inner-city districts. This conception corresponds to the notion of the "creative capital of cities" that stands at the center of our analysis (see above). Scott starts from the thesis that "dense production agglomerations are especially likely to be sites of insistent originality and inventiveness," and tries to measure the "output" of such creative fields, using the example of the recorded music industry in US cities. According to Scott (2000: 123), "we should expect to observe a non-linear increasing returns relation between the size of any music industry agglomeration and its ability consistently to produce records that appeal to consumers." Consumer appeal or market success is empirically operationalized by the number of "hit single records" (based on the US Billboard's Hot 100 charts) produced in any given agglomeration by *independent* record companies, which represent the industry's most important suppliers of innovative products. The empirical analysis confirmed an outstanding relative concentration of successful creative output (in terms of hit records) in New York and Los Angeles in relation to the total number of independent record companies, whereas other US cities fell far behind. Hence a comparatively high index of representation (similar to the "location quotient" measure of relative concentration) of successful creative output in a particular cultural economy subsector of a city indicates the specific creative capacities of the respective city's cultural economy. Nonetheless, due to the particular difficulties of operationalizing the "output" of creative work in the culture industries as compared to manufacturing industries (which can draw on the output of patents, the share of product and process innovations, etc.), the analysis of the urban cultural economies' creativity effects in empirical terms has scarcely been advanced.

We have also to take into account that the city *as a whole* can become a factor of creative success, in that the *symbolic quality* of the specific location is either incorporated into the products of the cultural economy or the origin of these products itself becomes a mark of quality (Scott 2000). Hence, production locations such as New York, Paris, and Berlin operate in cultural and media spheres as "brand names" that invoke the attractive social and cultural qualities of the city in question. The social and cultural milieus to which metropolitan areas owe their international reputation are exploited commercially in the marketing of the city as a brand. With regard to the content and design of products, cultural production and media industry firms have to contend with rapidly changing trends. Consequently, there is a wish to remain "on the pulse" of new cultural development – to stay in touch with subculture trends developing in metropolises such as New York, Paris, and Berlin. Cities of this kind are perceived as social and cultural spaces marked by great diversity, openness, and cultural dynamism (Krätke 2002a). This in turn enhances their attractiveness to "creative talents" and makes them a source of inspiration for cultural producers. Marked social and cultural diversity and openness, therefore, represents a specific "cultural capital" of the city that attracts specific economic activities and actors. This form of cultural capital is concentrated to a large extent in the premier metropoles and global cities of the culture industry, and functions as an additional agglomeration factor in the selective concentration process of the culture and media industries in the international urban system. The notion of "cultural capital" is related to sociocultural properties such as diversity and the vitality of "everyday culture" as a collective resource. This notion is grounded in a comprehensive sociological understanding of "culture" and might be used (like the notion of social capital) not only at the micro level (see Bourdieu 1982, 1983) but also at a meso level of societal development with regard to cities and regions. In this context, urban cultures and a city's sociocultural properties represent an important intangible resource in urban and regional economic development, a resource that particularly influences the development of the cultural economy. A city's cultural capital is a socially produced locational advantage for its culture and media industries.

This particular aspect of Berlin's attractiveness was emphasized by Tim Renner, the former head of the German branch of Universal Music, with regard to why the company relocated from Hamburg to Berlin in 2002. The global firm established its new German headquarters with 500 employees in a reconverted former factory building in the up-and-coming district of Friedrichshain-Kreuzberg. Renner explicitly related this locational choice to the district's place-specific cultural capital. He lauded the district as a *culturally vibrant* urban area where new developments were taking place. He also stated his preference for the location over other central areas of Berlin, "where tourists would presumably collect to gaze in awe at our firm logo. By contrast, there are plenty of 'young and wild' people living close to the industrial site in Friedrichshain" (*Tagesspiegel*, June 28, 2001; author's translation). A cultural economy firm like Universal Music needs to establish close ties to subcultures, as the music industry (like other branches of the cultural economy) does business on the basis of rapidly changing cultural trends. A proximity to a source of new trends – the subcultures which develop in culturally dynamic metropoles like Berlin – is vital to the economic success of the company. Universal Music moved from the city of Hamburg, which had been perceived as being "stiff," to the "dynamic" district Friedrichshain-Kreuzberg in order to take advantage of the creative atmosphere generated by its cultural capital. As Tim Renner comments:

> a media firm is dependent on a young, creative environment. And vice versa, a firm like ours must be able to send new ideas to the surrounding mass. We do need a highly active "sounding board" for new ideas. Furthermore, our new location will have the best companies around. On the other bank of the Spree River there are many new media firms with whom we have established cooperative ties, and other firms in the music industry will follow. (*Tagesspiegel*, July 8, 2001; author's translation)

Creative Cities and the Role of the Culture Industries in Urban Economic and Spatial Development: Implications for Urban Regeneration

The notion of the "creative city" based on flourishing creative industries has become particularly attractive to urban political decision makers because of the expectation that the culture industry will have a positive impact on urban economic development and spatial regeneration. That's the reason why Florida's theory of the "creative class" (see Chapter 2) has been taken up as a "message of hope" in many cities – in established urban centers of the culture industry as well as in cities that are confronted with economic decline in traditional manufacturing and service sectors and related labor-market pressures. Indeed, the culture industry might generally be characterized as one of the "lead industries" of the twenty-first century: changing consumption patterns are fostering a growing demand for cultural products and the culture industry is the central supplier of "content" for the development of information and communication technologies (e.g., the Internet), the capitalist economy's expanding marketing activities, and the accelerated proliferation of commercial entertainment in terms of the commodification of culture. Hence the culture industry is regularly included among the contemporary growth sectors of highly industrialized countries (alongside high-tech industries and advanced producer services). In addition, the culture industry belongs to the labor-intensive branches of industry whose growth can help to compensate for shrinking employment opportunities in various "traditional" manufacturing industries. The same argument has been used before in the propagation of a "post-industrial" society relying on labor-intensive service sectors (Bell 1974).

However, due to the specific sociocultural base of the cultural economy, the concentration of firms and creative actors within the urban system is highly selective (see above), so that only a limited number of particular cities and metropoles can make use of the cultural economy sector as a relevant focus of their development strategy. In recent times, many cities of Europe's old industrial regions (such as Bilbao, Glasgow, Manchester, etc.) have drawn on "cultural strategies" for economic regeneration, including support for the cultural economy sector as well as the extension of cultural facilities and selective "upgrading" of urban built environments. Comparative research demonstrates that cultural strategies can play a supportive role in regenerating cities of old industrial regions, but more as an image booster than as a job machine (Benneworth and Hospers 2009). The cultural economy's potential ability to make up for shrinking employment opportunities in various "old" industries is limited in quantitative terms, so that no city can solely count on the culture industries' growth to sustain its economy. Even a large metropolis such as Berlin, whose economy is characterized by a comparatively strong share of the cultural economy sector, cannot rely exclusively on this subsector in order to deal with the city's labor market problems. Focusing a city's economic development path on the expansion of the culture industry would represent a "Las Vegas option," since Las Vegas can be regarded as the unique example of a city whose economy is predominantly based on the entertainment industry and related services (such as tourism). Yet no urban political decision maker would explicitly propagate the highly unrealistic concept of becoming a second Las Vegas – a development path that predominantly relies on the cultural economy sector is not a promising choice. This contradicts many of the salvational promises made by the "creative industries" urban growth ideology.

According to Berlin's government report on the cultural economy (Senatsverwaltung für Wirtschaft 2008), the city was home to 22 900 cultural economy firms in 2006. Three-quarters of these firms were "micro firms" consisting of one or two people. Between 2000 and 2006, the number of firms increased by 5650. The sector's workforce (including employees, entrepreneurs, and self-employed freelancers) amounted to 160 000 persons in 2006 and had a share of 10% among the city's total workforce. In Berlin, the cultural economy sector has a comparatively strong share of the urban economy in terms of firm numbers and employment, yet with regard to the entire urban economy of the metropolis it represents a small "island of growth" alongside other knowledge-intensive high-tech sectors (such as biotechnology, medical engineering, and the software industry). These islands of growth are situated in a sea of job losses in other sectors, such as traditional manufacturing industries and low-skilled services.

An analysis of data maintained by the Federal Institute for Employment reveals that in Berlin between 1995 and 2005 the total number of employees decreased by 18%, which amounts to a loss of 229 000 jobs. This is for the large part made up of a loss of 136 000 jobs in manufacturing occupations (– 43%) and of 59 000 jobs in low-skilled service occupations. In the same period, the city's cultural economy sector recorded an increase of 5200 employees (+ 20%), which does not include the increasing number of self-employed freelancers and "free" acting artists. If the latter group is taken into account (see below), the cultural economy's job growth might be estimated to reach a total number of approximately 10 000. Other sectors of employment growth in Berlin were the knowledge-intensive technology-related services (including the software industry, data processing, technical laboratories, etc.) with an increase of 21 000 jobs, and the knowledge-intensive market-related services (such as business consulting and accountancy), with an increase of 27 000 jobs. In total, these growth sectors could compensate for just 25% of Berlin's total job losses (in quantitative terms). With regard to the cultural economy sector specifically, the potential for solving Berlin's overall labor market problem is even more restricted. Notwithstanding the fact that Berlin is a well-established prime center of the cultural economy, there is no foundation for expecting that the city's economic regeneration could primarily rely on this sector, even though the sector's positive quantitative contribution to the growth of job opportunities is acknowledged.

Furthermore, in contrast to affirmative conceptions of the creative industries' or the cultural economy's contribution to job growth and urban economic regeneration, we have to take into account that the contemporary culture industry primarily offers "low-quality" jobs in terms of precarious employment relations that lack social safeguards and benefits. A key aspect of the culture and media industries is that they have long taken a leading role in conforming with neoliberal conceptions of labor markets freed from social protections. Labor relations in these industries are dominated by permanent freelance work, temporary contract work, and one-person companies (Howkins 2001). The private sector, which accounts for the vast majority of job growth in the "creative economy," prefers short-term and part-time employment relations. With a view to the flexibilization of labor and the expanding ranks of the self-employed, the culture and media industries can be regarded as forerunners of a quite problematic trend which has been carried to extremes in the so-called "New Economy."

The culture and media industries are characterized by a pronounced polarization between flexible employees with a *privileged* status and flexible workers in *precarious* employment situations. In Florida's theory of the "creative class," job insecurity is advocated as a new freedom, neglecting the downsides of workforce flexibilization strategies. The creatives are portrayed as being at one with the neoliberal credo of a flexibilized labor market (see

Florida 2004: 115). According to Florida (2004: 135), "the old employment contract was group oriented and emphasized job security. The new one is tailored to the needs and desires of the individual." This glorification of a "free agent" economy doesn't pay attention to the divisions of labor within the artistically creative workforce and the fact that the majority of freelancers are forced into flexible work patterns. The privileged group of flexible employees in the culture and media industries was previously formed by the high-powered members of the entertainment branch, and now also includes highly skilled and specialized Internet and multimedia experts (Haaren and Hensche 1997; Gottschall and Schnell 2000). This fraction of flexible employees might enjoy chances for "individual self-determination" in their work life. For the majority of the media and culture industries' workforce, however, "regular" and socially protected forms of employment have been alien for a long time. The majority of artistically creative workers now constitute the "middle-class working poor" of the skilled service sector. These people have to accept multiple jobs in short-term contracts, excessive work hours, and poor payment.

In Berlin, many high-skilled creative workers, particularly freelancers, can scarcely survive on the payments received from contract work in the cultural economy and additionally apply for supplementary social support according to the "Hartz IV" legislation (*Tagesspiegel*, November 22, 2009). Precarious contract work, low earnings, and excessive working hours (frequently leading to "burn-out") underscore the ambivalence of chances for "individual self-determination" in the creative sector's work relations. These conditions have to be emphasized in view of accounts that tend to highlight the positive aspects of flexible "self-determination" of work hours and involvement in various projects, stressing a broad "acceptance" of the specific work–life combinations and the work culture among the actors of the creative industry (see Oßenbrügge, Pohl, and Vogelpohl 2009).

According to the recent report on Berlin's cultural economy, in 2006 the workforce of this sector consisted of 77 000 "regular" employees (accounting for a share of 48%), 12 000 workers with a "minor" employment relation (i.e., short-time work and low wage), and 70 000 self-employed freelancers and (mostly micro-) entrepreneurs, the latter group having a share of 44% of the entire sector's workforce (Senatsverwaltung für Wirtschaft 2008: 24). Between 2000 and 2006, the number of "regular" employees shrank in several subsectors of the cultural economy. Since 2006, the sector's "regular" employees as well as its entire workforce recorded new growth (which exceeded the average rate for Germany). Most important, however, is the finding that the majority (52%) of workers in this sector are self-employed freelancers or "minor" job holders (Senatsverwaltung für Wirtschaft 2008: 92). Most workers in Berlin's cultural economy are low-income earners, and in many subsectors (including the music industry, performing arts, publishing trade, photography, and design) the income levels of self-employed workers are far below that of regular, full-time employees (Senatsverwaltung für Wirtschaft 2008: 94–96). These findings indicate that the "new entrepreneurs" of the cultural economy are most accurately described as a highly flexibilized, low-income workforce.

In Berlin, the particularly strong growth of this sector might be interpreted as an expression of the city's overall shortage of employment opportunities (i.e., as a crisis symptom) rather than a unique "strength" of Berlin's economic development. Comparatively easy market access for new start-ups of micro firms, particularly in the cultural economy sector, contributes to this growth dynamic. Additionally, the sustained migration of artists and young creative workers to Berlin, due to the city's sociocultural attractiveness for artistically creative people and the size and diversity of Berlin's cultural economy, leads to the formation of a "culture-industrial reserve army" in terms of a flexible reservoir of cheap labor of skilled creative workers – which is both welcomed and accurately exploited by the capitalist corporations of the culture and media industries. These conditions are felt by the majority of creative freelancers in terms of increasing competition for temporary jobs and contracts, which in turn contributes to shrinking individual earnings in the freelance workforce. The Berlin government's report on the cultural economy highlights the fact that artistically creative workers have to cope with irregular and excessive working hours much more frequently than their colleagues in other sectors. The percentage of freelance workers in the cultural economy has doubled since 1998, and is now twice that of Berlin's economy on the whole (see Senatsverwaltung für Wirtschaft 2008: 97–98). Thus the cultural economy is spearheading a larger trend toward more deregulated, flexibilized, and precarious forms of employment, a trend that is to a large extent the product of neoliberal policy prescriptions. The cultural economy has not been a motor for the creation of full-time jobs, with their attendant social benefits and protections. In this regard, our analysis challenges the premise that the cultural economy could play a key role in shaping a successful and sustainable urban economic development path. The majority of the creative workforce of the cultural economy represents a highly flexibilized pool of skilled low-wage workers, whose growth in selected cities is amplified by a shortage of alternative employment opportunities.

Besides the implications for urban economic development and work relations, the culture industry and its creative workforce play a specific role in urban *spatial restructuring*: a flourishing cultural economy sector regularly triggers local "upgrading" and restructuring processes that contribute to increasing sociospatial inequality and polarization in cities. The local agglomeration of cultural producers and artistically creative workers in inner-city areas can be interpreted as a precarious reindustrialization within the metropolitan core (Hutton 2008), in which the economically less potent firms and the low-income strata of creative workers are constantly fraught with instability and displacement. This instability is particularly experienced by artists, due to the subsistence level of most artists' incomes and the "precarious tenure of artists in the steeply inflating property markets of the inner city" (Hutton 2008: 32). Local displacement of "creative industry" firms and workers can result both from processes of industrial "upgrading" within the sector – for example, new upscale media firms edging out less affluent artists – and from processes of residential gentrification. Furthermore, displacement occurs in the framework of large-scale inner-city redevelopment projects.

In a nutshell, the local agglomeration of artists and cultural economy activities at the intra-metropolitan scale functions as a "seedbed" for gentrification processes (see Smith and Williams 1986; Atkinson 2005; Lees, Slater, and Wyly 2008). Particularly in the inner-city districts, a concentration of cultural economy actors and artistically creative people is fuelling processes of sociospatial restructuring by which inner-city localities are revalued and gradually gentrified. This phenomenon has frequently been described (see Zukin 1982; Landry 2000; Catungal, Leslie, and Hii 2009). Inner-city districts with older buildings, lower prices, and a large element of mixed uses are usually home to local milieus of artistically creative people and the less well-established cultural economy firms. This local concentration contributes to the unfolding of gentrification processes in respective districts, in which the artistically creative people are functioning as a specific group among the "pioneers" of gentrification. The artists in effect are the explorers and regenerators that bring life to run-down areas and foster the development of support structures such as "cool" pubs and clubs, cafés and restaurants. They then attract a more middle-class clientele who like to live in such trendy, culturally attractive urban quarters. The incomers are particularly attracted by a neighborhood's "ambience of the artist's lifestyle" (Featherstone 1994). Markusen (2006a: 1936), however, has emphasized that "blaming artists for gentrification seems off the mark.... It is not their wealth that sets off markets and completes the process of neighborhood gentrification. In the crucial zoning and economic development decisions that shape this process, artists are not the protagonists and lobbyists."

On the supply side of gentrification, capitalist real estate developers and investors take their chance to invest in the upgrading of the respective urban districts' housing stock and built environment. The real estate business frequently involves the creative scene actors as temporary users of old factory buildings which are destined for upgrading, a practice which might also enhance the projects' "marketability" in terms of symbolic value. Moreover, the phenomenon of gentrification highlights the emergence of a competitive struggle for urban spaces among the different strata of the cultural economy's creative workforce. The classic pioneers of gentrification, to a large extent, are artistically creative people, low-income bohemians, and highly skilled young people at the bottom of the labor market food chain. These pioneers are subsequently dislocated in the gentrification process by the more affluent subgroups of the creative workforce and other sectors – high-income urban professionals who prefer to live in trendy inner-city districts in order to pursue yuppie or bobo (bourgeois bohemian) lifestyles. In this way, when creative artists and bohemians conglomerate in an "unexplored" district, they typically sow the seeds of their own displacement. The outmigration of creative workers with low income and precarious employment relations (i.e., the original explorers and regenerators of formerly neglected districts), however, leads to an impairment of the districts' "creative atmosphere" and reduces the potential for local cross-sectoral impulses as well as the districts' "subcultural capital." With time, the original creative scene is forced to relocate to another "low-value" location, and a new cycle of settlement and gentrification is set in motion.

In Berlin, the "movement" of creative milieus in the city's urban space has been clear to see over the last two decades. The most prominent "trendy district" before 1990 was Kreuzberg. In the next decade, which was shaped by the reunification of the city, this function was taken over by the districts of Prenzlauer Berg and Mitte. These districts have experienced the spread of gentrification processes, with a far-reaching displacement of the original population (Krätke and Borst 2000; Holm 2006; Bernt and Holm 2009) and the subsequent outmigration of artists and creative workers with low incomes and precarious job opportunities. Nonetheless, both districts are still characterized by an agglomeration of artistically creative workers and cultural economy firms. Gentrification has rather led to a changing social composition of the residing creative workforce. Over the last decade, the "creative scene" of explorers and regenerators has again relocated, moving on to the districts of Friedrichshain and (back) to Kreuzberg, from where it has recently also spread to the adjoining district of Neukölln (see Lange 2007).

The local agglomeration of "creative industries" in formerly neglected inner-city areas of Berlin has also been utilized by real estate developers for large-scale projects aimed at the conversion of old industrial waterfront sites into prime real estate, as the example of the "Media Spree" development project in the district Kreuzberg-Friedrichshain demonstrates (see Scharenberg and Bader 2009). The Media Spree project covers an area situated at the eastern edge of the city center on both sides of the river Spree (between the two bridges Jannowitzbrücke and Elsenbrücke). After the reunification of the formerly divided city, this old industrial area became a major local agglomeration district of Berlin's cultural industry. In this area, the prominent large firms MTV Europe and Universal Music Germany are located side by side with many small and medium-size firms of the music, fashion, and media industries (see above); at the same time, the area is home to the related creative milieus, a vibrant club culture, and subcultural scene. As Scharenberg and Bader (2009: 331) emphasize, "the creative and alternative image of the neighborhood played a crucial role in attracting enterprises to the area, and comprised a major aspect of the presentation of Media Spree in public discourse – a presentation that seems highly inappropriate given the project's size" (which, in spatial terms, far exceeds Berlin's previous largest redevelopment project, the "Potsdamer Platz"). The Media Spree project organization was founded in 2002 as a private sector marketing firm. In 2005, it was transformed into a "public–private partnership" with strong support from the city government. In 2009, Media Spree represented 19 large real estate companies and property owners, including public corporations. The area's potential for development is estimated at 2.5 million square meters of office space (offering working spaces for approximately 40 000 employees). With regard to the huge size of the intended construction project, it seems quite obvious that the area's creative scene and cultural economy firms are utilized by the real-estate-dominated association Media Spree for a large-scale development of office space and apartments at the edge of the city center – a development that would lead to the future displacement of the cultural economy's "creative periphery" firms and the "creative scene" of explorers and regenerators (i.e., the low-income strata of creative workers and artists). The Media Spree project has been challenged by a protest movement, at the center of which the group "Mediaspree Versenken" ("sink Media Spree") managed to receive broad media attention and mobilized a campaign that succeeded in achieving a renegotiation of the project. This renegotiation offers the chance for certain amendments (e.g., in favor of threatened alternative cultural projects); however, it cannot change the general orientation of the whole redevelopment project (see Scharenberg and Bader 2009).

This case can be regarded as a specific manifestation of the proliferation of gentrification as a *global* urban development strategy (Smith 2002). That strategy includes a broad range of "upgrading" projects in the built environment of cities beyond the well-known processes of residential gentrification, and particularly includes large-scale projects for the conversion of old industrial sites in inner-city areas. These large-scale development projects integrate spaces of production, consumption, and entertainment, as well as residence. The extended forms of contemporary gentrification (such as the Media Spree project) function "as a vehicle for transforming whole areas into new landscape complexes that pioneer a comprehensive class-inflected urban remake" (Smith 2002: 96). In this way, the growth of Berlin's cultural economy sector and its local agglomeration in particular inner-city districts are exploited for real-estate-based capital accumulation in the framework of extended gentrification, which has become a major strategy of urban restructuring.

Conclusion

The spatial organization of the cultural economy sector is characterized by a highly selective concentration of firms and actors in a limited number of large cities and metropoles. The German regional system contains a number of competing urban centers of the cultural economy, the leading centers of which are characterized by an extremely high concentration of employees across all subsectors of the culture and media industries. This allows optimal exploitation of cross-sectoral "impulses" and network relations within a city's territory.

Over the last two decades, Berlin has continuously strengthened its premier position among Germany's centers of the cultural economy. The analysis of the spatial organization of Berlin's economy underscored the fact that the city's inner-city area functions as a prime location for cultural-products industries. The existence of diverse local agglomerations of cultural economy firms and actors in the inner-city districts is an articulation of the rise of new "city industries" in the metropolitan region's economy.

As regards the determinants of the selective concentration of cultural economy actors in particular inner-city districts, several points have been emphasized. The actors of the culture and media scene regard the proximity of other cultural economy firms acting in the same subsector, or in complementary fields of activity, as the best environment for successful development. The local agglomeration in specific districts fosters communication links amongst the firms and actors and thus creates a "space of opportunities," which is welcomed particularly by the start-up firms and freelancers who are facing many uncertainties. Yet the local concentration of cultural economy activities in specific inner-city districts is not solely determined by the economic forces of cluster formation (in terms of localization economies, knowledge networking, and inter-firm cooperation in project-related networks). In Berlin – as in other metropoles of the cultural economy – culture and media firms specifically prefer "stimulating" inner-city locations in which working environments merge with everyday life activities. Local agglomerations of the cultural economy can thus be interpreted as constituting a specific overlap between the geographies of production and consumption. The flourishing of the "creative industries" or cultural economy sector is based on place-specific sociocultural milieus which positively combine with the dynamics of cluster formation in the urban economic space.

Creativity thus depends on the dynamic interplay of economic, sociocultural, and spatial factors. The notion of "urbanization economies" in cultural production emphasizes the positive stimulation of artistic creativity by a specific sociospatial environment. The cultural economy's creative actors are embedded in locally concentrated communities of practice which additionally benefit from interaction with a diversity of milieus and actors who are present in the same urban area. This diversity also encompasses a number of urban subcultures that make the city a source of inspiration for cultural producers. A city's social and cultural diversity, therefore, represents a specific form of "cultural capital" which attracts further economic activities and actors. Cultural economy districts create a favorable environment for artistically creative work – they encourage the exchange of knowledge and offer opportunities for inter-personal and interorganizational cooperation in the production of cultural goods and services.

However, concerning the widespread assumption that the culture industries could take on a leading role in urban economic regeneration, it has been emphasized that the spatial distribution of cultural economy firms and creative actors within the urban system is highly selective, so that only a limited number of particular cities and metropoles can make use of the cultural economy sector as a focus of their development strategy. Even in these established culture industry centers, the cultural economy only represents a particular local "island of growth," which is situated among a wide range of other subsectors with varying development prospects. Hence the cultural economy's potential ability to make up for shrinking employment opportunities in various "old" industries is limited in quantitative terms, so that no city can count solely on culture industries' growth. Furthermore, contemporary culture industries offer predominantly "low-quality" workplaces, with precarious employment relations and reduced social benefits and safeguards. The growth of a freelancer workforce with low income, excessive work hours, and discontinuous job flow can also be interpreted as a "crisis symptom" and an articulation of the post-Fordist restructuring of urban labor markets in prominent metropoles of the urban system.

Berlin's experiences offer a significant point of comparison for other cities' experiences in relation to creativity and economic growth. In the European and German context, Berlin is characterized by a particularly strong growth in its creative industries and qualifies as a major center of the cultural economy. Yet, with regard to Florida's claims about the positive relation between creativity and economic growth, Berlin represents a "critical" case – it is an example of a thriving cultural economy sector not only coexisting with, but also being enabled by and constituted through a weak economy. The local concentration and growth of an artistically creative workforce in Berlin has not triggered a process of economic regeneration at the aggregated level of the urban region's economy.

The cultural economy and its creative workforce also play a specific role in the restructuring of urban spaces. In inner-city districts in particular, the concentration of cultural economy actors and artistically creative people is contributing to a process by which inner-city localities are revalued and gradually gentrified. The artists and creative workers are explorers that bring new life to formerly neglected areas. Hence the artistically creative people are functioning as a specific group among the "pioneers" of gentrification. Real estate developers and investors take their chance to invest in the upgrading of the respective urban districts' housing stock and built environment. Moreover, the local agglomeration of cultural economy firms and creative scenes in previously "degraded" inner-city areas can also be utilized by real estate developers for large-scale projects aimed at the conversion of old industrial sites into prime real estate, as the example of the Media Spree development project in the Berlin district of Kreuzberg-Friedrichshain demonstrates. Such developments can be interpreted as a specific manifestation of the proliferation of gentrification as a *global* urban strategy that includes a broad range of large-scale "upgrading" projects in the built environment of cities beyond the well-known processes of residential gentrification.

6

Synthesis: The Creative
Capital of Cities

The preceding chapters aimed at establishing an alternative perspective to
the uncritical notions that currently dominate the debate on creativity and
cities. The alternative approach to the analysis of the role played by creative
workers in urban development focused on the relational dimension of urban
regions' innovation networks as well as on the urbanization economies of the
cultural economy sector. This chapter presents a short "synthesis" of our
main findings and an outline of some agendas for future research.

Urban theory is currently in the throes of a heated debate concerning
"creative industries" and the "creative class," which are said to form the
basis for the "creative city." This debate, however, has spawned a highly
questionable usage of the notion of creativity while encouraging the rise of
uncritical urban and social theory. The idea that cities – and in particular
the large metropoles of the urban system – function as major centers of creativity and innovation and thus play a decisive role in social and economic
development has long been a basic insight of urban theory. The recent surge
in scholarship on creativity and cities might be interpreted as the rise of a
new urban growth ideology that serves as a tool for interurban competition.
In particular the notion of the "creative class" as the most important human
resource of successful cities can be understood as a new place-marketing
slogan that is based on the glorification of specific functional elites in a
neoliberal social order.

The debate on creative industries and creative cities is focused on a specific
selection of creative subsectors. However, the definition of these subsectors
is contested. Most existing scholarship restricts the term "creative industries"
to the arts, media, and cultural industries. Research and development
activities, however, are also by nature creative, and are highly relevant in

*The Creative Capital of Cities: Interactive Knowledge Creation and the Urbanization Economies
of Innovation*, First Edition. Stefan Krätke.
© 2011 Stefan Krätke. Published 2011 by Blackwell Publishing Ltd.

numerous industries, particularly in the knowledge-intensive subsectors of the economy. In contradistinction to a narrow definition of creative industries limited to sectors that involve "artistic" creativity (i.e., the cultural economy in its traditional delimitation), we propose a wider delimitation that includes creative activities in the sphere of scientific and technological research. Both the cultural economy sector and industrial R&D activities represent components of the creative capital of cities and regions.

At the level of the city, the term "creative capital" denotes the ability of urban economic actors to generate scientific, technological, and artistic innovation on the basis of relational assets which are socially produced within a city or urban region. This understanding differs from the notion of creativity as a quality uniquely possessed by the individual, and concentrates on the socioeconomic context in which creative activities are embedded. The formation of interorganizational knowledge networks in a regional economy and the emergence of a locally bound creative milieu of cultural producers in the urban economic space are the expression of an urban and regional socioeconomic dynamism that enables creativity to flourish. While individual creativity is important, specific creative capabilities are inherently embedded in economic and social networks. The creative capital of cities or regions has to be understood as an expression of the aggregated collective capability of economic and social actors to generate new ideas, designs, and solutions. The "creative capital of cities" thus denotes a capacity to create value from interactive knowledge generation in urban economic settings which are at the same time characterized by the geographic clustering of specific subsectors and by the presence of a diversity of manufacturing activities and knowledge resources.

The preceding chapters dealt with the role of creativity at different levels of analysis. Figure 6.1 presents an outline of the different analytical layers of our investigation and its main lines of argumentation. The analysis focused on economically acknowledged creative work that is geared toward the creation of innovations. In contemporary times, this kind of creative work has become the task of a specialized and skilled workforce of scientists, engineers, designers and artists, and so forth. Creativity and innovation are closely interrelated or "symbiotic," since creative capabilities are a prime source of innovative capacity. Hence creativity functions as an essential "input" in the process of innovation. It denotes the capability of individuals and of interacting groups of workers (both at the intra-firm level and the level of interorganizational cooperation) to create new knowledge that entails the variation of existing forms or the creation of novel forms which are applied to generate new technologies, products, and organizational forms. The creation of new knowledge essentially requires a recombination or novel combination of complementary "pieces of knowledge" in terms of either specific competencies residing within a particular field of activity or

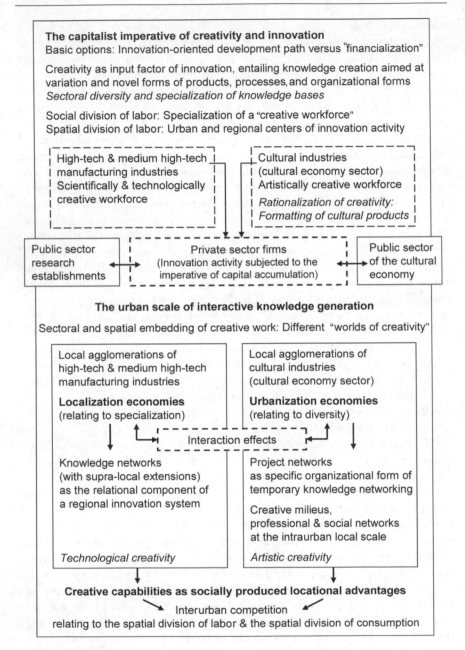

Figure 6.1 The creative capital of cities – analytical layers of investigation.

different knowledge bases of particular economic sectors, scientific disciplines etc. Hence interactive knowledge generation through the collaboration of creative workers is of key importance in the innovation process. Interactive knowledge creation, on the other hand, entails a shared learning process that strengthens or expands the involved actors' creative capabilities. The unfolding of creative capabilities is based both on specifically skilled human resources and on social resources in terms of the organized interaction amongst creative workers.

The critical discussion of the contemporary hype around the notion of "creativity" does not lead the author to an outright rejection of the term "creative." Long before the recent spread of shallow and uncritical contributions to "creativity and cities" and the emergence of a related new urban growth ideology, many outstanding scholars of urban theory (such as Jane Jacobs) have referred to the terms of creativity and innovative capability as essential features in urban economic development. The critique of the idea of a "creative class" as an all-encompassing construct (as presented in Chapter 2) does not imply that we should avoid analyzing the economic impact of particular "creative" occupational groups in urban economic development. Since the concept of social "classes" and the concept of "occupational groups" represent quite different levels of theory and analysis, there is no contradiction between rejecting the idea of an all-encompassing "creative class" and using specifically delimited "creative occupational groups" for the purpose of an analysis that shows to what extent these specific groups of the workforce have a positive impact on urban economic development.

Our deconstruction of the new "creative city" growth ideology started from a critique of Florida's "creative class" theory, highlighting its affirmation of neoliberal economic and social trends and poor recognition of relevant economic development factors at the urban level. The critique emphasized the need to disaggregate Florida's questionable grouping of occupations because of its categorical imprecision within the framework of contemporary capitalist development. We presented a macro-level analysis of the impact of creative occupational groups on regional economic success and stressed that an analysis of the positive impact exerted by the creative workforce on regional economic success can also be conducted without resorting to the questionable "creative class" category. However, in the framework of a knowledge-based and innovation-oriented development path, regional economic success does not rest solely on the mere concentration of workers in technologically or artistically creative occupations. Rather, it depends on the development of a highly networked regional innovation system that integrates these occupations as well as other groups of skilled workers.

This book has dealt with the unfolding of creativity and innovation activity in urban regions, yet the included sectors represent different "worlds of creativity." These different worlds may exist side by side within a particular city or metropolis. The analysis highlights the different functioning and socioeconomic context of creative work in innovation-oriented industrial sectors and in the cultural economy. In both sectors, agglomeration economies and the formation of interorganizational networks are relevant common aspects of the unfolding of creative capabilities. Yet this point does not justify a general theory of creativity. An advanced understanding of the relationship between "creativity and cities" would rather be based on knowledge of the diversity and differences of urban "worlds of creativity." Since creativity represents quite an "open" term with regard to its functioning and impacts, it is important to relate this term to specific spatial and sectoral contexts (as suggested by the distinction between technological and artistic creativity). Moreover, it should be emphasized that creative work and innovation activities are embedded in the economy of historically specific social formations.

Our analysis started from the observation that the contemporary debate on creativity is characterized by a tendency to decontextualize the issues of creativity and innovation from their embeddedness in a capitalist society and the imperatives of capital accumulation. This decontextualization has fostered the emergence of new growth ideologies that entail a glorification of capitalism as a socioeconomic formation essentially based on knowledge creation and superior innovative capacities. In the framework of a capitalist economy, the unfolding of creativity and innovation activity takes place "under the command of capital." Technological and artistic innovation is dominated by the private sector's profit-making institutions, even though national or regional innovation systems involve cooperative links between private sector firms and public sector establishments. Private sector dominance leads to the privileging of those fields and modes of innovation activity that promise entrepreneurial and commercial success. Creativity and innovation are thus embedded in the basic imperatives of capitalist economies which subordinate creative work and innovation activity to the continued race for competitive advantage and the appropriation of surplus profits.

With regard to the current phase of capitalist development, we emphasized the rise of a finance-dominated regime of accumulation. In this model of capitalist development, the imperative to enhance capital accumulation through technological and organizational innovation in the sphere of manufacturing processes is increasingly subject to *competing strategic choices*. Investment in real sector innovation and technological change is no longer functioning as the major pathway to increased capital accumulation, since financial sector deals and speculative financial investment activities can take on the role of an equally relevant or even superior strategy. While technological innovation and the related processes of knowledge creation remain significant sources of competitive advantage and surplus profits, the capitalist economy can privilege different pathways and investment options that comply with the imperatives of capital accumulation. On the level of cities and regions, too, there are different pathways to "economic success." Besides an innovation-oriented path that focuses on the development of innovative capabilities, the space economy of capitalism offers – at least for a number of major urban regions – the option of relying on economic command and control relations for attaining superior competitiveness in the urban system. The unfolding of creativity and innovation activity thus represents a *particular* strategic option in the framework of increasing interurban competition.

Since a general outline of the role of creativity and innovation in capitalist development doesn't grasp the specific mechanisms that are at work in the formation of urban centers of creative and innovative activity, we needed to proceed toward a more detailed account of creativity and innovation – one that employs relevant concepts of economic geography such as the concepts of agglomeration economies and knowledge networks – in order to investigate the unfolding of creative work and innovative capabilities in their *specific* sectoral and spatial contexts. At the urban scale (see Figure 6.1), a variety of different "worlds of creativity" have emerged, which may coexist in the same local space. The different "worlds of creativity" and local innovation systems are related to specific subsectors of economic activity. Chapter 3 started from the phenomenon of local agglomerations of high-tech and medium high-tech manufacturing industries, in which innovative capacities rely on the unfolding of technological creativity in regional knowledge networks, whereas Chapter 5 concentrated on local agglomerations of the culture industry (or the cultural economy), whose innovative capacities are based on the unfolding of artistic creativity in specific forms of collaborative organization and "milieus" of interaction at the intra-urban local scale.

In order to interpret the geographic clustering of creative occupations and to advance the understanding of the "creative capital of cities," we employed two basic theoretical concepts of economic geography: (1) "localization economies," i.e., economic externalities derived from specialization, and (2) "urbanization economies," i.e., economic externalities stemming from diversity. Technological creativity and the innovative capacity of research-intensive manufacturing sectors are strongly based on knowledge networking and spillovers between the knowledge bases of networked firms and research establishments (see Figure 6.1). Yet in metropolitan regions these firms also take advantage of a diversified economic structure that enables them to combine knowledge resources from other industries. In the realm of technological innovation, creativity appears to be a socially produced locational advantage that rests on the knowledge networks maintained by regional actors in particular sectors. These knowledge networks constitute "creative capital" as a specific source of innovative capacity.

With regard to the unfolding of artistic creativity, we demonstrated that the metropolitan regions' cultural economy clusters make use in similar ways of externalities that stem from both specialization and diversity. However, due to its specific properties, artistically creative work seems to derive greater benefit from urbanization economies, that is, the stimulating effects of a pronounced variety of cultural economy actors and urban sociocultural diversity. In the culture and media industries in particular, where production is frequently carried out by temporary project networks and relies on a highly flexibilized, freelance workforce, knowledge and innovative ideas are not only exchanged between firms, but also to large extent outside the sphere of inter-firm interaction, in the sphere of locally concentrated professional milieus and social networks (see Figure 6.1). Furthermore, large cities and metropoles are characterized by a co-location of diverse subsectors and clusters, so that the actors of an urban cluster may benefit from agglomeration economies arising from co-location with other local clusters. In conclusion, we might say that the creative capital of major cities and metropolitan regions is based on the interactive effects of localization and urbanization economies.

As regards the specific *urban dimension* of creative potential, we emphasized the formation of local agglomerations of cultural economy firms and artistically creative workers at the intra-metropolitan scale. The local clustering of artistically creative workers in particular inner-city districts of a large city or metropolis, and the related emergence of a locally bound creative milieu of cultural producers, underscore the point that creativity to a large extent represents a socially produced asset. The local creative milieu – in which the cultural economy's creative actors interact – is a key asset of the creative capital of cities, as it provides networking opportunities amongst firms, whether in work or non-work settings. Culture industry firms and the artistically creative workforce specifically prefer "trendy" inner-city districts that are home to diverse subcultural scenes, because they provide *stimulating environments* for the unfolding of artistic creativity. A flourishing culture industry requires urban settings that provide openness and diversity in terms of opportunities for social exchange and cross-fertilization between various actors and branches of activity. The notion of "urbanization economies" of cultural production emphasizes the positive stimulation of artistic creativity by a specific sociospatial environment.

This book aimed at a contribution to critical urban theory in terms of analyzing the role of creativity and innovation in the urban world of a *capitalist society*. According to this perspective, the implications of "creative industries" for urban labor markets, social polarization, and urban regeneration have to be considered. With particular reference to the role of the culture industry in urban development, three points have been emphasized. Firstly, the contemporary culture industry takes a leading role in conforming with neoliberal conceptions of labor markets. With a view to the flexibilization of labor and the expanding ranks of self-employed freelancers, the culture industry can be regarded as a forerunner of neoliberalization. By spreading precarious employment relations and intermittent project work, the cultural economy sector represents the vanguard of the trend toward deregulated and flexibilized forms of employment. Today, the majority of artistically creative workers can be characterized as the "middle-class working poor" of the skilled service sector. The creative workforce of the cultural economy represents a highly flexibilized pool of low-wage workers, whose growth in selected cities might be additionally amplified by a shortage of other employment opportunities. In this regard, our analysis challenges the premise that the cultural economy could play a key role in shaping a successful urban economic development path.

Secondly, only a limited number of particular cities and metropoles offer the conditions suitable for privileging the cultural economy sector as a main focus of the city's development strategy. Due to the specific sociocultural base of the cultural economy, the concentration of firms and creative actors within the urban system is highly selective. Long-established urban clusters of the cultural economy (that are for the most part concentrated in prominent metropolises) cannot be voluntarily "copied" by other cities trying to jump on the "creative cities" bandwagon. Moreover, even in the established prominent urban centers of the cultural economy, the sector's potential ability to make up for shrinking employment opportunities in traditional manufacturing industries and low-skilled services is limited in quantitative terms. Our analysis of the cultural economy in the Berlin metropolis might be taken here as an exemplary case. This city's experiences offer a significant comparator for other city experiences in relation to creativity and economic growth. In the European and German context, Berlin represents a prominent center of the cultural economy and is characterized by particularly strong growth in its creative industries. Yet with regard to Florida's claims about the positive relation between creativity and economic growth, Berlin is a "critical" case – it may be one of the best examples of a thriving cultural economy sector not only coexisting with, but also being enabled by and constituted through a weak economy. The local concentration and growth of an artistically creative workforce has not triggered a process of economic regeneration at the aggregated level of the urban region's economy. An urban economic development strategy which predominantly relies on the cultural economy sector in order to fix the urban region's labor market problems does not appear to be a promising choice. Nonetheless, many European cities confronted with industrial decline and related labor market problems have drawn on "cultural strategies" for economic regeneration, including support for the cultural economy sector as well as the extension of cultural facilities. Indeed, this approach has been utilized for the reconstruction of a "positive" urban image that might enhance a city's competitiveness. Yet these strategies have not led to a sufficient recovery of employment opportunities at the aggregate level of the urban economy.

Thirdly, our analysis concentrated on the impact of "creative industries" on urban *spatial restructuring* processes. We emphasized that the cultural economy's development is closely related to increasing sociospatial inequality. This includes several aspects. Within the urban space, the less well-established cultural economy firms and the low-income strata of creative workers are constantly fraught with displacement. Thus the local clustering of cultural producers and artistically creative workers in inner-city areas represents a *precarious* form of reindustrialization within the metropolitan core (Hutton 2008). On the one hand, local displacement of "creative industry" firms can result from the sector's internal "upgrading" processes (in terms of new upscale firms edging out economically less potent firms). On the other hand, displacement occurs in the framework of residential gentrification and large-scale inner-city redevelopment projects. Particularly in the inner-city districts, a concentration of cultural economy actors and artistically creative people regularly contributes to gentrification processes, in which artistically creative people are functioning as "pioneers" that bring new life to formerly neglected areas. Capitalist real estate developers take up the chance offered by this "grassroots" revitalization and invest in the upgrading of the respective urban districts' housing stock and built environment. The original creative scene is subsequently dislocated in the gentrification process by the more affluent urban professionals who prefer to live in these new, trendy districts. In many cases, the local agglomeration of "creative industries" in formerly neglected inner-city areas has also been utilized by real estate developers for large-scale redevelopment projects aimed at the conversion of old industrial sites and mixed-use areas with older buildings and lower prices into prime real estate. In this way, the local growth of the cultural economy is exploited for real-estate-based capital accumulation in the framework of the extended forms of contemporary gentrification, which include a broad range of "upgrading" projects in the urban space beyond the well-known processes of residential gentrification.

On a more general level, the notion of the "creative capital of cities" should be linked to the unfolding of interurban competition in contemporary capitalism. Within a capitalist economy, whose major spatial anchoring points are cities and metropolitan regions, the socially produced "creative capital" of cities represents a specific force of accumulation in the framework of innovation-related economic development paths. Due to the socially interactive character of most innovation processes, the urban context is of particular significance for generating innovative capacities. At the same time, capitalist development has led to the formation of a strongly networked urban system that is characterized by a pronounced spatial division of labor and that extends beyond the level of national urban systems to form a global urban system. Within this urban system, the concentration of capital and economic control functions in a number of outstanding urban centers has increased the economic power and "competitiveness" of some cities, while many other urban regions are functioning in supra-regional and global production networks as "executive" manufacturing locations, or are even left outside the multi-local capitalist production system. Accumulation of capital in particular places does not rely solely on innovation activity and technological change. It can as well proceed by means of the creation of "privileged" places that are able to benefit from the appropriation of value produced at diverse locations within the urban system. Against this background, we should consider cities and urban regions "as competitive economic and geopolitical units within a capitalist geography of seesawing uneven development" (Harvey 1989: 45). Harvey emphasized that "those urban regions that achieve a superior competitive position survive, at least in the short run, better than those that do not" (ibid.). At the intra-urban level, however, a "superior competitive position" might be achieved at the expense of particular groups of the urban population (i.e., the losers of urban economic and sociospatial restructuring). At the level of urban systems, interurban competition entails a (changing) mix of winners and losers.

It is essential to underline the point that there are different paths to attaining competitiveness and "successful" urban economic development. An innovation-oriented development path that focuses on the enhancement of a city's creative capital represents just one specific path. This path might lead to an urban economy that rests on superior innovation capabilities in the realm of real economy sectors. A different path would, for example, bet on the enhancement of financial sector activities and corporate control over geographically extended value chains, supplemented by the extension of specialized corporate services. Furthermore, many cities strive to improve their competitive position with regard to attracting capital, affluent citizens, and "high rank" professionals by investment in the environmental or cultural "qualities of place," or by of fostering sociospatial restructuring through gentrification and ambitious redevelopment projects. Other cities improve their competitive position by consolidating a given manufacturing base through cluster promotion policies in both "new industries" and traditional sectors. Different approaches might as well be selectively combined.

In general, interurban competition increases the pressures toward product innovation and technological change. Some cities are able to develop or consolidate particularly strong functions of an innovation center that positively contribute to their economic development. Nevertheless, the competitiveness of urban regions may stem from quite different sources (including different functional and sectoral structures as well as different development paths). The "creative city" growth ideology ignores the fact that urban economic development is embedded in a capitalist economy that offers a variety of approaches to improving competitive positioning. Creativity and innovation activity represent a particular strategic asset in the framework of increasing interurban competition. In the present phase of capitalist development, this interurban competition takes on three main forms: competition for command and control functions, competition within the spatial division of labor, and competition within the spatial division of consumption (see Harvey 1989).

From this perspective, creative work that leads to technological innovation is functional to interurban competition within the spatial division of labor. In global production networks and value chains, the particular urban nodes of advanced R&D capacities and functions can attain a considerably high proportion of value-added. Creative work that results in artistic innovation, on the other hand, strengthens an urban region's positioning as a center of the cultural economy sector and contributes to the expansion of employment opportunities, particularly in flexibilized freelancer positions. It might additionally be regarded as a functional ingredient of urban competitiveness within the spatial division of consumption, since a flourishing cultural economy positively contributes to a city's attractiveness and appeal to consumers in the realms of culture, fashion, and lifestyle. Cities that develop strong technological innovation capacities might attain a comparatively privileged position within the spatial division of labor, and cities that qualify as centers of cultural production activity and artistic innovation might additionally improve their competitive position by attracting cultural tourists and new inhabitants, including affluent "high rank" professionals of diverse sectors of activity. There might be a contrast as well as a productive interplay between cities as workshops for advanced industrial production and technological innovation and cities as centers for cultural innovation and conspicuous consumption. However, the downsides of growth in the cultural economy with regard to employment structures and sociospatial restructuring processes (as outlined above) need to be considered.

As a socially produced regional advantage, creativity and innovative capacity contribute to uneven development in the urban and regional system. Interurban competition in its diverse forms will remain fundamental to uneven development in the urban system of capitalism, which includes "shifts in fortune" of individual cities and a continued structuration of spaces of advantage and disadvantage at all spatial scales. The "creative capital of cities" represents a particular form of regional advantage that is relevant for the capitalist economy in the realm of technological change, interurban competition, and the restructuring of urban spaces.

However, in recent times, the capitalist economy has increasingly developed its destructive forces – based on the interplay of deregulation, financialization, and the rise of the "dealer class" – at the expense of the development of society's productive forces and investments in the infrastructures of knowledge generation. A "knowledge-based" economic development path focusing on scientific, technological, and artistic innovation activity would only be a potential solution if "Main Street" instead of "Wall Street" could regain a leading role in capitalist economies – a prerequisite of which would be appropriate measures for disarming the "dealer class." Beyond the sphere of "real sector" innovation activity, human creativity is most urgently needed for inventing broader social innovations that could transform neo-liberalized capitalist societies in order to create a more responsible, equitable, and sustainable framework for economic development.

This book aimed to present a multi-layered and critical perspective on the role of creativity and innovation in urban development. Yet this complex subject should be further investigated with regard to the economic, sociospatial, and political dimensions of the creative capital of cities and their impact on uneven development in the urban and regional system. Relevant agendas for future research include topics that are situated at different levels of analysis. At the most general level, research on the impact of the current world economic crisis on real sector innovation activity in capitalist economies would advance a more realistic view of the prospects of a knowledge-intensive and innovation-driven economic development path in contemporary capitalism. The work on this topic should be supplemented by research on the distribution of investment flows between "secondary" financial circuits of a dealer economy and investment in real sector innovation activity. This kind of analysis might oppose the proliferation of unrealistic or affirmative generalizing conceptualizations of the current phase of capitalist development (such as the notion of an economy that is essentially based on creativity and knowledge).

Moreover, in the realm of political economy research it would be relevant to perform analyses of the "Florida syndrome" in terms of its spread in different countries in the arena of neoliberal urban policy agendas (following the line of research initially presented by Peck 2005 and 2009). This should be complemented by comparative urban studies on the impact of creative industries and urban cultural regeneration strategies on regional "economic success." Comparative urban studies at the national and international scale can detect different pathways of urban regions in contemporary capitalism and inform us about which cities are concentrating (to which extent) on creative and knowledge-intensive real sector innovation activities. As most previous analyses of the cultural economy of cities have concentrated on case studies of large cities and prominent metropolises of the urban system, particular research efforts should be directed at comparative urban studies on the role of the cultural economy in small and medium-sized cities, and the outcome of "creative city" regeneration strategies in these kinds of places. As research on creativity and cities has for the most part concentrated on the experience of cities in the traditional core countries of capitalism, future research should also be directed at the role of creative industries (and their specific sectoral composition) in cities of the "global South," particularly in the "emerging" economies of the BRIC states (Brazil, Russia, India and China).

A third line of future research could be directed at comparative research on the relationship between the local concentration and growth of "creative industries" and urban social and sociospatial inequality. This line of research is of particular relevance in the realm of "critical urban theory." While there is much evidence that prominent large urban centers of the "creative industries" display a particularly pronounced inequality in their social and sociospatial structure, the specific causal relationships among these pheno-mena have to be further investigated. Indeed, there exist articulations of urban social and spatial inequality that cannot be attributed to the growth of creative industries or a particular kind of creative workforce. With regard to the "direct" impacts of creative sectors on urban social and sociospatial inequality, further research on the flexibilization of creative workers in a freelance economy and its impact on specific life–work combinations could advance our understanding of contemporary restructuring processes of labor relations and their articulation in urban space. Research on the sociospatial restructuring of contemporary cities, which has been focused on the proli-feration of (classical and new, extended forms of) gentrification processes, could be advanced and detailed by case studies on the displacement of firms and creative workers within the cultural economy districts as a result either of internal "upgrading" or gentrification pressures stemming from real-estate-based strategies of capital accumulation in urban space. Furthermore, the voluntary or compulsory movement and relocation of "creative scenes" in urban space and their impact on sociospatial restructuring seems to offer a relevant focus of detailed research.

Another research topic, which is of interest specifically in the field of economic geography and regional economic research, would be studies of the relationship between urban clusters, knowledge networks, and "creative performance." While this kind of research has been advanced with regard to technological creativity, it seems particularly complicated to analyze the relationship with regard to the outcome of creative work in the diverse subsectors of the cultural economy. Future research can draw on Scott's notion of the "creative field" and his comparative analysis of creative performance in different urban regions.

Despite the criticism of contemporary "creative city" strategies' insertion in neoliberal urban policy agendas (see above), it seems relevant to analyze which urban policies might be appropriate for harnessing a city's creative potential. The creative capital of cities will remain an important develop-ment resource of urban regions, regardless of which general direction a city's political strategy takes. Beyond the familiar prescriptions of neoliberalized urban politics, the discussion of appropriate strategies for supporting the creative capital of cities could be directed at (a) the sphere of technological innovation, by assessing policies that support the improvement of the urban innovation system; and (b) the sphere of artistic innovation, by assessing policies for strengthening a city's cultural economy. Here, policies for fostering the development of the cultural economy's creative periphery of non-profits, and policies directed at preserving urban spaces for the unfolding of non-profit creative scenes and activities are of particular relevance. Such policies could offer an alternative approach to oppose the transformation of spaces inhabited by artistically creative workers by real-estate-based "upgrading" strategies.

Beyond the agenda for future research outlined above, more emphasis should also be put on approaches that depart from the debate on market-led models of technological and artistic innovation in order to explore notions of community-based *social innovations* as an alternative vision of a city's creative capabilities. This might widen the perspective and lead to a broader conception of "social creativity," one which calls for sustained endeavor to enhance economic prospects and quality of urban life *in an inclusive way* for all of the city's inhabitants.

Appendix: Grouping of Occupations and Subsectors

Delimitation of the sectoral aggregate of "knowledge-intensive industrial activities" (code numbers of subsectors based on the sectoral classification WZ 2003 by the German Federal Office of Statistics 2003):

(a) High-technology industries: 30 Manufacturing of electronic data processing machines, office machines; 321–323 Electronics, communications engineering; 331–335 Medical engineering, measurement technology
(b) Medium high-technology industries: 242–247 Production of chemical products; 291–293, 294–295, 296–297 Mechanical engineering; 311–315, 316 Electrical engineering, electric equipments; 34–35 Construction of vehicles
(c) Knowledge-intensive technology-related services: 64 Communications services; 72 Data processing and databases; 73 Research and development; 74204–74206, 74208, 743 Technical engineering offices

Grouping of Occupations

(Code numbers of professions based on the classification of occupations by the Federal Office of Statistics 1992)

1 Manufacturing occupations

10–11 Stone processors, building material manufacturers; 12–13 Ceramics and glass manufacturers; 14–15 Chemistry workers, plastic goods manufacturers;

The Creative Capital of Cities: Interactive Knowledge Creation and the Urbanization Economies of Innovation, First Edition. Stefan Krätke.
© 2011 Stefan Krätke. Published 2011 by Blackwell Publishing Ltd.

16–17 Paper manufacturers, printers; 18, 50 Wood manufacturers, carpenters, joiners; 19–24 Metal producers, molders, metal processors; 25–27, 29, 32 Smiths, plumbers, locksmiths, toolmakers, and associated professions; 313 Electric motor manufacturers; 32 Assemblers and other metal professions; 33–36 Spinning occupations, textile manufacturers; 37 Leather manufacturers; 39, 40 Pastries manufacturers, meat and fish manufacturers; 42, 43 Manufacturers of drinks, other food occupations; 44–47 Bricklayers, carpenters, civil engineering workers; 48–49 Interior decorators, upholsterers; 51 Painters, varnishers, and related professions; 53 Laborers without activity specification; 28, 311.2 Mechanics, electricians; 314–315, 54 Electric equipments manufacturers, machinists, and related professions

2 Scientifically and technologically creative occupations

032, 60–65, 774–779, 881 Engineers, chemists, scientists, technicians, data processing experts, economic and social scientists

3 Artistically creative occupations

82, 83 Journalists, artists, and related professions

4 Skilled professionals of the education and health service sector

84, 87, 88 Teachers, doctors, chemists, other health service occupations

5 Skilled professionals of the finance and real estate business

69, 704, 705, 771 Finance and insurance business experts, real estate business experts, real estate agents, and property managers

6 The "political class" and state organization management

76, 81 Members of legislative bodies, political functionaries, managers of public administration, managers of associations, legal consultants

7 Firm management and economic consulting

750–757 Entrepreneurs, firm managers, management consultants, accountants

8 The service class

66–68, 701–703, 706, 71–74, 772, 773, 78–80, 85, 86, 90–93, 97–99 Office clerks, telephonists, data typists, sales clerks, transport occupations, postal distributors, warehouse managers, house servants and cleaning occupations, security service occupations

Grouping of Economic Subsectors

(Numbering of subsectors based on the sectoral classification WZ 2003 by the Federal Office of Statistics 2003)

1 High-technology industries

30 Manufacturing of electronic data processing machines, office machines; 321–323 Electronics, communications engineering; 331–335 Medical engineering, measurement technology

2 Medium high-technology industries

242–247 Production of chemical products; 291–293, 294–295, 296–297 Mechanical engineering; 311–315, 316 Electrical engineering, electric equipments; 34–35 Construction of vehicles

3 Low-technology and medium low-technology industries

15 Food processing; 16 Tobacco processing; 17 Textile industry; 18 Clothing industry; 19 Leather industry; 20 Wood processing (without furniture industry); 21 Paper industry; 22 Publishing and printing, duplication of recorded data carriers; 23 Coking plants, mineral oil processing; 25 Manufacturing of plastic products; 26 Manufacturing of glass, ceramics, processing of stones; 27 Manufacturing of metal; 28 Manufacturing of metal products; 36 Manufacturing of furniture, jewelry, musical instruments, sports equipment, and toys; 37 Recycling

4 Knowledge-intensive technology-related services

64 Communications services; 72 Data processing and databases; 73 Research and development; 74204–74206, 74208, 743 Technical engineering offices

5 Knowledge-intensive market-related business services

7411–7412 Legal and tax consultancy; 7413–7415 Management consultancy; 744 Advertising; 74201–74203, Architectural offices; 74207, 74209, 745–748 Other business services; 61, 62, 6322–6323 Navigation, air traffic

6 Financial sector

65, 66, 671–672 Credit and insurance business

7 Real estate sector

70, 71 Real estate trade and management, renting

8 Knowledge-intensive education- and health-services

801–802, 8042, 803 Education; 851–852, 853 Health services, welfare services

9 Media and cultural economy

221–222 Publishing trade; 921–925 Culture and entertainment

10 Public administration

751–753, 990, 911–913 Public administration

11 Other services

50, 51, 52 Wholesale and retail trade, repair of motor vehicles; 55, 60, 631 Gastronomy, land transport; 634, 900, 8041, 926–927, 93, 95 Storekeeping, other public and personal services

Table A.1 Different "occupational profiles" of German regions with a comparatively high share of employees in creative occupations, 2005.

Content of table columns:

OG234	Total share of occupational groups nos. 2–4: Creative occupational groups
OG2	Share of scientifically and technologically creative workforce
OG3	Share of artistically creative workforce (employed)
OG3+Art	Share of artistically creative workforce (employed and self-employed artists)
OG4	Share of skilled professionals of the education and health service sector
OG567	Total share of occupational groups nos. 5–7: Other "high ranking" professionals
OG5	Skilled professionals of the finance and real estate business
OG6	The "political class" and management of state organizations
OG7	Firm management and economic consulting

Shares of employees in selected occupational groups in total employment, 2005. Selection of the 50 highest ranks (of a total number of 439 districts) according to the share of the creative workforce:

Code no.	Name	OG234	OG2	OG3	OG3 +Art	OG4	OG567	OG5	OG6	OG7
9562	Erlangen	31.5	24.7	0.7	1.0	5.7	9.6	3.6	0.5	5.5
9184	Munich (district)	28.0	20.6	3.1	3.8	3.6	10.5	5.0	0.8	4.6
6411	Darmstadt	26.5	20.6	1.4	2.3	3.6	6.3	2.2	1.4	2.7
7314	Ludwigshafen Rhein	25.8	22.8	0.6	0.8	2.3	3.8	2.3	0.3	1.2
8221	Heidelberg	23.3	11.4	1.6	2.6	9.2	6.1	2.7	1.0	2.4
16053	Jena	23.1	13.7	1.5	1.9	7.5	9.2	1.9	4.4	2.8

(Continued)

Table A.1 *(cont'd)*

Code no.	Name	OG234	OG2	OG3	OG3 +Art	OG4	OG567	OG5	OG6	OG7
8111	Stuttgart	22.7	16.0	1.9	2.8	3.8	13.0	7.9	1.3	3.7
5316	Leverkusen	22.7	19.0	0.7	1.0	2.7	5.4	2.5	0.6	2.4
5313	Aachen	22.6	15.2	1.2	2.2	5.3	7.5	4.5	1.1	1.9
9162	Munich (city)	22.5	14.1	2.5	4.5	3.9	13.7	7.6	1.4	4.7
9188	Starnberg	21.4	14.3	0.8	3.4	3.6	6.9	2.9	0.5	3.4
14262	Dresden	21.1	13.4	1.4	2.4	5.3	7.8	2.8	2.6	2.4
8115	Böblingen	20.8	17.8	0.7	1.1	2.0	4.9	2.4	0.3	2.1
7315	Mainz	20.8	9.3	4.8	5.6	5.9	9.2	5.4	1.4	2.3
12054	Potsdam	20.1	8.8	3.8	4.8	6.4	8.6	3.9	2.5	2.1
16055	Weimar	19.8	9.0	3.4	5.2	5.6	6.8	1.8	3.0	2.1
6413	Offenbach am Main	19.5	14.3	0.9	1.9	3.4	9.8	6.6	0.6	2.5
8212	Karlsruhe	19.5	14.1	1.3	2.1	3.2	9.7	6.6	0.8	2.3
8421	Ulm	19.4	13.4	1.2	1.8	4.2	5.4	3.1	0.4	1.9
8311	Freiburg im Breisgau	19.3	9.1	1.6	3.7	6.5	7.5	3.7	1.6	2.2
8211	Baden-Baden	19.0	6.2	9.8	10.7	2.1	5.9	2.9	0.8	2.2
14365	Leipzig	18.5	8.8	2.5	3.5	6.2	8.1	4.2	1.5	2.4
8416	Tübingen	18.2	8.1	1.3	2.7	7.5	5.1	2.7	0.6	1.7
5314	Bonn	18.2	9.0	2.1	3.2	6.0	9.5	4.3	2.8	2.4
3101	Braunschweig	18.2	12.7	1.3	1.8	3.6	6.7	3.3	0.9	2.5
8435	Bodenseekreis	18.1	14.9	0.6	1.2	2.0	5.7	3.0	0.4	2.3
3103	Wolfsburg	18.1	15.9	0.7	0.8	1.4	6.5	1.4	1.0	4.1
11000	Berlin	18.0	8.6	2.0	5.2	4.3	7.5	3.1	1.7	2.7
5315	Cologne	17.6	9.5	2.6	4.8	3.3	12.0	7.1	1.2	3.7
9362	Regensburg	17.5	12.5	0.9	1.5	3.5	6.3	3.5	0.9	2.0

(Continued)

Table A.1 (cont'd)

Code no.	Name	OG234	OG2	OG3	OG3 +Art	OG4	OG567	OG5	OG6	OG7
13001	Greifswald	17.4	7.9	1.0	1.2	8.3	5.3	2.4	1.3	1.6
6436	Main-Taunus-Kreis	17.3	13.8	0.6	1.3	2.2	12.2	5.5	0.9	5.8
2000	Hamburg	17.2	10.5	2.2	4.2	2.5	10.1	5.6	1.2	3.3
6433	Groß-Gerau	17.1	14.5	0.5	0.9	1.7	5.9	2.5	0.3	3.1
6434	Hochtaunuskreis	17.1	12.1	0.9	1.9	3.1	13.4	5.4	0.8	7.1
8226	Rhein-Neckar-Kreis	17.1	13.7	0.7	1.4	1.9	5.6	2.3	0.4	3.0
6414	Wiesbaden	17.0	11.9	1.4	2.5	2.6	13.1	9.0	1.3	2.8
9572	Erlangen-Höchstadt	16.5	13.7	0.6	1.2	1.6	4.5	1.9	0.3	2.3
8222	Mannheim	16.4	11.5	1.2	1.7	3.3	8.2	4.7	0.8	2.7
8116	Esslingen	16.4	13.3	0.7	1.3	1.8	5.3	2.5	0.5	2.3
9190	Weilheim-Schongau	16.2	12.0	0.4	1.4	2.8	5.9	3.5	0.6	1.8
5515	Münster (Westf.)	16.1	9.7	1.4	2.4	4.1	11.2	6.8	2.1	2.3
8215	Karlsruhe	15.9	13.1	0.5	1.0	1.8	4.6	2.3	0.3	2.0
9564	Nuremberg	15.8	11.9	1.0	1.7	2.2	9.1	5.9	0.9	2.4
5913	Dortmund	15.8	10.4	1.0	1.8	3.7	8.0	5.0	0.7	2.3
13003	Rostock	15.8	7.6	1.3	1.7	6.5	6.3	2.9	1.2	2.3
5114	Krefeld	15.7	11.8	1.0	1.6	2.3	5.2	2.7	0.5	2.1
6412	Frankfurt am Main	15.6	10.6	1.5	2.4	2.6	17.3	11.7	1.6	4.0
14161	Chemnitz	15.6	9.6	1.0	1.4	4.6	7.6	2.7	2.0	2.9
3152	Göttingen	15.6	7.8	0.9	1.6	6.2	5.5	3.6	0.5	1.4
439 distr.	German average	13.5	8.8	1.0	1.8	2.9	6.5	3.4	0.8	2.3

Table A.2 Different "sectoral profiles" of German regions with a comparatively high share of employees in knowledge-intensive subsectors, 2005.

Content of table columns:

SEC1	Share of high-tech industries
SEC2	Share of medium high-tech industries
SEC4	Share of knowledge-intensive technology-related services
SEC124	Total share of research-intensive manufacturing and technology-related services
SEC9	Share of the culture and media economy
SEC5	Share of knowledge-intensive market-related business services
SEC67	Share of the finance and real estate sector
SEC8	Share of knowledge-intensive education- and health services
KISEC	Total share of knowledge-intensive subsectors

Shares of selected subsectors in total employment, 2005. Selection of the 75 highest ranks (of a total number of 439 districts) according to the share of knowledge-intensive subsectors:

Code no.	Name	SEC1	SEC2	SEC4	SEC124	SEC9	SEC5	SEC67	SEC8	KISEC
3103	Wolfsburg	0.3	63.3	3.7	67.4	1.3	4.1	1.5	5.9	80.2
9161	Ingolstadt	2.2	45.9	2.1	50.3	0.8	9.1	2.6	10.7	73.5
9279	Dingolfing-Landau	0.1	59.7	0.9	60.7	0.3	3.9	2.3	5.8	73.0
9562	Erlangen	3.6	29.7	4.7	37.9	0.4	8.5	3.0	20.1	69.8
3402	Emden	0.5	43.1	1.3	44.9	0.5	11.4	2.3	10.4	69.4
9662	Schweinfurt	2.3	41.2	1.4	44.9	0.2	9.3	3.6	11.5	69.4
6412	Frankfurt am Main	1.8	4.3	7.5	13.6	2.4	24.9	17.7	9.5	68.1

(Continued)

Table A.2 (*cont'd*)

Code no.	Name	SEC1	SEC2	SEC4	SEC124	SEC9	SEC5	SEC67	SEC8	KISEC
8221	Heidelberg	2.1	9.1	8.6	19.8	2.5	8.7	5.5	31.0	67.4
9463	Coburg	1.0	22.4	1.5	24.8	1.6	7.5	19.2	13.9	67.1
9362	Regensburg	5.4	23.3	3.0	31.7	1.2	10.8	4.4	16.8	64.9
16053	Jena	10.0	3.7	8.4	22.2	0.6	9.2	3.6	28.7	64.3
8111	Stuttgart	1.2	17.6	6.9	25.8	3.3	12.2	10.6	12.3	64.2
6413	Offenbach am Main	2.2	15.5	8.3	25.9	0.8	13.1	9.1	14.6	63.5
13001	Greifswald	3.7	3.3	8.1	15.1	1.1	11.8	3.6	31.7	63.3
8115	Böblingen	7.0	31.5	8.9	47.4	0.5	5.7	2.9	6.3	62.8
9162	Munich (city)	2.5	11.2	7.7	21.4	4.0	13.4	10.5	13.4	62.7
7320	Zweibrücken	0.4	26.7	3.9	31.0	0.5	11.2	2.0	17.8	62.4
8435	Bodenseekreis	5.8	28.3	3.8	38.0	0.6	5.3	3.6	14.0	61.5
6411	Darmstadt	2.0	12.9	11.9	26.8	2.5	11.9	3.9	15.9	61.1
3102	Salzgitter	1.2	36.6	1.9	39.6	0.1	9.5	1.5	9.8	60.6
16056	Eisenach	2.0	24.6	1.5	28.1	1.4	12.8	3.0	14.8	60.1
3101	Braunschweig	4.8	10.2	8.9	23.9	2.0	9.9	7.5	16.4	59.8
14167	Zwickau	0.5	21.6	3.9	26.0	1.1	11.4	3.4	16.7	58.6
8211	Baden-Baden	1.0	11.2	2.5	14.6	16.4	7.8	4.2	15.5	58.4
6434	Hochtaunuskreis	3.5	10.1	5.6	19.2	1.1	15.8	10.1	11.8	58.0
9761	Augsburg	3.5	12.0	3.7	19.2	3.3	11.7	5.6	18.1	58.0
5313	Aachen	2.4	4.5	9.4	16.2	1.2	11.1	5.1	24.3	57.9
14365	Leipzig	0.8	4.1	7.6	12.5	4.0	14.4	6.5	20.5	57.8
9461	Bamberg	2.1	23.4	4.2	29.8	1.6	8.5	3.4	14.5	57.8
8222	Mannheim	2.7	17.2	4.9	24.8	1.2	12.0	6.5	13.0	57.6
8311	Freiburg im Breisgau	5.3	4.2	4.5	14.1	2.4	9.4	5.0	26.7	57.5
6633	Kassel	2.6	30.3	2.6	35.5	0.2	6.3	2.1	13.6	57.5

(*Continued*)

Table A.2 (*cont'd*)

Code no.	Name	SEC1	SEC2	SEC4	SEC124	SEC9	SEC5	SEC67	SEC8	KISEC
5111	Düsseldorf	2.4	7.6	4.7	14.7	1.8	19.2	11.4	10.4	57.5
14263	Görlitz	1.1	13.0	2.7	16.8	2.0	11.5	3.6	23.5	57.4
12054	Potsdam	0.7	0.3	7.1	8.1	6.5	13.6	6.1	22.9	57.2
9184	Munich (district)	6.7	7.7	14.1	28.5	5.8	8.1	7.1	7.7	57.2
14262	Dresden	6.5	4.2	7.8	18.5	2.5	11.1	4.7	20.0	56.8
9188	Starnberg	6.3	11.4	9.1	26.8	1.7	7.1	3.8	17.1	56.6
9564	Nuremberg	3.3	10.8	5.9	19.9	1.9	16.6	7.6	10.2	56.3
6433	Groß-Gerau	0.6	23.5	7.6	31.7	0.3	13.3	3.2	7.6	56.1
8416	Tübingen	2.2	10.1	3.6	15.9	1.1	4.1	3.5	31.6	56.0
5515	Münster (Westf.)	0.9	4.9	8.7	14.5	2.7	11.4	9.1	18.4	56.0
10045	Saarpfalz-Kreis	0.7	24.8	4.5	30.0	0.2	5.3	2.8	17.7	56.0
2000	Hamburg	1.9	6.5	5.9	14.3	3.6	17.2	8.3	12.5	55.8
1002	Kiel	1.5	7.9	5.4	14.9	1.8	9.8	8.7	20.6	55.7
3152	Göttingen	7.4	3.2	5.2	15.9	1.2	6.2	4.6	27.5	55.4
5315	Cologne	0.9	6.9	5.2	13.0	4.3	14.2	10.6	13.2	55.3
15202	Halle/Saale	0.6	1.3	5.4	7.3	3.0	13.4	4.4	27.1	55.2
8135	Heidenheim	0.6	30.7	2.1	33.4	0.6	6.6	3.4	11.0	55.0
8421	Ulm	5.6	9.0	5.1	19.7	1.3	12.2	3.9	17.7	54.8
9663	Würzburg	0.6	7.0	5.0	12.5	2.1	8.9	5.2	25.9	54.7
9190	Weilheim-Schongau	4.6	23.9	1.7	30.1	0.5	4.2	4.4	15.4	54.7
12053	Frankfurt/Oder	1.1	0.6	4.7	6.4	2.2	12.7	3.6	29.9	54.6
9178	Freising	3.3	8.0	5.3	16.7	0.4	26.4	2.3	8.7	54.5
9572	Erlangen-Höchstadt	1.2	32.5	2.9	36.6	0.1	4.4	2.4	10.9	54.5
8216	Rastatt	3.2	32.0	1.6	36.9	1.0	5.2	2.5	8.8	54.3
7334	Germersheim	1.7	33.1	3.2	38.0	0.1	4.1	2.2	9.8	54.2
5314	Bonn	0.3	2.1	9.5	12.0	3.2	11.8	6.3	20.4	53.6
11000	Berlin	1.7	4.7	5.9	12.3	3.0	13.0	6.1	19.1	53.5

(*Continued*)

Table A.2 (cont'd)

Code no.	Name	SEC1	SEC2	SEC4	SEC124	SEC9	SEC5	SEC67	SEC8	KISEC
8426	Biberach	3.2	28.8	2.2	34.2	0.3	3.3	3.3	12.3	53.4
16055	Weimar	0.5	3.9	5.5	9.9	5.0	10.8	3.2	24.2	53.3
7315	Mainz	1.0	1.0	6.5	8.6	8.5	8.5	7.9	19.6	53.2
8212	Karlsruhe	4.9	3.8	9.1	17.8	2.0	9.6	8.5	15.3	53.2
6414	Wiesbaden	1.3	5.1	4.9	11.3	1.9	12.5	14.5	12.9	53.0
13006	Wismar	1.0	11.2	3.4	15.6	0.3	8.4	4.8	24.0	53.0
13005	Stralsund	0.4	5.8	2.8	9.1	1.8	11.8	4.8	25.5	52.9
4011	Bremen	2.4	12.1	4.6	19.2	1.7	11.8	4.7	15.6	52.9
5913	Dortmund	2.8	4.2	7.1	14.1	1.3	11.5	8.0	17.9	52.7
3241	Hanover	1.8	8.5	5.3	15.6	1.7	12.6	6.5	16.3	52.7
5113	Essen	1.6	3.3	7.5	12.4	1.8	14.6	5.5	18.3	52.6
3403	Oldenburg	1.0	2.4	6.7	10.1	1.4	13.2	6.5	21.1	52.4
9261	Landshut	5.6	5.8	3.0	14.4	1.3	12.0	5.2	19.5	52.4
13003	Rostock	0.9	3.9	4.3	9.2	2.1	14.1	5.2	21.7	52.3
6611	Kassel	0.8	10.0	3.2	14.0	3.2	11.5	5.6	17.7	52.0
439 distr.	German average	2.3	9.7	4.2	16.2	1.4	9.2	4.9	15.5	47.2

References

Acs, Z., de Groot, H., and Nijkamp, P. (eds.) (2002) *The Emergence of the Knowledge Economy*. Berlin: Springer.

Adorno, T. (1991) *The Culture Industry: Selected Essays on Mass Culture*. London: Routledge.

Aglietta, M. (1979) *A Theory of Capitalist Regulation*. London: New Left Books.

Aglietta, M. (2000) *Ein neues Akkumulationsregime: Die Regulationstheorie auf dem Prüfstand*. Hamburg: VSA.

Amin, A. (ed.) (1994) *Post-Fordism: A Reader*. Oxford: Blackwell.

Amin, A. and Cohendet, P. (2004) *Architectures of Knowledge: Firms, Capabilities and Communities*. Oxford: Oxford University Press.

Amin, A. and Thrift, N. (eds.) (1994) *Globalization, Institutions and Regional Development in Europe*. Oxford: Oxford University Press.

Amin, A. and Thrift, N. (eds.) (2003) *The Blackwell Cultural Economy Reader*. Oxford: Blackwell.

Anderson, C. (1974) *The Political Economy of Social Classes*. New York: Prentice Hall.

Anderson, G. (2008) *Cityboy: Beer and Loathing in the Square Mile*. London: Headline.

Arauzo-Carod, J.-M. and Viladecans-Marsal, E. (2009) Industrial location at the intra-metropolitan level: The role of agglomeration economies. *Regional Studies*, 43 (4), 545–558.

Asheim, B. and Coenen, L. (2005) Knowledge bases and regional innovation systems: Comparing Nordic Clusters. *Research Policy*, 34, 1173–1190.

Asheim, B. and Gertler, M. (2005) The geography of innovation: Regional innovation systems. In J. Fagerberg, D. Mowery, and R. Nelson (eds.), *The Oxford Handbook of Innovation* (pp. 291–317). Oxford: Oxford University Press.

Atkinson, R. (2005) *Gentrification in a Global Context: The New Urban Colonialism*. New York, London: Routledge.

Attali, J. (1984) *Noise – The Political Economy of Music*. Minneapolis: Minnesota University Press.

The Creative Capital of Cities: Interactive Knowledge Creation and the Urbanization Economies of Innovation, First Edition. Stefan Krätke.
© 2011 Stefan Krätke. Published 2011 by Blackwell Publishing Ltd.

Aydalot, P. and Keeble, D. (eds.) (1988) *High-technology Industry and Innovative Environments: The European Experience*. London: Routledge.

Baldwin, T., McVoy, D., and Steinfield, C. (1996) *Convergence – Integrating Media, Information and Communication*. London: Sage.

Banks, M., Lovatt, A., O'Connor, J., and Raffo, C. (2000) Risk and trust in the cultural industries. *Geoforum*, 31 (4), 453–464.

Bastian, D. (2006) Modes of knowledge migration: Regional assimilation of knowledge and the politics of bringing knowledge into the region. *European Planning Studies*, 14, 601–619.

Bathelt, H., Malmberg, A., and Maskell, P. (2004) Clusters and knowledge: Local buzz, global pipelines and the process of knowledge creation. *Progress in Human Geography*, 28, 31–56.

Beaverstock, J.V., Smith, R.G., and Taylor, P.J. (1999) A roster of world cities. *Cities*, 16 (6), 445–458.

Bell, D. (1974) *The Coming of Post-industrial Society. A Venture in Social Forecasting*. London: Heinemann.

Belussi, F. and Sedita, S.R. (2008) The management of "events" in the Veneto performing music cluster: Bridging latent networks and permanent organizations. In P. Cooke and L. Lazzeretti (eds.), *Creative Cities, Cultural Clusters and Local Economic Development* (pp. 237–257). Cheltenham: Edward Elgar.

Benneworth, P. and Hospers, G.-J. (eds.) (2009) *The Role of Culture in the Economic Development of Old Industrial Regions*. Münster, Hamburg, London: LIT.

Berlin-Institut für Bevölkerung und Entwicklung (2007) *Talente, Technologie und Toleranz – wo Deutschland Zukunft hat*. Berlin: Berlin-Institut für Bevölkerung und Entwicklung, www.berlin-institut.org

Bernt, M. and Holm, A. (2009) Is it, or is it not? The conceptualization of gentrification and displacement and its political implications in the case of Berlin-Prenzlauer Berg. *City*, 13 (2–3), 312–324.

Biswas, R.K. (ed.) (2000) *Metropolis Now! Urban Cultures in Global Cities*. Vienna: Springer.

Bittner, R. (ed.) (2001) *Urbane Paradiese: Zur Kulturgeschichte des modernen Vergnügens*. Frankfurt-Main, New York: Campus.

Blasius, J. (1993) *Gentrification und Lebensstile*. Wiesbaden: Deutscher Universitätsverlag.

Boschma, R. (2005) Proximity and innovation. A critical assessment. *Regional Studies*, 39 (1), 61–74.

Boschma, R. and Fritsch, M. (2009) Creative class and regional growth. Empirical evidence from seven European countries. *Economic Geography*, 85 (4), 391–423.

Bourdieu, P. (1982) *Die feinen Unterschiede*. Frankfurt-Main: Suhrkamp.

Bourdieu, P. (1983) Ökonomisches Kapital, kulturelles Kapital, soziales Kapital. In R. Kreckel (ed.), *Soziale Ungleichheiten*. Göttingen: Soziale Welt-Sonderheft 2, pp. 183–198.

Boyer, R. (1990) *The Regulation School: A Critical Introduction*. New York: Columbia University Press.

Braczyk, H.-J., Cooke, P., and Heidenreich, M. (eds.) (1998) *Regional Innovation Systems*. London: UCL Press.

Braczyk, H.J., Fuchs, G., and Wolf, H.-G. (eds.) (1999) *Multimedia and Regional Economic Restructuring*. London: Routledge.

Brandt, A., Hahn, C., Krätke, S., and Kiese, M. (2009) Metropolitan regions in the knowledge economy: Network analysis as a strategic information tool. *Journal of Economic and Social Geography*, 100 (2), 236–249.

Brandt, A., Krätke, S., Hahn, C., and Borst, R. (2008) *Metropolregionen und Wissensvernetzung. Eine Netzwerkanalyse innovationsbezogener Kooperationen in der Metropolregion Hannover-Braunschweig-Göttingen*. Münster, Hamburg, London: LIT.

Brenner, N. (2009) What is critical urban theory? *City*, 13 (2–3), 198–208.

Brenner, N. and Theodore, N. (eds.) (2002) *Spaces of Neoliberalism: Urban Restructuring in North America and Western Europe*. Oxford: Blackwell.

Breschi, S. and Lissoni, F. (2004) Knowledge networks from patent data: Methodological issues and research targets. In H. Moed, W. Glänzel, and U. Schmoch (eds.), *Handbook of Quantitative Science and Technology Research: The Use of Publication and Patent Statistics in Studies of S&T Systems* (pp. 613–643). Berlin: Springer.

Brooks, D. (2000) *Bobos in Paradise: The New Upper Class and How They Got There*. New York: Simon and Schuster.

Bryson, J.R. and Daniels, P.W. (eds.) (2007) *The Handbook of Service Industries*. Cheltenham: Edward Elgar.

Burt, R. (1992) *Structural Holes: The Social Structure of Competition*. Cambridge, MA: Harvard University Press.

Burt, R. and Minor, M.J. (eds.) (1983) *Applied Network Analysis*. Beverly Hills: SAGE.

Butterwegge, C., Lösch, B., and Ptak, R. (2008) *Kritik des Neoliberalismus*. Wiesbaden: VS Verlag.

Camagni, R. (ed.) (1991a) *Innovation Networks. Spatial Perspectives*. London: Belhaven.

Camagni, R. (1991b) Local "milieu", uncertainty and innovation networks: Towards a dynamic theory of economic space. In R. Camagni (ed.), *Innovation Networks. Spatial Perspectives* (pp. 121–144). London: Belhaven.

Camagni, R. (1999) The city as a milieu: Applying the GREMI approach to urban evolution. *Revue d'Economie Régionale et Urbaine*, 3, 591–606.

Cappellin, R. and Wink, R. (2009) *International Knowledge and Innovation Networks. Knowledge Creation and Innovation in Medium-technology Clusters*. Cheltenham: Edward Elgar.

Catungal, J.P., Leslie, D., and Hii, Y. (2009) Geographies of displacement in the creative city: The case of Liberty Village, Toronto. *Urban Studies*, 46 (5/6), 1095–1114.

Caves, R. (2002) *Creative Industries: Contracts between Art and Commerce*. Cambridge, MA, London: Harvard University Press.

Chesnais, F. (2004) Das finanzdominierte Akkumulationsregime: theoretische Begründung und Reichweite. In C. Zeller (ed.), *Die globale Enteignungsökonomie* (pp. 217–254). Münster: Westfälisches Dampfboot.

Cinti, T. (2008) Cultural clusters and districts: The state of the art. In P. Cooke and L. Lazzeretti (eds.), *Creative Cities, Cultural Clusters and Local Economic Development* (pp. 70–92). Cheltenham: Edward Elgar:

Clark, T.N. (ed.) (2003) *The City as an Entertainment Machine*. Bingley, UK: Emerald Group.

Coe, N. (2000) The view from out West: Embeddedness, inter-personal relations and the development of an indigenous film industry in Vancouver. *Geoforum*, 31 (4), 391–407.

Coe, N. (2001) A hybrid agglomeration? The development of a satellite-Marshallian industrial district in Vancouver's film industry. *Urban Studies*, 38 (10), 1753–1775.

Coenen, L., Moodysson, J., and Asheim, B.T. (2004) Nodes, networks and proximities: On the knowledge dynamics of the Medicon Valley biotech cluster. *European Planning Studies*, 12, 1003–1018.

Cohen, W.M. and Levinthal, D.A. (1990) Absorptive capacity: A new perspective on learning and innovation. *Administrative Science Quarterly*, 35 (1), 128–152.

Cooke, P. (2002) *Knowledge Economies: Clusters, Learning and Cooperative Advantage*. London: Routledge.

Cooke, P. (2006) Global bioregional networks: A new economic geography of bioscientific knowledge. *European Planning Studies*, 14 (9), 1265–1285.

Cooke, Ph. and Lazzeretti, L. (eds.) (2008a) *Creative Cities, Cultural Clusters and Local Economic Development*. Cheltenham: Edward Elgar.

Cooke, P. and Schwartz, D. (eds.) (2007) *Creative Regions*. London: Routledge.

Crane, D. (1992) *The Production of Culture: Media and the Urban Arts*. London: Sage.

Daniels, P.W. and F. Moulaert (eds.) (1991) *The Changing Geography of Advanced Producer Services: Theoretical and Empirical Perspectives*. London, New York: Belhaven Press.

Dicken, P. (2007) *Global Shift: Mapping the Changing Contours of the World Economy*, 5th edition. London: Sage.

Diez, J.R. (2002) *Betrieblicher Innovationserfolg und räumliche Nähe. Zur Bedeutung innovativer Kooperationsverflechtungen in metropolitanen Verdichtungsregionen*. Münster: LIT.

Dörre, K. and Holst, H. (2009) Nach dem Shareholder Value? Kapitalmarktorientierte Unternehmenssteuerung in der Krise. *WSI-Mitteilungen*, 62 (12), 667–674.

Dunford, M. (1990) Theories of regulation. *Environment and Planning D*, 8, 297–321.

Dunning, J.H. (ed.) (2000) *Regions, Globalization, and the Knowledge-based Economy*. Oxford: Oxford University Press.

Ebert, R. and Kunzmann, K. (2007) Kulturwirtschaft, kreative Räume und Stadtentwicklung in Berlin. *DISP*, 171 (4), 64–79.

Ernst, D. and Kim, L. (2002) Global production networks, knowledge diffusion, and local capability formation. *Research Policy*, 31, 1417–1429.

Evans, G. (2009) Creative cities, creative spaces and urban policy. *Urban Studies*, 45 (5–6), 1003–1040.

Fagerberg, J., Mowery, D., and Nelson, R. (eds.) (2005) *The Oxford Handbook of Innovation*. Oxford: Oxford University Press.

Featherstone, M. (1994) City cultures and post-modern lifestyles. In A. Amin (ed.), *Post-Fordism: A Reader* (pp. 387–408). Oxford: Blackwell.

Firestone, S. (2008) Diverse cities and knowledge spillovers. *The Annals of Regional Science*, DOI 10.1007/s00168-008-0246-7. Published online June 14, 2008.

Florida, R. (2004) *The Rise of the Creative Class*. New York: Basic Books.

Florida, R. (2005) *Cities and the Creative Class*. New York: Routledge.

Florida, R. (2008) *Who's Your City? How the Creative Economy Is Making Where to Live the Most Important Decision of Your Life*. New York: Basic Books.

Florida, R., Mellander, C., and Stolarik, K. (2008) Inside the black box of regional development. Human capital, the creative class, and tolerance. *Journal of Economic Geography*, 8 (5), 615–649.

Florida, R. and Tinagli, J. (2004) *Europe in the Creative Age*. Milan: Demos.

Fornahl, D. and Brenner, T. (eds.) (2003) *Cooperation, Networks and Institutions in Regional Innovation Systems*. Cheltenham: Edward Elgar.

Friedmann, J. (1986) The world city hypothesis. *Development and Change*, 17 (1), 69–84.

Friedmann, J. (1995) Where we stand: A decade of world city research. In P.L. Knox and P.J. Taylor (eds.), *World Cities in a World-system* (pp. 21–47). Cambridge: Cambridge University Press.

Friedmann, J. and Wolff, G. (1982) World city formation: An agenda for research and action. *International Journal of Urban and Regional Research*, 6 (3), 309–344.

Fritsch, M. and Kauffeld-Monz, M. (2008) The impact of network structure on knowledge transfer: An application of social network analysis in the context of regional innovation networks. *The Annals of Regional Science*, DOI 10.1007/s00168-008-0245-8. Published online May 28, 2008.

Fritsch, M. and Stützer, M. (2007) Die Geographie der kreativen Klasse in Deutschland. *Raumforschung und Raumordnung*, 65, 15–29.

Fromhold-Eisebith, M. (2009) Space(s) of innovation: Regional knowledge economies. In P. Meusburger, J. Funke, and E. Wunder (eds.), (2009) *Milieus of Creativity: An Interdisciplinary Approach to Spatiality of Creativity* (pp. 201–218). Heidelberg: Springer Science.

Garnham, N. (2005) From cultural to creative industries. *International Journal of Cultural Policy*, 11 (1), 15–29.

Garreau, J. (1991) *Edge City: Life on the New Frontier*. New York: Doubleday.

Gereffi, G. and Korzeniewicz, M. (eds.) (1994) *Commodity Chains and Global Capitalism*. Westport, CT, London: Praeger.

Gertler, M.S. (1995) "Being There": Proximity, organization, and culture in the development and adoption of advanced manufacturing technologies. *Economic Geography*, 71, 1–26.

Gertler, M. (2003) Tacit knowledge and the economic geography of context, or the undefinable tacitness of (being) there. *Journal of Economic Geography*, 3, 79–99.

Gibson, C. and Kong, L. (2005) Cultural economy: A critical review. *Progress in Human Geography*, 29 (5), 541–561.

Giuliani, E. (2005) Cluster absorptive capacity: Why do some clusters forge ahead and others lag behind? *European Urban and Regional Studies*, 12, 269–288.

Giuliani, E. (2007) The selective nature of knowledge networks in clusters: Evidence from the wine industry. *Journal of Economic Geography*, 7 (2), 139–168.

Glaeser, E.L., Kolko, J., and Saiz, A. (2001) Consumer city. *Journal of Economic Geography*, 1, 27–50.

Goodall, B. (1972) *The Economics of Urban Areas*. Oxford: Pergamon Press.

Gostomski, C.B. v., Küpper, B., and Heitmeyer, W. (2006) Fremdenfeindlichkeit in den Bundesländern. Die schwierige Lage in Ostdeutschland. Deutsche Zustände, Folge 5, Thematische Einzelanalysen in 2006. Bielefeld: Universität Bielefeld.

Gottschall, K. and Schnell, C. (2000) "Alleindienstleister" in Kulturberufen – Zwischen neuer Selbständigkeit und alten Abhängigkeiten. *WSI-Mitteilungen*, 12, 804–810.

Gräber, H., Holst, M., Schackmann-Fallis, K.-P., and Spehl, H. (1987) *Externe Kontrolle und regionale Wirtschaftspolitik*. Berlin: Edition Sigma.

Grabher, G. (1993) The weakness of strong ties: The lock-in of regional development in the Ruhr area. In G. Grabher (ed.), *The Embedded Firm: On the Socioeconomics of Industrial Networks* (pp. 255–277). London: Routledge.

Grabher, G. (2001) Ecologies of creativity: The village, the group, and the heterarchic organization of the British advertising industry. *Environment and Planning A*, 33 (2), 351–374.

Graf, H. (2006) *Networks in the Innovation Process: Local and Regional Interactions*. Cheltenham: Edward Elgar.

Granovetter, M. (1973) The strength of weak ties. *American Journal of Sociology*, 78, 1360–1380.

Grotz, R. and Braun, B. (1997) Territorial or trans-territorial networking: Spatial aspects of technology-oriented co-operation within the German mechanical engineering industry. *Regional Studies*, 31 (6), 545–557.

Grotz, R. and Schätzl, L. (eds.) (2001) *Regionale Innovationsnetzwerke im internationalen Vergleich*. Münster: LIT.

Haaren, K.v. and Hensche, D. (eds.) (1997) *Arbeit im Multimedia-Zeitalter. Die Trends der Informationsgesellschaft*. Hamburg: VSA.

Hall, P. (1966) *The World Cities*. London: Heinemann.

Hall, P. (1998) *Cities in Civilization*. London: Phoenix.

Hall, P. (2000) Creative cities and economic development. *Urban Studies*, 37 (4), 639–649.

Hall, P. (2001) Global city-regions in the twenty-first century. In A.J. Scott (ed.), *Global City-Regions: Trends, Theory, Policy* (pp. 59–77). Oxford: Oxford University Press.

Hannigan, J. (1998) *Fantasy City: Pleasure and Profit in the Postmodern Metropolis*. New York, London: Routledge.

Hartley, J. (ed.) (2005) *Creative Industries*. Oxford: Blackwell.

Harvey, D. (1982) *The Limits to Capital*. Oxford: Blackwell.

Harvey, D. (1989) *The Urban Experience*. Baltimore, MD: Johns Hopkins University Press.

Harvey, D. (2003) *The New Imperialism*. Oxford: Oxford University Press.

Harvey, D. (2004) Die Geographie des "neuen" Imperialismus: Akkumulation durch Enteignung. In C. Zeller (ed.), *Die globale Enteignungsökonomie* (pp. 183–216). Münster: Westfälisches Dampfboot.

Harvey, D. (2005) *A Brief History of Neoliberalism*. Oxford: Oxford University Press.

Harvey, D. (2006) *Spaces of Global Capitalism: A Theory of Uneven Geographical Development*. New York, London: Verso.

Helbrecht, I. (2005) Geographisches Kapital – Das Fundament der kreativen Metropolis. In H.-J. Kujath (ed.), *Knoten im Netz. Zur neuen Rolle der Metropolregionen in der Dienstleistungswirtschaft und Wissensökonomie* (pp. 121–156). Münster, Hamburg, London: LIT.

Held, D., McGrew, A., Goldblatt, D., and Perraton, J. (1999) *Global Transformations: Politics, Economics and Culture*. Cambridge: Polity Press.

Henderson, J., Dicken, P., Hess, M., Coe, N., and Yeung, H. (2002) Global production networks and the analysis of economic development. *Review of International Political Economy*, 9 (3), 436–464.

Herr, H. (2009) Vom regulierten Kapitalismus zur Instabilität. *WSI-Mitteilungen*, 62 (12), 635–642.

Heßler, M. and Zimmermann, C. (eds.) (2008) *Creative Urban Milieus: Historical Perspectives on Culture, Economy, and the City*. Franfurt-Main: Campus.

Hoekman, J., Frenken, K., and van Oort, F. (2008) The geography of collaborative knowledge production in Europe. *The Annals of Regional Science*, DOI 10.1007/s00168-008-0252-9. Published online July 31, 2008.

Holm, A. (2006) *Die Restrukturierung des Raumes. Stadterneuerung der 90er Jahre in Ostberlin Interessen und Machtverhältnisse.* Bielefeld: Transcript.

Howkins, J. (2001) *The Creative Economy: How People Make Money from Ideas.* London, New York: Penguin Press.

Hübner, K. (ed.) (2005) *The New Economy in Transatlantic Perspective: Spaces of Innovation.* New York, London: Routledge.

Huffschmidt, J. (2002) *Politische Ökonomie der Finanzmärkte.* Hamburg: VSA.

Huffschmidt, J., Köppen, M., and Rhode, W. (eds.) (2007) *Finanzinvestoren: Retter oder Raubritter? Neue Herausforderungen durch die internationalen Kapitalmärkte.* Hamburg: VSA.

Hutton, T. (2006) Spatiality, built form, and creative industry development in the inner city. *Environment and Planning A*, 38 (10), 1819–1841.

Hutton, T. (2008) *The New Economy of the Inner City.* New York, London: Routledge.

IMF (International Monetary Fund) (ed.) (2009) *Global Financial Stability Report. A Report by the Monetary and Capital Markets Department.* Washington, DC: IMF.

Indergaard, M. (2004) *Silicon Alley.* New York, London: Routledge.

Jacobs, J. (1969) *The Economy of Cities.* New York: Random House.

Jacobs, J. (1984) *Cities and the Wealth of Nations.* New York: Random House.

Jansen, D. (1999) *Einführung in die Netzwerkanalyse. Grundlagen, Methoden, Anwendungen.* Opladen: Leske and Budrich.

Kalsø Hansen, H., Vang, J., and Asheim, B. (2005) The Creative Class and Regional Growth: Towards a Knowledge Based Approach. *CIRCLE Electronic Working Paper Series*, Paper no. 2005/15, Lund University. Retrieved June 15, 2008 from: http://www.circle.lu.se/publications.

Kaplinsky, R. (2004) Spreading the gains from globalization. What can be learned from value-chain analysis? *Problems of Economic Transition*, 47 (2), 74–115.

KEA (Kern European Affairs) (2006) *The Economy of Culture in Europe. Study prepared for the European Commission.* Brussels: KEA.

Kearns, G. and Philo, C. (eds.) (1993) *Selling Places: The City as Cultural Capital, Past and Present.* Oxford: Pergamon Press.

Keeble, D. and Wilkinson, F. (eds.) (2000) *High-technology Clusters, Networking and Collective Learning in Europe.* Aldershot: Ashgate.

Ketzler, R. and Schäfer, D. (2009) Drohende Finanzierungsklemme bei Innovationen: Rechtzeitig entgegensteuern. *DIW Wochenbericht*, 76 (45), 772–783.

Kirchberg, V. (1992) *Kultur und Stadtgesellschaft. Empirische Fallstudien zum kulturellen Verhalten der Stadtbevölkerung und zur Bedeutung der Kultur für die Stadt.* Wiesbaden: Deutscher Universitäts-Verlag.

Kirchberg, V. and Göschel, A. (eds.) (1998) *Kultur in der Stadt. Stadtsoziologische Analysen zur Kultur.* Opladen: Leske and Budrich.

Klaus, P. (2006) *Stadt, Kultur, Innovation. Kulturwirtschaft und kreative innovative Kleinstunternehmen in Zürich.* Zürich: Seismo.

Klein, N. (2001) *No Logo! Der Kampf der Global Players um Marktmacht: Ein Spiel mit vielen Verlierern und wenigen Gewinnern.* München: Riemann.

Knoke, D. and Kuklinski, J.H. (1982) *Network Analysis.* Sage University Papers No. 28. London: Sage.

Knox, P.L. (2002) World cities and the organization of global space. In R.J. Johnston, P.J. Taylor, and M.J. Watts (eds.), *Geographies of Global Change*, 2nd edition (pp. 328–338). Oxford: Blackwell.

Knudsen, B., Florida, R., Stolarik, K., and Gates, G. (2008) Density and creativity in U.S. regions. *Annals of the Association of American Geographers*, 98 (2), 461–478.

Kong, L. (ed.) (2009) *Creative Economies, Creative Cities: Asian-European Perspectives.* Heidelberg: Springer.

Koschatzky, K. (2001) *Räumliche Aspekte im Innovationsproze_: Ein Beitrag zur neuen Wirtschaftsgeographie aus der Sicht der regionalen Innovationsforschung.* Münster, Hamburg, London: LIT.

Krätke, S. (1992) Urban land rent and real estate markets in the process of social restructuring: The case of Germany. *Environment and Planning D*, 10 (3), 245–264.

Krätke, S. (1995) *Stadt – Raum – Ökonomie. Einführung in aktuelle Problemfelder der Stadtökonomie und Wirtschaftsgeographie.* Basel, Boston, Berlin: Birkhäuser.

Krätke, S. (1999) A regulationist approach to regional studies. *Environment and Planning A*, 31, 683–704.

Krätke, S. (2000) Berlin – the metropolis as a production space. *European Planning Studies*, 8 (1), 7–27.

Krätke, S. (2001) Institutionelle Ordnung und soziales Kapital der Wirtschaftsregionen: Zur Bedeutung von Raumbindungen im Kontext der Globalisierung. *Geographische Zeitschrift*, 89, 145–166.

Krätke, S. (2002a) *Medienstadt: Urbane Cluster und globale Zentren der Kulturproduktion.* Opladen: Leske und Budrich.

Krätke, S. (2002b) Network analysis of production clusters: The Potsdam/Babelsberg film industry as an example. *European Planning Studies*, 10 (1), 27–54.

Krätke, S. (2002c) Urbanität heute: Stadtkulturen, Lebensstile und Lifestyle-Produzenten im Kontext der Globalisierung. In A. Mayr, M. Meurer, and J. Vogt (eds.), *Stadt und Region: Dynamik von Lebenswelten* (pp. 224–235). Leipzig: Deutsche Gesellschaft für Geographie.

Krätke, S. (2003) Global media cities in a worldwide urban network. *European Planning Studies*, 11 (6), 605–628.

Krätke, S. (2004a) Kreatives Wissen in stadtregionaler Perspektive – Medienwirtschaft im Metropolenraum Berlin. In U. Matthiesen (ed.), *Stadtregion und Wissen: Analysen und Plädoyers für eine wissensbasierte Stadtpolitik* (pp. 93–109). Opladen: Leske and Budrich.

Krätke, S. (2004b) City of talents? Berlin's regional economy, socio-spatial fabric and "worst practice" urban governance. *International Journal of Urban and Regional Research*, 28 (3), 511–529.

Krätke, S. (2005a) City of talents? Die Kulturökonomie von Berlin. In I. Bader and A. Scharenberg (eds.), *Der Sound der Stadt: Musikindustrie und Subkultur in Berlin.* Münster: Westfälisches Dampfboot.

Krätke, S. (2005b) Wissensintensive Wirtschaftsaktivitäten im Regionalsystem der Bundesrepublik Deutschland. Clusterpotenziale und Beitrag zur regionalen Wirtschaftsleistung. In H.-J. Kujath (ed.), *Knoten im Netz: Zur neuen Rolle der Metropolregionen in der Dienstleistungswirtschaft und Wissensökonomie* (pp. 159–202). Münster, Hamburg, London: LIT.

Krätke, S. (2007) Metropolization of the European economic territory as a consequence of increasing specialization of urban agglomerations on the knowledge economy. *European Planning Studies*, 15 (1), 1–28.

Krätke, S. and Borst, R. (2000) *Berlin – Metropole zwischen Boom und Krise.* Opladen: Leske & Budrich.

Krätke, S. and Brandt, A. (2009) Knowledge networks as a regional development resource: A network analysis of the interlinks between scientific institutions and regional firms in the metropolitan region of Hannover, Germany. *European Planning Studies,* 17 (1), 43–63.

Krätke, S. and Scheuplein, C. (2001) *Produktionscluster in Ostdeutschland: Methoden der Identifizierung und Analyse.* Hamburg: VSA.

Krätke, S. and Taylor, P.J. (2004) A world geography of global media cities. *European Planning Studies,* 12 (4), 459–477.

Krugman, P. (1991) *Geography and Trade.* Cambridge, MA: MIT Press.

Landry, Ch. (2000) *The Creative City: A Toolkit for Urban Innovators.* London: Earthscan.

Lange, B. (2007) *Die Räume der Kreativscenen: Culturepreneurs und ihre Orte in Berlin.* Bielefeld: Transcript.

Lash, S. and Urry, J. (1994) *Economies of Signs and Space.* London, Thousand Oaks, CA: Sage.

Leborgne, D. and Lipietz, A. (1991) Two social strategies in the production of new industrial spaces. In G. Benko and M. Dunford (eds.), *Industrial Change and Regional Development – The Transformation of New Industrial Spaces* (pp. 27–50). London: Belhaven Press.

Lees, L., Slater, T., and Wyly, E. (2008) *Gentrification.* New York, London: Routledge.

Leyshon, A. (2001) Time-space (and digital) compression: Software formats, musical networks, and the reorganization of the music industry. *Environment and Planning A,* 33, 49–77.

Leyshon, A. (2009) The software slump?: Digital music, the democratisation of technology, and the decline of the recording studio sector within the musical economy. *Environment and Planning A,* 41, 1309–1331.

Leyshon, A., Matless, D., and Revill, G. (eds.) (1998) *The Place of Music.* New York: Guilford Press.

Lipietz, A. (1993) The local and the global: Regional individuality or interregionalism? *Transactions of the Institute of British Geographers,* 18 (1), 8–18.

Lloyd, R. (2006) *Neo-Bohemia: Art and Commerce in the Postindustrial City.* New York and Abingdon: Routledge.

Lo, V. and Schamp, E.W. (eds.) (2003) *Knowledge, Learning, and Regional Development.* Münster: LIT.

Lorenzen, M. and Frederiksen, L. (2008) Why do cultural industries cluster? Localization, urbanization, products and projects. In P. Cooke and L. Lazzeretti (eds.), *Creative Cities, Cultural Clusters and Local Economic Development* (pp. 155–179). Cheltenham: Edward Elgar.

Lundvall, B.A. (1988) Innovation as an interactive process: From user–producer interaction to the national system of innovation. In G. Dosi, C. Freeman, and R. Nelson (eds.), *Technical Change and Economic Theory* (pp. 349–369). London: Pinter.

Lundvall, B.A. (ed.) (1992) *National Systems of Innovation: Towards a Theory of Innovation and Interactive Learning.* London: Pinter.

Luxemburg, R. (1951) *The Accumulation of Capital.* New Haven, CT: Yale University Press.

Maggioni, M. and Uberti, T.E. (2006) International networks of knowledge flows: An econometric analysis. *Papers on Economics and Evolution* 2005–19, Max Planck Institute of Economics, MPI Jena. Retrieved April 30, 2009 from: http://ideas. repec. org./p/esi/evopap/2005-19.html

Maggioni, M., Nosvelli, M., and Uberti, T.E. (2007) Space versus networks in the geography of innovation: A European analysis. *Papers in Regional Science*, 86 (3), 471–493.

Malecki, E. and Oinas, P. (eds.) (1999) *Making Connections: Technological Learning and Regional Economic Change*. Aldershot: Ashgate.

Malerba, F. and Vonortas, N. (eds.) (2009) *Innovation Networks in Industries*. Cheltenham: Edward Elgar.

Marcuse, P. and van Kempen, R. (eds.) (2000) *Globalizing Cities: A New Spatial Order?* Oxford: Blackwell.

Markusen, A. (1996) Sticky places in slippery space. A typology of industrial districts. *Economic Geography*, 72 (3), 293–313.

Markusen, A. (2006a) Urban development and the politics of a creative class: Evidence from a study of artists. *Environment and Planning A*, 38 (10), 1921–1940.

Markusen, A. (2006b) Cultural Planning and the Creative City. Retrieved October 30, 2008 from: www.hhh.umn.edu/projects/prie.

Markusen, A. (2008) *Organizational Complexity in the Regional Cultural Economy*. Retrieved May 30, 2009 from: www.hhh.umn.edu/projects/prie.

Marshall, A. (1920) *Principles of Economics*. London: Macmillan.

Martin-Brelot, H., Grossetti, M., Eckert, D., Gritsai, O., and Kovács, Z. (2010) The spatial mobility of the "creative class": A European perspective. *International Journal of Urban and Regional Research*, 34 (4), 854–870.

Marx, K. (1981) *Capital. A Critique of Political Economy*. Harmondsworth: Penguin Books.

Maskell, P. and Malmberg, A. (1999a) Localised learning and industrial competitiveness. *Cambridge Journal of Economics*, 23, 167–185.

Maskell, P. and Malmberg, A. (1999b) The competitiveness of firms and regions. "Ubiquitification" and the importance of localized learning. *European Urban and Regional Studies*, 6, 9–25.

Massey, D. (1984) *Spatial Divisions of Labour: Social Structures and the Geography of Production*. London: Macmillan.

Matthiesen, U. (ed.) (2003) *Stadtregion und Wissen: Analysen und Plädoyers für eine wissensbasierte Stadtpolitik*. Opladen: Leske & Budrich.

Medienhandbuch (Media Handbook) (2009) Hamburg: Medienhandbuch Publikationsgesellschaft. Retrieved on 15 November 2009 from: www.medienhandbuch.de

Meusburger, P. (2009) Milieus of creativity: The role of places, environments, and spatial contexts. In P. Meusburger, J. Funke, and E. Wunder (eds.), *Milieus of Creativity: An Interdisciplinary Approach to Spatiality of Creativity* (pp. 97–154). Heidelberg: Springer Science.

Meusburger, P., Funke, J., and Wunder, E. (Eds.) (2009) *Milieus of Creativity: An Interdisciplinary Approach to Spatiality of Creativity*. Heidelberg: Springer Science.

Milios, J. (2000) Social classes in classical and Marxist political economy. *American Journal of Economics and Sociology*, 59 (2), 283–302.

Molotch, H. (2003) *Where Stuff Comes From: How Toasters, Toilets, Cars, Computers and Many Other Things Come to Be as They Are*. New York, London: Routledge.

Moodysson, J., Coenen, L., and Asheim, B. (2008) Explaining spatial patterns of innovation: Analytical and synthetic modes of knowledge creation in the Medicon Valley life science cluster. *Environment and Planning A*, 40, 1040–1056.

Morrison, A. and Rabellotti, R. (2009) Knowledge and information networks in an Italian wine cluster. *European Planning Studies*, 17 (7), 983–1006.

Mossig, I. (2006) *Netzwerke der Kulturökonomie*. Bielefeld: Transcript.

Moulaert, F. and Nussbaumer, J. (2005) The social region – Beyond the territorial dynamics of the Learning Economy. *European Urban and Regional Studies*, 12 (1), 45–64.

Moulaert, F. and Sekia, F. (2003) Territorial innovation models: A critical survey. *Regional Studies*, 37, 289–302.

Müller, A. (2005) *Die Reformlüge: 40 Denkfehler, Mythen und Legenden, mit denen Politik und Wirtschaft Deutschland ruinieren*. Munich: Droemer Knaur.

Müller, L. (2010) *Bank-Räuber: Wie kriminelle Manager und unfähige Politiker uns in den Ruin treiben*. Berlin: Econ.

Mundelius, M. (2006) *Die Bedeutung der Kulturwirtschaft für den Wirtschaftsstandort Pankow, Berlin*. Berlin: DIW.

Murmann, J.P., Jones, G., and Galambos, L. (eds.) (2006) *Knowledge and Competitive Advantage: The Coevolution of Firms, Technology, and National Institutions*. Cambridge: Cambridge University Press.

Musgrave, R.A. (1969) *Finanztheorie*, 2nd edition. Tübingen: Mohr.

Neckel, S. (2000) Leistung versus Erfolg. Der Zufall von Reichtum und Ruhm – zur symbolischen Ordnung der Marktgesellschaft. *Frankfurter Rundschau* 233 (7.10. 2000), 21.

Noller, P. (1999) *Globalisierung, Stadträume und Lebensstile: Kulturelle und lokale Repräsentationen des globalen Raums*. Opladen: Leske & Budrich.

Noller, P., Prigge, W., and Ronneberger, K. (eds.) (1994) *Stadt-Welt: Über die Globalisierung städtischer Milieus*. Frankfurt-Main, New York: Campus.

Nonaka, I. and Takeuchi, H. (1995) *The Knowledge-creating Company: How Japanese Companies Create the Dynamics of Innovation*. New York: Oxford University Press.

Nooteboom, B. (1999) The dynamic efficiency of networks. In A. Grandori (ed.), *Inter-firm Networks: Organization and Industrial Competitiveness* (pp. 91–119). New York, London: Routledge.

Nooteboom, B. (2003) Problems and solutions in knowledge transfer. In D. Fornahl and T. Brenner (eds.), *Cooperation, Networks and Institutions in Regional Innovation Systems* (pp. 105–127). Cheltenham: Edward Elgar.

Oakey, R., Kipling, M., and Wildgust, S. (2001) Clustering among firms in the non-broadcast visual communications (NBVC) sector. *Regional Studies*, 35 (5), 401–414.

Oßenbrügge, J., Pohl, T., and Vogelpohl, A. (2009) Entgrenzte Zeitregime und wirtschaftsräumliche Konzentrationen. Der Kreativsektor des Hamburger Schanzenviertels. *Zeitschrift für Wirtschaftsgeographie*, 53 (4), 249–263.

Owen-Smith, J. and Powell, W.W. (2004) Knowledge networks as channels and conduits: The effects of spillovers in the Boston biotechnology community. *Organization Science*, 15, 5–21.

Peck, J. (1996) *Work-Place: The Social Regulation of Labour Markets*. New York, London: Guilford Press.

Peck, J. (2005) Struggling with the creative class. *International Journal of Urban and Regional Research*, 24 (4), 740–770.

Peck, J. (2009) The cult of urban creativity. In R. Keil and R. Mahon (eds.), *Leviathan Undone? Towards a Political Economy of Scale* (pp. 159–176). Vancouver: University of British Columbia Press.

Peck, J. and Tickell, A. (1994) Searching for a new institutional fix: The after-Fordist crisis and the global-local disorder. In A. Amin (ed.), *Post-Fordism. A Reader* (pp. 280–315). Oxford: Blackwell.

Pilon, S. and DeBresson, C. (2003) Local culture and regional innovation networks: Some propositions. In D. Fornahl and T. Brenner (eds.), *Cooperation, Networks and Institutions in Regional Innovation Systems* (pp. 15–37). Cheltenham: Edward Elgar.

Polanyi, M. (1967) *The Tacit Dimension*. London: Routledge.

Porter, M.E. (1993) *Nationale Wettbewerbsvorteile. Erfolgreich konkurrieren auf dem Weltmarkt*. Wien: Ueberreuter.

Porter, M.E. (1998) Clusters and competition: New agendas for companies, governments, and institutions. In M.E. Porter, *On Competition* (pp. 197–287). Boston, MA: Harvard University Press.

Porter, M.E. (2001) Regions and the new economics of competition. In A.J. Scott (ed.), *Global City-Regions: Trends, Theory, Policy* (pp. 139–157). Oxford: Oxford University Press.

Power, D. and Scott, A.J. (eds.) (2004) *Cultural Industries and the Production of Culture*. New York, London: Routledge.

Pratt, A. (1997) The cultural industries production system: A case study of employment change in Britain, 1984–91. *Environment and Planning A*, 29, 1953–1974.

Pratt, A. (2000) New media, the new economy and new spaces. *Geoforum*, 31 (4), 425–436.

Pratt, A. (2009) Urban regeneration: From the arts "feel good" factor to the cultural economy: A case study of Hoxton, London. *Urban Studies*, 45 (5–6), 1041–1061.

Pred, A. (1977) *City Systems in Advanced Economies*. New York: John Wiley.

Raspe, O. and van Oort, F. (2006) The knowledge economy and urban economic growth. *European Planning Studies*, 14 (9), 1209–1234.

Ratti, R., Bramanti, A., and Gordon, R. (eds.) (1997) *The Dynamics of Innovative Regions*. London: Ashgate.

Rehfeld, D. (1999) *Produktionscluster. Konzeption, Analysen und Strategien für eine Neuorientierung der regionalen Strukturpolitik*. München: Hampp.

Rehfeld, D. (2001) Global strategies compared: Firms, markets and regions. *European Planning Studies*, 9, 29–46.

Robins, K. (1995) The new spaces of global media. In R.J. Johnston, P.J. Taylor, and M.J. Watts (eds.), *Geographies of Global Change: Remapping the World in the Late Twentieth Century*. Oxford: Blackwell.

Romer, P. (1990) Endogenous technological change. *Journal of Political Economy*, 98 (5), 71–102.

Roost, F. (2000) *Die Disneyfizierung der Städte. Großprojekte der Entertainmentindustrie am Beispiel des New Yorker Times Square und der Siedlung Celebration in Florida.* Opladen: Leske & Budrich.

Roth, R. (2001) Kreatives Handeln von Eliten und Bewegungen. Überlegungen am Beispiel des "Reformstaus" in der Bundesrepublik. In H. Bluhm and J. Gebhardt (eds.), *Konzepte politischen Handelns. Kreativität, Innovation, Praxen* (pp. 315–334). Baden-Baden: Nomos.

Ryan, B. (1992) *Making Capital from Culture: The Corporate Form of Capitalist Cultural Production.* Berlin, New York: Walter de Gruyter.

Sassen, S. (1991) *The Global City: New York, London, Tokyo.* Princeton, NJ: Princeton University Press.

Sassen, S. (1996) New employment regimes in cities: The impact on immigrant workers. *New Community*, 22 (4), 579–594.

Sassen S. (2000) *Cities in a World Economy.* London: Sage.

Schamp, E.W. (2000) *Vernetzte Produktion: Industriegeographie aus institutioneller Perspektive.* Darmstadt: Wissenschaftliche Buchgesellschaft.

Schamp, E.W. (2002a) Evolution und Institution als Grundlagen einer dynamischen Wirtschaftsgeographie: Die Bedeutung von externen Skalenerträgen für geographische Konzentration. *Geographische Zeitschrift*, 90: 40–52.

Schamp, E.W. (2002b) Globalization and the reorganization of a metropolitan knowledge system: The case of research and development in Frankfurt/Rhein-Main, Germany. In R. Hayter (ed.), *Knowledge, Industry and Environment* (pp. 355–375). Aldershot: Ashgate.

Scharenberg, A. and Bader, I. (2009) Berlin's waterfront site struggle. *City*, 13 (2–3), 325–335.

Schmiedl, D. and Niedermeyer, G. (2006) *Patentatlas Deutschland. Regionaldaten der Erfindungstätigkeit.* München: Deutsches Patent- und Markenamt.

Schumpeter, J.A. (1952) *Theorie der wirtschaftlichen Entwicklung: Eine Untersuchung über Unternehmergewinn, Kapital, Kredit, Zins und den Konjunkturzyklus.* 5. Aufl., Berlin: Duncker and Humblot.

Scott, A.J. (1988a) *New Industrial Spaces.* London: Pion.

Scott, A.J. (1988b) *Metropolis: From the Division of Labour to Urban Form.* Berkeley: University of California Press.

Scott, A.J. (1996) The craft, fashion, and cultural-products industries of Los Angeles: Competitive dynamics and policy dilemmas in a multisectoral image-producing complex. *Annals of the Association of American Geographers*, 86 (2), 306–323.

Scott, A.J. (1997) The cultural economy of cities. *International Journal of Urban and Regional Research*, 21 (2): 323–339.

Scott, A.J. (2000) *The Cultural Economy of Cities: Essays on the Geography of Image-producing Industries.* New York, London: Sage.

Scott, A.J. (ed.) (2001) *Global City-Regions: Trends, Theory, Policy.* Oxford: Oxford University Press.

Scott, A.J. (2006) Creative cities: Conceptual issues and policy questions. *Journal of Urban Affairs*, 28 (1), 1–17.

Scott, A.J. (2008) *Social Economy of the Metropolis: Cognitive-cultural Capitalism and the Global Resurgence of Cities.* Oxford: Oxford University Press.

Scott, A.J. and Storper, M. (2009) Rethinking human capital, creativity and urban growth. *Journal of Economic Geography*, 9 (2), 147–167.

Senatsverwaltung für Wirtschaft, Technologie und Frauen (ed.) (2008) *Kulturwirtschaft in Berlin: Entwicklungen und Potenziale.* Berlin: Senatsverwaltung für Wirtschaft, Technologie und Frauen, Senatsverwaltung für Stadtentwicklung.

Short, J.R., Kim, Y., Kuus, M., and Wells, H. (1996) The dirty little secret of world cities research: Data problems in comparative analysis. *International Journal of Urban and Regional Research*, 20 (4), 697–718.

Siebel, W. (2008) Talent, Toleranz, Technologie. Kritische Anmerkungen zu drei neuen Zauberworten der Stadtpolitik. *RegioPol, Zeitschrift für Regionalwirtschaft*, 1 (1), 31–39.

Simmie, J. (2003) Innovation and urban regions as national and international nodes for the transfer and sharing of knowledge. *Regional Studies*, 37 (6–7), 607–620.

Smith, N. (1996) *The New Urban Frontier: Gentrification and the Revanchist City.* New York, London: Routledge.

Smith, N. (2002) New globalism, new urbanism: Gentrification as global urban strategy. In N. Brenner and N. Theodore (eds.), *Spaces of Neoliberalism: Urban Restructuring in North America and Western Europe* (pp. 80–103). Oxford: Blackwell.

Smith, N. and Williams, P. (eds.) (1986) *Gentrification of the City.* London: Allen & Unwin.

Soja, E. (2000) *Postmetropolis: Critical Studies of Cities and Regions.* Oxford: Blackwell.

Söndermann, M. and Fesel, B. (2007) *Culture and Creative Industries in Germany.* Bonn: German Commission for UNESCO.

Sternberg, R. (1999) Innovative Netzwerke und Regionalentwicklung. In ARL (ed.), *Europäische Einflüsse auf die Raum- und Regionalentwicklung* (pp. 78–105). Hannover: ARL-Verlag.

Stolarick, K. and Florida, R. (2006) Creativity, connections and innovation: A study of linkages in the Montréal region. *Environment and Planning A*, 38 (10), 1799–1817.

Storper, M. (1995) The resurgence of regional economies, ten years later: The region as a nexus of untraded interdependencies. *European Urban and Regional Studies*, 2 (3), 191–221.

Storper, M. (1997) *The Regional World: Territorial Development in a Global Economy.* New York: Guilford Press.

Storper, M. and Venables, A.J. (2004) Buzz: Face-to-face contact and the urban economy. *Journal of Economic Geography*, 4, 351–370.

Storper, M. and Walker, R. (1989) *The Capitalist Imperative: Territory, Technology, and Industrial Growth.* Oxford: Blackwell.

Taylor, P.J. (2004) *World City Network: A Global Urban Analysis.* New York, London: Routledge.

Taylor, P.J. and Aranya, R. (2008) A global "urban roller coaster"? Connectivity changes in the world city network, 2000–04. *Regional Studies*, 42, 1–16.

Taylor, P.J., Catalano, G., and Walker, D.R.F. (2002) Measurement of the world city network. *Urban Studies*, 39, 2367–2376.

Taylor, P.J. and Hoyler, M. (2000) The spatial order of European cities under conditions of contemporary globalization. *Journal of Economic and Social Geography*, 91 (2), 176–189.

Taylor, P.J., Ni, P., Derudder, B., Hoyler, M., Huang, J., Lu, F., Pain, K., Witlox, F., Yang, X., Bassens, D., and Shen, W. (2009) Measuring the world city network: New developments and results. *GaWC Research Bulletin*, No. 300. Loughborough: GaWC. Retrieved April 30, 2009 from: www.lboro.ac.uk/gawc/rb/rb300.html

Taylor, P.J. and Walker, D.R.F. (2001) World cities: A first multivariate analysis of their service complexes. *Urban Studies*, 38 (1), 23–47.

Thiel, J. (2005) *Creativity and Space: Labour and the Restructuring of the German Advertising Industry*. Aldershot: Ashgate.

Throsby, D. (2001) *Economics and Culture*. Cambridge: Cambridge University Press.

Tödtling, F., Lehner, P., and Trippl, M. (2006) Innovation in knowledge-intensive industries. The nature and geography of knowledge links. *European Planning Studies*, 14, 1035–1058.

Waitt, G. and Gibson, C. (2009) Creative small cities: Rethinking the creative economy in place. *Urban Studies*, 46 (5/6), 1223–1246.

Wall, R.S. and van der Knaap, G.A. (2009) Centrality and structure within contemporary worldwide corporate networks. *GaWC Research Bulletin*, No. 295. Loughborough: GaWC. Retrieved April 30, 2009 from: www.lboro.ac.uk/gawc/rb/rb295.html

Wassermann, S. and Faust, K. (1994) *Social Network Analysis: Methods and Applications*. Cambridge: Cambridge University Press.

Watson, A. (2009) The world according to iTunes: Creative project ecologies and the global urban networks of digital music production. *GaWC Research Bulletin*, No. 317. Loughborough: GaWC. Retrieved October 30, 2009 from: www.lboro.ac.uk/ gawc/rb/rb317.html

Watson, A., Hoyler, M., and Mager, C. (2009) Spaces and networks of musical creativity in the city. *Geography Compass*, 3 (2), 856–878.

Weber, A. (1914) *Industrielle Standortslehre*. Grundriss der Sozialökonomik, VI. Abteilung: Industrie, Bauwesen, Bergwesen. Tübingen: J.C.B. Mohr, pp. 54–83.

Whitley, R. (1999) *Divergent Capitalisms*. Oxford: Oxford University Press.

Wilson, D. and Keil, R. (2008) The real creative class. *Social and Cultural Geography*, 9 (8), 841–847.

Windolf, P. (ed.) (2005) *Finanzmarktkapitalismus: Analyse zum Wandel von Produktionsregimen*. Opladen: VS Verlag für Sozialwissenschaften.

Wynne, D. (ed.) (1992) *The Culture Industry*. Aldershot: Avebury.

Zeller, C. (ed.) (2004) *Die globale Enteignungsökonomie*. Münster: Westfälisches Dampfboot.

Zukin, S. (1982) *Loft Living: Culture and Capital in Urban Change*. Baltimore, MD: Johns Hopkins University Press.

Zukin, S. (1995) *The Cultures of Cities*. Oxford: Blackwell.

Index

Aachen 63
absorptive capacity 101–2, 103
accumulation
    capitalism 6, 7, 14, 15, 17, 93, 203
    by dispossession 27
    finance dominated 23, 30, 198
    research and development 29
Adlershof technology district,
    Berlin 168, 169, 170–1
Adorno, T. 142–3
advanced manufacturing sectors 93
advanced producer services 19–20, 28,
    31, 161, 166
advertising industry 129, 135, 144–5
agglomeration
    artistically creative workers 187–8,
    189, 200
    Berlin 167, 169, 170–2, 173–4,
    190
    communication 168, 191
    cultural economy 85, 187–8,
    191–3
    knowledge generation 96, 104, 109
    local industries 170
    multimedia 173–4
    recruitment 142
    scale economies 30, 93
    social advantages 175
    specialization 109, 159, 181

    urban economic development 88, 94
    see also cluster dynamics
agricultural class 40
American Prospect 90
Amin, A. 94
Amsterdam 153
Anderson, G. 43
Arauzo-Carod, J.-M. 168
architecture 129, 166
artistic creative work 5, 9, 14–15,
    133–4, 142–6, 171
artistically creative occupations
    clustering 47–8, 49, 61, 159–60,
    199
    creative class 41, 42, 197, 209–11
    cultural production 130–1
    Germany 212
    regional distribution 47–51, 79, 80
artistically creative workers
    agglomeration 187–8, 189, 200
    Berlin 163, 180
    categories of 39
    concentrations of 178–9
    inner-cities 188, 202
    low mobility 85
    middle-class working poor 186,
    201
    regional development 46, 47–51
    role of 42

The Creative Capital of Cities: Interactive Knowledge Creation and the Urbanization Economies of Innovation, First Edition. Stefan Krätke.
© 2011 Stefan Krätke. Published 2011 by Blackwell Publishing Ltd.